CAMEL PILOT SUPREME

CAPTAIN D.V. ARMSTRONG DFC

To Rob Fletcher, who inspired this centenary tribute, and whose contributions have been inestimable.

By the same author

Flight Unlimited (with Eric Müller) Müller & Carson, London, 1983.

Flight Unlimited '95 (with Eric Müller) Carson, Morningside, 1995.

Flight Fantastic: The Illustrated History of Aerobatics, Foulis/Haynes, Sparkford, 1986.

Welgevonden: Wilderness in the Waterberg, Lapalala, Johannesburg, 1995.

Jeff Beck: Crazy Fingers, Backbeat Books, San Francisco, 2001

Richard III: The Maligned King, The History Press, Stroud, 2008 and 2013.

Richard III: A Small Guide to the Great Debate, Imprimis, Norwich, 2013.

Finding Richard III: The Official Account of the Retrieval and Reburial Project (Ed.) (with J. Ashdown-Hill, D. Johnson, W. Johnson and P.J. Langley), Imprimis, Norwich, 2014.

Richard Duke of Gloucester as Lord Protector and High Constable of England, Imprimis, Norwich, 2015.

CAMEL PILOT SUPREME
CAPTAIN D.V. ARMSTRONG
DFC

To Phil
best wishes

ANNETTE CARSON

Annette Carson

27 Oct 2019
Tunveston

AIR WORLD

AIR WORLD

CAMEL PILOT SUPREME
Captain D.V. Armstrong DFC

First published in Great Britain in 2019 by
Air World
An imprint of
Pen & Sword Books Ltd
Yorkshire – Philadelphia

ISBN 978 1 52675 267 3

Printed and bound in England by TJ International, Padstow, Cornwall, PL28 8RW

Typeset by Aura Technology and Software Services, India

Pen & Sword Books Limited incorporates the imprints of Atlas, Archaeology,
Aviation, Discovery, Family History, Fiction, History, Maritime, Military, Military
Classics, Politics, Select, Transport, True Crime, Air World, Frontline Publishing, Leo
Cooper, Remember When, Seaforth Publishing, The Praetorian Press, Wharncliffe
Local History, Wharncliffe Transport, Wharncliffe True Crime and White Owl.

For a complete list of Pen & Sword titles please contact

PEN & SWORD BOOKS LIMITED
47 Church Street, Barnsley, South Yorkshire, S70 2AS, England
E-mail: enquiries@pen-and-sword.co.uk
Website: www.pen-and-sword.co.uk

Or
PEN AND SWORD BOOKS
1950 Lawrence Rd, Havertown, PA 19083, USA
E-mail: Uspen-and-sword@casematepublishers.com
Website: www.penandswordbooks.com

CONTENTS

INTRODUCTION

A hundred years ago, the art of aerobatics was a great wonder. As soon as aviators had machines they could control in all dimensions, their urge was to explore the freedom of flight without limits. Not content with straight-and-level, as early as 1908 Wilbur Wright stunned Europe with daring displays of diving, banking and circling in his unwieldy wing-warping boxkite biplane. The first loops were performed in 1913 and, in the same year, Louis Blériot's test pilot Adolphe Pégoud experimented with negative *g* and flew upside-down in his graceful wing-warping Blériot XI monoplane.

Incredibly, wing-warping was still employed in such early war machines as the Morane-Saulniers flown at the battle of the Somme by young Second Lieutenant D.V. Armstrong, in 1916, as a member of the legendary No. 60 Squadron of Britain's Royal Flying Corps. Soon the relentless impetus of war produced an onrush of new designs, all of them experimental, and most of them demanding consummate skills from airmen required to adapt to a succession of different airframes, power plants, armament and equipment. How striking, then, that the Sopwith Camel, famed for its intolerance of so many unwary pilots, emerged from the Great War so beloved by its handlers. 'What a glorious machine it was,' wrote one, nearly forty years later. 'So trigger-finger sensitive, although a pig to land in really gusty weather. Compared with some engines, the rotary ran like a sewing machine – but with big gusts of warm and (to me) perfect-smelling castor oil fumes giving memories of early Hendon aromas. I can never forget the Camel.'

Young Armstrong's exceptional virtuosity in aerobatting the formidable little beast was such that his exploits were still recounted with awe after the passage of several generations. He shone bright in the recollections of those who knew him, and lived on in the esteem of those who heard of him. Keenest of all were the memories of those who saw him at his finest, cleaving the air and disturbing the grass of fields once farmed but now given over to the gods of battle. COs were known to emerge demanding furiously who was indulging in such sensational and hazardous flying, but soon melted and invited the culprit into the mess. In a corps of men devoted to flight, Armstrong reminded them that aeroplanes were destined to be more than weapons of war, and brought back a brief taste of that joyful exuberance forever associated with life among the clouds.

CHAPTER 1

SOUTH AFRICA: FAMILY, HOME & MILITARY SERVICE

The Great War of 1914-19 threw together countless numbers of youthful servicemen from innumerable different backgrounds and many far-flung lands. Among those who served His Majesty King George V in Europe was D'Urban Victor Armstrong, a lad of 18 who arrived in England in the bracing cold of November 1915 having left behind his native sub-tropical clime of Natal, South Africa. His sights were set on learning to fly.

D'Urban Armstrong was the second son and youngest child of George Shearer Armstrong, one of that restless breed of adventurers and pioneers whose desire was always to be seeking new horizons. George's father, William, was a Scot from the tiny hamlet of Arnprior in Perthshire, who married Elizabeth Shearer from nearby Stirling. William's family claimed descent from the infamous sixteenth-century Border reiver John Armstrong of the Mangerton clan: 'Johnnie of Gilnockie' had held the Anglo-Scottish Borderlands in thrall, amassing great riches by means of the time-honoured reiver activities of ravaging, destruction and plunder, to which was added protection money from those who hoped to be spared. His career ended with a noose at the command of James V of Scotland (father of Mary, Queen of Scots), but the king's faithless default on a promise of safe-conduct had the effect of rendering the notorious raider something of a folk hero, at least to his fellow Borderers.

William Armstrong, born to the stock-raising life, decided to leave Scotland to seek his fortune in Australia, where Elizabeth gave birth to D'Urban's father, George Shearer Armstrong, on their farm in August 1855. Despite his success there, William's wanderlust induced him to sample other lands including New Zealand. He was then attracted to try his hand at stock-farming in South Africa, emigrating to the Colony of Natal in 1862 where he established farms at Oakford and Redcliff.

1

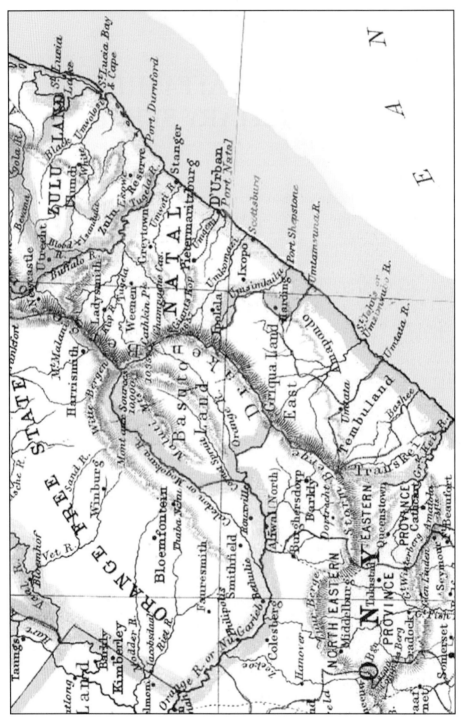

Natal in the late 19th century.

The aim of the British authorities was to foster agriculture, but few areas were at all suitable and, like many other settlers, William found the available land too rugged and lacking in essential resources like water. The hunting was good and the coastal position was conducive to trade, and many immigrants took to a life of trading and/or transport-riding into the vast interior with sixteen-span ox wagons. But sugar-cane plantations were also beginning to thrive in Natal, so after establishing himself as a stock-farmer William Armstrong took to sugar-planting, settling on a homestead a few miles from Verulam, just north of Durban.

At this point George's freedom came to an end and he was sent to Verulam School, aged 12, subsequently serving an apprenticeship at a general engineering works. When old enough he joined the local volunteer corps, the Victoria Mounted Rifles, later to become the Natal Mounted Rifles. As a youngster he well remembered the coronation of the Zulu King Cetshwayo. When in 1869 the news arrived of diamonds being discovered on the Vaal river west of Bloemfontein, the first party to organize systematic digging was one formed in Natal. George, too, was eager to try his luck and, as soon as his apprenticeship was over, he set out for Kimberley by ox-drawn postcart to join the hordes of diamond prospectors descending from all over the world.

In the ensuing years his diamond-mining friends and business associates would include Cecil Rhodes and many other notable pioneers of the industry. It was during George's days in the diamond fields, in 1879, that Cetshwayo roused the Zulu nation against British demands, culminating in the terrible bloodshed of Isandlwana and Rorke's Drift, and ending with the king's final defeat at Ulundi. George's family was moved to the safer Durban area but, though he attempted to return, every able-bodied man at the diamond fields was ordered to remain and protect the all-important mining concerns.

His diamond enterprises flourished and during this time he married an American girl, Ethyl Langford, and started a family; their daughter Betty arrived in 1881 and eldest son Athol was born in 1885; two daughters, Edie and Frances, followed in 1886 and 1887. Eventually George sold up for a large sum in the early 1890s and headed back to Natal ... only to sell up and leave for America ... only to return at the end of the Second Anglo-Boer War when he settled at last on the family farm at Phoenix, between Durban and Verulam.

After trying his hand at gold mining, stock raising and tea planting, he turned to the sugar industry and in 1910 founded a sugar-cane farming company, Umhlatuzi Valley Sugar Co. Ltd, to raise funds for sugar-cane cultivation on reclaimed swamplands (this was the first attempt to drain in Zululand). Next he established the Zululand Sugar Milling Co. Ltd at Empangeni in partnership with Athol in 1911, but operations commenced only in 1913 owing to delays with machinery and building work.[1]

G.S. Armstrong.

By now his second son had been born in the Durban area on 26 July 1897 and named after Sir Benjamin D'Urban, in whose honour the town itself had been named. He was known in the family as 'Urban'.

Had D.V. Armstrong set down his experiences of early childhood in as much detail as his father

4

described his own, he would have painted a picture of local rural Africa at the turn of the twentieth century which had remained recognizably similar for generations. On the land in Natal it was a picture of farms and crops intimately meshed into the cycle of the seasons, with life and livelihood at the mercy of pests and diseases that bred in the searing, humid heat, able to decimate a crop or wipe out entire herds of livestock. Mosquitoes were a constant menace, and floods would sometimes lay waste to the plantations. In terms of basic existence it was a story of supplies sometimes plentiful, sometimes scarce, sometimes non-existent through loss or damage or disaster. Until the roads were surfaced and tarred, ox-wagons were still the most reliable means of transporting heavy loads in a country so enormous that railway links could initially serve only a few urban centres.

As a young boy growing up on a farmstead in Natal, D'Urban would hardly notice such adult concerns, given his free run of the land and the abundance of adventure and exploration at hand. A settler family would have a variety of live-in farm hands as well as domestic workers whose tasks included cleaning and caring. As they grew, the children would have a dedicated child-carer or nanny who was often closer than their natural mother; for a wife whose family was not wealthy had a full daily workload of her own. Boys were often taken under the wing of a reliable, retired or senior estate worker who became an informal teacher of the Zulu customs; this *umngane* would be a regular travel companion and minder when oversight was needed. D'Urban had older siblings, of course: three sisters and a brother; but young ladies of that era were closely constrained by convention, not to mention attire. In any case his nearest sister Frances was ten years older; and with Athol twelve years his senior their pastimes hardly coincided.

The farm's Zulu workers had family and clan members living in or nearby and boys of similar age, black and white, would play and explore together. White children would learn from their Zulu counterparts the simple skills of living on the land and making use of natural resources; how to glean and gather, fashion and mend, seek for spoor, and track the signs of living things. The Armstrong family would be widely known to the Zulus in the area, and to embed the family in the community a son would be encouraged to learn and respect local customs and speak the Zulu language fluently.

The Zulu were a hunting nation, and the boy would sometimes be permitted to join their hunts; they had scant interest in cultivating crops and a huge and fearsome appetite for meat. George Armstrong's reminiscences tell of their elaborate preparations when a major hunt was planned: 'They were

Rural Zululand in the early 1900s.

splendid fellows in those days, and I expect in the remote districts these are still carried out.' A propitious day would be agreed, and messengers would be sent from kraal to kraal until a radius of up to twenty miles had been alerted as to time and place. They came in groups each ranging from ten to fifty men, carrying assegais, small shields and sticks. The day would start at an encampment with singing and ceremonies designed to bring good fortune; then strategies would be set and at intervals of a few minutes the separate companies would move out stealthily to their allotted positions at the hunting-ground. 'When the wings of the hunting army converged, the word was whispered back: "*Ihlangeni*" – "we have met". For hunt or war, the procedure was the same.'

D'Urban, like his father, would in time have his own rifle and with practice hone his marksmanship. To go out hunting on his own, without those expert trackers and helpers, demanded an intimate understanding of bird and branch, donga and reed bed, anthill and boulder, and the skill to interpret every stir and flicker in an otherwise immobile scene. 'Nothing pleased me more than to get away out in the bush,' said his father's account, 'and have a small hunt all to myself or with some of my friends.'

Aside from horse- and stock-husbandry, D'Urban's rudimentary home-schooling probably comprised little more than the 'three Rs'. His father must have been away from home to a large extent, while the family remained based in Victoria County at their farmstead in Inanda, with the

Hilton College in the early 1900s – the classroom block where D'Urban was taught.

town of Durban within easy reach. When in 1910 George and Athol went into sugar production and processing in the Empangeni area of Zululand, their business interests were about 100 miles farther along the coast north-eastwards from Durban. The family moved there soon afterwards, Athol setting up home with Edith Emily Burns whom he married in November 1911 (they had no children). Their first enterprise, Umhlatuzi Valley Sugar (UVS) is still flourishing today, while Zululand Sugar Milling was acquired in 1957 by the larger nearby Felixton Mill, owned by Sir James Liege Hulett & Sons, to become one of the premier sugar manufacturers in South Africa. Meanwhile, presumably while they were still living in the vicinity of Durban, the Armstrong homestead was not too remote to prevent the younger boy from being sent off for formal education, an inevitable shock to the system as it had been for his father before him.

D'Urban was fortunate indeed to be enrolled at an excellent school, Hilton College, in the Pietermaritzburg area. Established in 1872, Hilton would become probably the best private school for boys in South Africa. He was sent there as a boarder, entering the preparatory school at the age of 8 in August 1905: he can be seen at the far left in the photograph below, listed by the school as taken in his first year, on a visit to the nearby spectacular rocky outcrop known as Pinnacles. This is clearly a robust boy who has led an active life. He completed the prep stage in 1908, whereupon he entered Pearce House.

By the turn of the century a railway line was well established from Durban which he could take at the start and finish of every term, stopping at Hilton Road for the village of Hilton. It was less than ten miles west of Pietermaritzburg but in the rainy season the route was virtually impassable except by rail; presumably the College would arrange transport between station and school for the younger boys and his trusted Zulu *umngane* would help with luggage and sports equipment. When he was older, and the family had moved to Empangeni, there was also a rail connection there.

Now, for the first time, D'Urban comes to life as an individual through the pages of his school reports and attainments. It emerges that he excelled at languages: in addition to English and Zulu he spoke Dutch/Afrikaans and French and was good at Latin. Hilton College closely paralleled the English style of public school and its educational courses were based on the Cambridge examination curriculum. In December 1910, aged 13, he came second in the scholarship examination and was made an honorary scholar of the school. He was appointed a school prefect in 1912, and from then onwards took an increasingly prominent part in the life of the College. Of other scholastic progress there is little detail revealed by his school reports, although he generally did well.

In terms of sporting achievements the picture is much more colourful. Hilton was the first Natal school to play rugby football, and in 1910 DVA was reported as 'conspicuous' as a forward in the Pearce rugby team. He is seen below at the right-hand end of the middle row.

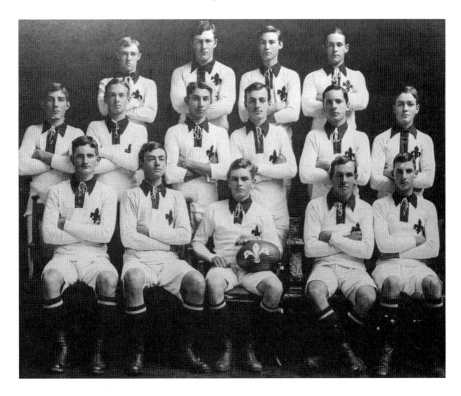

1912 heralded a landmark when he was made a prefect at the unusually early age of 14 years. In the group photograph of prefects below he is second from right in the back row, visibly junior to the others who are all some years older.

At cricket aged 14 he was a promising medium bowler, poor bat but good catch although inclined to be slow. This last may perhaps be explained by a spurt in growth: the report in the following year's rugby season (1913) says he weighed in at 11st 4lbs, a not inconsiderable size for a 15/16-year-old (his height at that age is unknown, but in wartime photographs he easily matches the height of his tallest companions). In rugby he was always prominent in the pack, 'a good kick but weak tackler: good in the line-out and uses his weight to advantage; played an excellent game throughout the season'. As vice-captain of rugby in 1914 (and captain of Pearce's XV) he weighed a couple of pounds less and had improved his tackling. In a fixture against local rivals Michaelhouse, 'the one noticeable feature of the Hilton game was the splendid kicking of Armstrong'. The overall verdict: 'An excellent kick and medium tackler, shows plenty of dash but is inclined to be rather rough' – a quality reflected in a friend's later recollection of 'the beloved Bruiser (D'Urban) Armstrong, about whom one could write reams'.

His cricket report for 1913 (age 15/16) is outstanding: 'Vice-Captain for the first half of the season, Captain for the second half. Best all-round man on the side. Good forcing bat with not enough patience. Very safe field.' He remained captain of the 1st XI in his final year at Hilton, taking five wickets with his bowling in three of their fixtures, but the College team had several disappointments: 'In the first half of the season Bazley and Armstrong were the only two who showed any true 1st XI form.' In the second half he was again singled out: 'Armstrong ... was most useful with bat and ball'. As well as remaining vice-captain of the XV in his last year he was also Head of Pearce House.

The Hilton No. 1 Defence Corps had been established from the school's very beginning, as had its military band. D'Urban was a sergeant, a bandsman

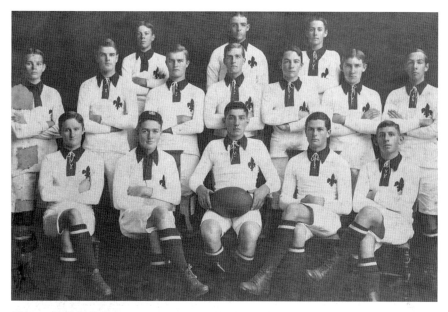

Hilton College Rugby 1st XV, 1914, with DVA at left of the Captain, both capped having received rugby honours

and member of the rifle shooting team. They regularly paraded in Queen Victoria's birthday reviews, and one of his contemporaries remembered him 'on a march from Pietermaritzburg Station to Mountain Rise down Church Street led by their enthusiastic drum and pipe band, in which Armstrong and Len Randles were the chief kettle-drummers'.

D'Urban left school having matriculated second class in December 1914, and by January 1915 had already registered in the Durban Military District for 'peace training' under the South Africa Defence Act of 1912, for which the cadet corps was designed to equip the boys. Among later personal reminiscences he was described as always a central figure: 'No name is written so widely across the records of our school. ... Bright and happy by nature, he was very popular amongst his companions. ... Few boys have left Hilton with a brighter promise of a great career.'[2]

Yet even before we leave his school-days we must take note of a significant if not life-changing event for D'Urban Armstrong which took place in late 1911. A Hilton Old Boy, Evelyn Frederick Driver, arrived in the Cape with a Blériot XI monoplane shipped from England where that August he had gained his Aviator's Certificate No. 110 at Hendon. He had formed a syndicate with English fellow-pilot Cecil Compton Paterson, who brought over his own Farman-based design of biplane. In earlier years a few tentative

Evelyn 'Bok' Driver with Blériot XI monoplane in 1911

demonstrations of flying had been seen in South Africa, but had tended to be fleeting and unimpressive. By contrast Driver and Paterson had arranged a three-month tour, witnessed by thousands, that took them from the Cape to Johannesburg to Kimberley, concentrating on public racecourse venues. Never before had the crowds seen flights so sustained and of such altitude, agility and élan. Reuters reported their exploits at Cape Town on 18 December:

> Following upon flights at heights sometimes reaching two thousand feet at Kenilworth yesterday, the two aviators, Driver and Paterson, made a considerable number of trial flights at Kenilworth to-day. Driver, in his monoplane, made a circular flight of some twenty miles at an elevation of about one thousand feet, whilst Paterson made eight or nine small ascents in his biplane of ten minutes each, and on one occasion took up his mechanic.

> This afternoon, about four o'clock, Driver in his monoplane made a somewhat sensational spiral flight rising to a height of over three thousand feet, coming over Adderley Street, where he attracted a deal of attention, and descending again at Kenilworth.

Towards the end of their fortnight in the Cape, Paterson set a South African record by staying in the air for thirty-five minutes and reaching a height of nearly 2,000 feet, only to crash his biplane the next day. 'Bok' Driver, a Natalian from Pietermaritzburg, had been one of the three-man 'first aerial post' team in England to fly a consignment of mail that September from Hendon to Windsor; he now proceeded to fly the first airmail in South Africa from Kenilworth to Muizenberg on 27 December 1911. Reuters reported again:

> The first South African aerial post was inaugurated this evening by Mr Driver, who in his monoplane started from Kenilworth for Muizenberg at 7.15 p.m., with one bag of mails. He covered the journey of five miles in seven and a half minutes. A large crowd awaited his arrival, when a number of congratulatory speeches were made. Mr Driver arrived back at Kenilworth at 8.10, taking twelve minutes on the return journey, during which he took a big sweep out to sea, rising to an altitude of over 2,500 feet.

This was sensational news for Hilton College, and several pages of press cuttings about the exploits of 'Flying Driver' were quoted with pride in the March 1912 issue of the College's journal, *The Hiltonian*. For the lads of the school it brought very close the thrilling revelation of successful conquest of the skies – and by one of their own! Such an astounding achievement could not fail to make a deep impression, and we may well conjure with the idea that the 14-year-old D'Urban Armstrong's head was filled with dreams of flight.

Athol Armstrong, Natal Mounted Rifles and 8th South African Horse

We have already met DVA's elder brother, Athol Langford Armstrong, who was born on 11 February 1885 in Jagersfontein, Orange Free State, while his father, George Shearer Armstrong, was occupied in the diamond industry. He would have been aged about seven on George's return to Natal, and is known to have attended Durban High School from age 9 to 12 (1894–1897), his later education being unrecorded. Important relationships were being forged at this time between the Armstrong family and that of the distinguished Natal Senator Sir Marshall Campbell, who also had sons at Durban High School and Hilton College. Thanks to marriage links, these two prominent families produced common descendants.

Initially enrolled, like his father, with the volunteer Natal Mounted Rifles (3rd Mounted Rifles), Athol commenced service in the military that would eventually span ten years. He first saw action aged 21 against the Zulu rebellion of 1906-7, the abortive uprising led by Chief Bambatha in opposition to the British imposition of a poll tax on the Zulu nation. He was a lieutenant with the Verulam Troop, the first NMR troop to be mobilized (on 15 April 1906) as mounted infantry attached to the Durban Light Infantry and later to the Umvoti Field Force.

We next find Athol reporting as a lieutenant with the NMR on 10 August 1914, again in the suppression of a rebellion, in the course of which he was wounded. This time it was the Maritz rebellion whose outbreak led to martial law being imposed in October 1914. It was a revolt by a section of the Boer population against the SA government's participation in the First World War on the British side, on the grounds that they had received German sympathy for the Afrikaner

cause in the Anglo-Boer hostilities. The opposite photograph outside his house, with Athol on the left (with cane) and D'Urban on the right, was probably taken around the time of his recuperation at the end of 1914.

On recovery from his injuries Athol volunteered once more and was transferred on 8 February 1915 to the reserve list which led to active service in East Africa from May 1916 as a member of the South African Overseas Expeditionary Force.

The Expeditionary Force had been raised in July 1915 to contribute to the British war effort, since South African legislation restricted its own Union Defence Force to operating in southern Africa; hence an entirely new force, made up of volunteers, had to be raised for service in other theatres of war. Athol was duly appointed temporary lieutenant in the 8th South African Horse (Mounted Rifles) with seniority from 1 November 1914, which may reflect the date of his break in service due to injury. (These wartime appointments were prefixed 'Temporary' for the duration of the war; this prefix will be generally omitted below.)

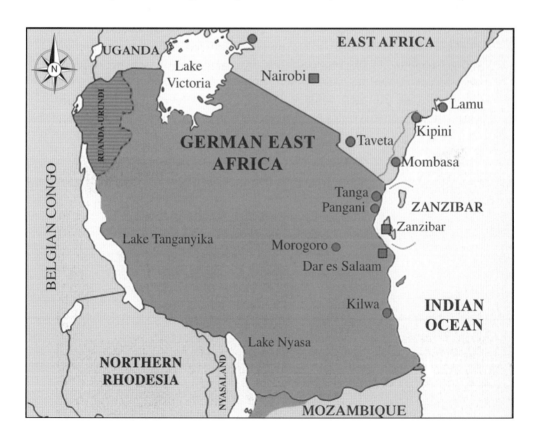

Athol probably had a wretched time of it, fighting in 1916 with the Expeditionary Force in the British campaign in tropical German East Africa (now Tanzania) where the terrain was hostile and horrific numbers of troops were being struck down by virulent disease. His unit disembarked from HMS *Professor* at Kilindini Harbour, Mombasa (Kenya), on 31 May and was involved in engagements in German East Africa that ran through to September and beyond. But Athol's active service was cut short by gunshot wounds sustained in August including one, listed as accidental, that severely injured his right hand. He was hospitalized but unable to be invalided out until 11 October.

Arriving in Durban on 27 October, he was given leave which allowed him to pick up the threads of home life with Edith. Initially it lasted to the end of the year, but then he had a further spell of recuperative leave extended to 26 April 1917, i.e. a period of six months in all, so it is likely that his injuries were exacerbated in some way, quite possibly by the fever that hospitalized so many of his comrades. He was recorded as 'relinquishing his temporary Imperial Commission on ceasing to be employed with effect from 26 April 1917', effectively retiring from service with the rank of lieutenant.

For a while, until April 1918, Athol resumed his interests in the family's sugar industry, but his injuries from the German East Africa campaign were so severe that he went over to England for treatment. Sadly, it was not successful. He died while undergoing an operation at a hospital in Marylebone, London, on 25 November 1918, aged 33. He was listed as 'died on service', as a result of injuries received. Athol was buried in England at St Denys' Church in Little Barford, Bedfordshire, the home of his elder sister, Betty Royds. The headstone was erected by his widow, Edith, with the inscription to his memory saying, simply, 'Brave to a fault'.

D'Urban Armstrong, Natal Mounted Rifles, South African Aviation Corps

In September 1914, immediately after the outbreak of war, D'Urban had signed up for voluntary service with the Natal Mounted Rifles like his brother and father before him – this was even before he left school at the end of the year, and while his elder brother was engaged in countering the Maritz rebellion in which he was wounded. The two are seen below (D'Urban on the right) with a steam plough on the family's sugar farm, probably while Athol was still recuperating.

On leaving school aged 17 D'Urban had anticipated serving with the Union Defence Force, which in September had invaded German South West Africa (now Namibia) at the request of the British government, the first time the UDF had been deployed operationally, and a deployment which occasioned the Maritz rebellion in which Athol had been wounded.

However, D'Urban was rejected on account of a lingering weakness in one knee, acquired from a rugby injury in his last season at Hilton. Nothing daunted, he then passed all tests for the Motor Transport Service but was again disappointed, being turned down as under-age. In fact this line of service would have suited him well, with an engineer for a father and a familiarity with the development and maintenance of machinery in the sugar industry; photographs also show the family had a motorcycle and at least one car. Such a background would later be put to good use in handling the intricacies of aeroplane engines and airframes, a skill which many leading pilots acknowledged they lacked. The Motor Transport Service performed signally in German South West Africa, and it is likely his name was marked down to join this sector on his 18th birthday, but by then the Union forces had already won a worthy victory and the campaign was over. Whichever the division he was eventually posted to, D'Urban underwent training and service between December 1914 and October 1915 at the rank of second lieutenant.

Meanwhile aviation had made a great impact in the German South West Africa campaign, being regarded by some as a decisive factor. Two years earlier the South African government had the foresight to recognize the significant role it could play in military operations. The Driver/Paterson syndicate having dissolved, Compton Paterson had opened a flying school at Kimberley and in September 1913 signed a contract to provide pilot training to military pupils. The government prudently declined responsibility for any personal injuries or accidents sustained during tuition, but hundreds applied and ten were chosen. From these, six were gazetted on 22 April 1914 as probationary lieutenants in the Active Citizen Force of the Union Defence Force. They were then sent over to England to gain military training with the Royal Flying Corps, the aviation arm of the British Army. Still in England when the Great War broke out in August 1914, their request to the South African authorities to volunteer for service with the RFC was granted and they joined some of the first British squadrons to be mobilized and sent to the Western Front in France.

Soon after this came the South African intervention in German South West Africa, and before the year was out it was decided their services were needed back in the African continent again. Until now they were still members of the UDF, but on 29 January 1915 the official formation of the South African Aviation Corps (SAAC) was gazetted, and the small cadre of men experienced in aerial warfare in France returned to face

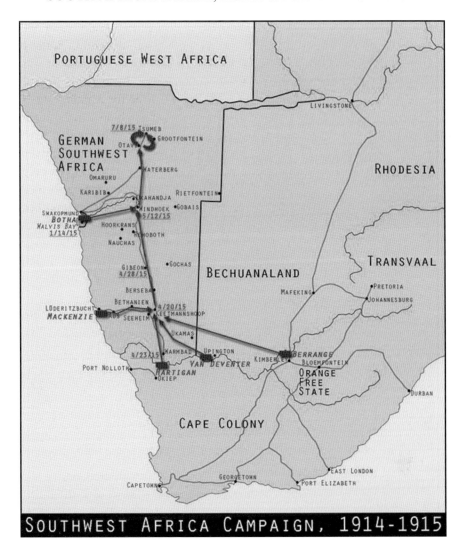

PORTUGUESE WEST AFRICA

GERMAN
SOUTHWEST
AFRICA

RHODESIA

TRANSVAAL

BECHUANALAND

ORANGE
FREE
STATE

CAPE COLONY

SOUTHWEST AFRICA CAMPAIGN, 1914-1915

the daunting prospect of organizing the embryonic SAAC to serve in African skies. Of the original six pioneer students, Kenneth van der Spuy became South Africa's first qualified military pilot and was among the small band tasked with procuring equipment and preparing machines for the arid, drought-ridden climate of German South West Africa. Their role being to provide aerial support for South African land forces, they were principally employed in aerial reconnoitring, including location of water sources. Van der Spuy made their first reconnaissance flight on 6 May 1915 around the Walvis Bay area, and would continue his

Insignia of the South African Aviation Corps (Zuidafrikaanse Vliegenierskorps)

career in aviation for several decades rising to the rank of major general. The tactical benefit derived from these airborne operations proved a revelation to General Louis Botha, Prime Minister and Commander-in-Chief of the Union's force in German South West Africa. After experiencing a reconnaissance flight for himself he declared, 'Now I can see for hundreds of miles'.

The SAAC's invaluable work in South West Africa ensured the South Africans constantly outmanoeuvred the Germans, who were forced to surrender on 9 July 1915. It was a victory greeted with great acclaim at home, and a success that proved the incalculable superiority of aerial support in roles traditionally performed by light horse and mounted infantry.

The 150 or so personnel of the SA Aviation Corps were now stood down, sent back to South Africa, and moved to a base in Cape Town. Frustrated by inactivity, most of the men volunteered for war service back in England with the Royal Flying Corps, among them Bok Driver. By this time the British government had concluded an agreement with the Dominions, as a matter of economy, that all their separate aerial units should be incorporated into the RFC. It was decided the SAAC would become the nucleus of a wholly South African RFC squadron, which the men set off to join in three detachments, embarking on 31 July, 18 September and 8 November. No. 26, which became known as the South African Squadron, was officially formed at the Netheravon aerodrome on Salisbury Plain, Wiltshire, on 8 October 1915. Although the SA Aviation Corps was not officially disbanded until 1921, for all practical purposes it ceased to exist independently on this date.

Badge of No 26 Army Co-operation
Squadron when incorporated into the
RAF. The motto in Afrikaans means
'A guard in the sky'.

By the time the squadron's pilots were combat ready, supported by a full complement of 209 personnel recruited and trained (a large number of supporting staff were drawn from advertisements in the South African press), it was now the end of 1915. But at this point fate stepped in and redirected their efforts. On Christmas Day, with snow falling, No. 26 Squadron embarked at Southampton for their new destination, which they reached on 31 January 1916: Mombasa, where they were needed against the common enemy in German East Africa. This was where Athol Armstrong was to serve with the 8th Mounted Horse from May to October that year. Springboks from No. 26 Squadron remained fighting there for the rest of the war.

At the same time as the trained and experienced airmen of the SAAC were forming up into No. 26 Squadron, D'Urban Armstrong was recorded on 23 October 1915 as a member of the SA Aviation Corps with the rank of second lieutenant. Any details of his service in South Africa seem to have disappeared without trace.

CHAPTER 2

ROYAL FLYING CORPS: EARLY DAYS

Soon after the German surrender in South West Africa, and with his 18th birthday approaching on 26 July 1915, young D'Urban Armstrong made his way to Cape Town to apply for transfer to aviation service overseas. Probably his impetus was knowing that, after their success in the South West Africa campaign, nearly all the men of the SAAC had immediately volunteered for the Royal Flying Corps that very month.

A faded retrospective note in the South African archives gives his rank on 23 October as probationary second lieutenant, South African Aviation Corps. Another record, this time dated 1915, states that on 26 October he was 'seconded to SA Squad RFC' with the SA Expeditionary Force in the rank of second lieutenant. His RFC transfer papers also describe him as a member of the SAAC. Beyond this, no prior record has been found and although Armstrong's RFC card correctly notes his service in SA with 'Sth African Natal Mounted Rifles', it also accords him the rank of second lieutenant with the non-existent 'Sth African Defence Corps', which must be an error for South African Aviation Corps. Whether he had already been introduced to flying is not known, but evidently he was as yet unqualified because he was not posted to No. 26 Squadron but was sent for flight training, on a list that totalled ten names.

When D'Urban Armstrong sailed for England he was probably among the third SAAC detachment, which sailed on 8 November aboard the RMS *Saxon* arriving at Plymouth on 28 November 1915. Departing from Cape Town, he was accompanied by his recently widowed sister, Betty Royds, and her two small children, Ted and Nat, whose father had shortly before been killed in a car accident at a tragically early age. The opportunity of travelling with D'Urban allowed the young widow the chance to get away from painful memories and to spend some time with family and friends in England. All his life Nat still remembered the perils of that sea journey and the constant fear of attack from enemy shipping. On arrival, the address given for Betty Royds as one of DVA's next-of-kin was 70 Lancaster Gate, West London.

Basic Training, November 1915 to February 1916

D'Urban's military flying career officially commenced on the day of his departure, 8 November, his commission in the South African military being paralleled in the RFC with the rank of second lieutenant, General List, Royal Flying Corps Special Reserve (PI 1869). On 16 December he was posted to No. 1 Reserve Aeroplane Squadron at South Farnborough. He was also given machine-gun training at the School of Musketry, Hythe, on the Kent south coast.

On Boxing Day, 26 December 1915, he was transferred to No. 9 Reserve Aeroplane Squadron in Norwich and commenced flying training three days later. At the formation of the RFC the Central Flying School had been established at Upavon, Wiltshire, but the Army significantly underestimated the military potential of aeroplanes and its preparations to train pilots were erratic to say the least. In general, recruits who had not already learnt to fly privately underwent *ab initio* training of a few weeks conducted by the Royal Aero Club to gain their licence, then continued training with the Corps to gain their RFC wings. On 27 July 1915 No. 9 Reserve Aeroplane Squadron[1] was formed at Mousehold Heath Aerodrome, Norwich, as part of the 6th Wing of the RFC.

Better known as a site of civil aviation between the wars, the aerodrome has now disappeared under the Heartsease Estate and is scarcely documented or remembered as it was in the First World War, when in October 1914 the War Office took over the Cavalry Drill Ground at Mousehold Heath, locally known as Four-Mile Square. There had been cavalry barracks on the west of the heath since 1791, later named Nelson Barracks after Norfolk's celebrated admiral. The adjacent Britannia Barracks, built for the Norfolk Regiment at the end of the nineteenth century, remain standing, but of the older Nelson Barracks there remains no recognizable trace. Most cavalry regiments of the British Army had been stationed there at some point, and one that returned several times was the 7th (Princess Royal's) Dragoon Guards, reflected in a small byway named Dragoon Street, still marked on maps. This was one of the tracks that led eastward from the site of Nelson Barracks to cross the heath to the old drill ground.

The aerodrome first became operational when set up for flying training squadrons in 1915, the first being No. 18 which arrived in August and left

King Edward VII visits Norwich, 1909: King's Own Norfolk Imperial Yeomanry, Cavalry Drill Ground, Mousehold Heath. [Image courtesy of Norfolk County Council Library and Information.]

for France in November. They were followed by No. 9, DVA's training squadron. Norwich manufacturers Boulton & Paul Ltd had already been commissioned by the War Office to build FE.2bs, the first of which was rolled out on the aerodrome in October 1915. The company later claimed credit for making Mousehold Heath an early flying centre by way of a wry story. Under their original contract they had been permitted only to construct aircraft, not to flight-test them at the heath which was on their doorstep. This was because the War Office's outdated maps indicated as available for use only a small section of the rented Drill Ground (which had duly been allocated to the RFC), owing to the presence on their maps of several smallholdings depicted around the area. Only when officials were induced to inspect the site had Boulton & Paul been able to prove to them that the smallholdings had long disappeared and the large acreage of ground was fully grassed, thereby persuading them it was perfect for aeronautic activities. From FE.2bs they moved to more advanced designs, and eventually produced 1,550 Sopwith F.1 Camels, more than any other manufacturer.

All flying on training aircraft at this time was weather-dependent, being ruled out if there was any kind of wind. 'They were wonderfully easy-going and happy-go-lucky days,' according to Captain W.M. (Willie) Fry MC, who learnt to fly with the RFC at about this time. 'The great thing was to do all flying in as still air as possible and if the wind-socks stood out at all from their masts it was a very keen instructor who carried on. As a result, most of the flying was done in the early morning or evening.'[2]

Initial dual instruction was given on the Maurice Farman Longhorn, an already outmoded pusher biplane design powered by a 70hp V-8 Renault engine. It had a large forward (canard) elevator, reminiscent of the Wright Flyer of 1903, carried between a pair of gigantic skids from which it derived its nickname. The mainplanes had a span of some 50 feet and on the lower mainplane rested the nacelle which carried two passengers in tandem, with a primitive system of dual control which allowed the trainee in the rear to have his feet on duplicate rudder pedals but required him to reach forward around his instructor's body to grab hold of extensions branching out either side of the control column.

It was liberally festooned with piano wire, tied and braced in every direction with turnbuckles for rigging and adjustment. The standing joke, told and re-told to every new trainee, was that one would know if a Longhorn was properly rigged by whether a canary could escape if released amid the forest of wires. But it was a forgiving aeroplane to learn on, well behaved and with no vices, and the air-cooled Renault was reliable and sweet-running. For a novice like Fry the Longhorn was a reassuringly predictable creature: she climbed at forty-five, flew level at sixty, and on landing 'settled down like a kite'. With the four-wheeled undercarriage and giant skids there was so much of the contraption underneath that the pilot was unlikely to be seriously hurt if he hit the ground in a crash.

After a few hours on Longhorns the trainee would graduate to the Maurice Farman Shorthorn, a more versatile machine which went through an upgrade from the 80hp to the 100hp version of the same Renault V-8. Instructor and student sat in tandem in a nacelle roughly the size and shape of a bathtub, a dual-control system providing both parties with their own sets of linked controls, with the pusher engine and airscrew clattering away behind them and no means of vocal communication. Known fondly as the Rumpty or Rumpety for the noise made by its twin pairs of bicycle-type wheels when taxiing, it had dispensed with the canard design and carried its elevator more conventionally at the rear. In the early war years the

Above: *Maurice Farman MF7 'Longhorn'.*

Below: *Maurice Farman MF11 'Shorthorn'.*

Shorthorn performed effectively enough to be employed for observation over the enemy on the Western Front – spotting artillery positions, anti-aircraft batteries and troop and transport movements – and for defensive patrols to deter German aircraft from crossing the lines; an observer sat in the forward seat, equipped with a Lewis gun (although with a seriously restricted field of fire). It was a little more difficult to fly than the Longhorn, though like its sister it was a faithful and safe conveyance, and it remained in use as a trainer for several years.

A Royal Aero Club Flying Certificate was still a requirement at this point in the air war, and Armstrong gained his ticket, No. 2461, on 12 February

1916, after successfully completing the required number of set tasks on a 'Maurice Farman Biplane' [Shorthorn] at the Military School, Norwich, Mousehold Heath Aerodrome, Norfolk. The record gave his nationality as British because, although his family had settled in South Africa and were well-established residents, the status of British subject was conferred by birth within the Crown's dominions, among which was the Union of South Africa at this time.

It will be noticed that he is still wearing regimental-style service dress uniform from his original unit, as used by early transferees into the RFC, but with RFC insignia – badges and buttons – and soon, in his case, wings. The introductory process would involve assessment during an operational flying tour, with the option of a permanent transfer for those who wished to make a career in aviation; if not, they could return to their parent regiment or corps. The RFC, being made up of its own core officers plus large numbers of attached officers from other regiments, was very pragmatic about continued use of pre-existing uniforms, and Armstrong was one of those who used the old and the new interchangeably.

22 and 45 Squadrons, February to May 1916

On 19 February 1916 D'Urban went to receive further training at Gosport, Hampshire, later the home of the famous Instructors' School. Here in the Instructional Squadron he transitioned to tractor biplanes, the 80hp rotary Gnome-powered Avro and the Royal Aircraft Factory-built BE.2c which

Early BE2c manufactured by the British Aircraft Factory. (70hp Renault)

employed the familiar air-cooled Renault V-8. The BE.2c trainers in use at Gosport since 1915 were the early models with the 70hp Renault: when the BE.2c went to war it lost its skids and gained more power. Stable and easy to fly from the pilot's point of view, it had genuinely effective ailerons, as opposed to the wing-warping retained in earlier BE models (BE signifying 'Blériot Experimental' tractor types). He would soon discover that it was actually capable of vertically banked turns! But it was far from ideal for the observer in the front whose task was reconnaissance and artillery range-finding, as he could see very little apart from the centre-section above and the wings below. Any photography had to be done by the pilot. And although the observer had a gun for defence, he was prevented from firing forward by the propeller while all other directions were impeded by struts, wires and tailplane.

Willie Fry also trained on (later version) BE.2cs and recalled them as follows:

> The BE.2c, although much criticized, chiefly on account of its indifferent performance, was delightful to fly. One sat half out of the cockpit, which was half way down the fuselage and

behind the centre section, quite exposed, with the observer in front under the centre section and the 90hp Royal Aircraft Factory [RAF 1a] air-cooled engine purring like a sewing machine if all was going well, with two vertical exhaust pipes, one for each cylinder block, smoking like chimneys over the top wings, and the machine, with its dihedral set wings, so stable that it almost flew itself.[3]

Although most ambitious young pilots hoped to take the war to the enemy flying armed fighter aircraft (known as scouts), at this date it was the two-seat observation aeroplane that the RFC relied on for its essential army support role, and indeed the BE.2c remained a stalwart in use for that task, together with ground-strafing and light bombing, for most of the war. D'Urban was well remembered during their time on BE.2cs by his fellow-student H.H. (Harold) Balfour, nephew of Prime Minister Arthur Balfour, who trained with him at Gosport. He recalled DVA as 'a very enterprising pupil who rivalled us all by being the first to loop a BE.2c, to our admiration'.[4] It later became something of an initiation rite to loop the more advanced types to which you graduated after gaining your ticket, but these were very early days for any kind of stunting.

Ever since its inception the aviation corps had been viewed in much the same role as the Army's light horse and mounted infantry (scouting, reconnoitring, range-finding, etc.), and it was also believed that to control an aeroplane involved skills not unlike controlling a horse. It is a well-known truism that the pilots of the RFC, certainly at the outset, were selected from the officer class and usually from a public-school background. Though it has become fashionable to disparage the public-school system and all its works, there is no denying its pupils in that era were there to learn hard lessons in discipline and the ethos of stiff-upper-lip self-mastery; there was also the opportunity to gain a sense of military conduct through cadet training. Clearly the Army was heavily reliant for its commissioned officers on lads with this early preparation. Most, as we see from the numbers who flocked to volunteer, were ardently patriotic and pitifully keen to serve, unknowingly, in a war that would soon descend into unimaginable carnage.

Those who could afford public-school places could also afford to own and ride horses, the standard means of transport and source of manly recreation such as hunting, breeding and racing; thus providing yet more skills indispensable to the Army's understanding of warfare as it had always

Our Dumb Friends League
(A SOCIETY FOR THE ENCOURAGEMENT OF KINDNESS TO ANIMALS)
PRESIDENT.
THE RIGHT HON. THE EARL OF LONSDALE.

BLUE CROSS FUND
TO HELP HORSES IN WAR TIME

PRESIDENT
LADY SMITH-DORRIEN.

CHAIRMAN
SIR ERNEST FLOWER.

I Have done my Bit!

A FRENCH HORSE, who has done his bit!
Won't YOU do YOURS by helping
his SICK and WOUNDED Comrades?

British, French, Italian and Belgian.

ARTHUR J. COKE, Secretary,
58, VICTORIA STREET, LONDON, S.W.

been fought. Many reasons prompted officers who had served their time on the Western Front to seek transfer to the RFC and among them, unsurprisingly, was the horrific slaughter of horses – animals that they had learnt to train and trust in earlier lives – that held companionable memories of leather and tack and hay and warm breath on a cold morning – and that were suffering terror and death on an industrial scale. A small charity, Our Dumb Friends League, tried to offer what care it could.[5]

If anyone personified the concept of horsemanship translated to airmanship it was young D'Urban Armstrong who had spent a lifetime with horses and, like his father and brother, had volunteered for the Natal Mounted Rifles. The many aspects of mounted infantry work in the bush included patrolling, reconnaissance, pursuit, hit-and-run and hand-to-hand skirmishing. In these varied circumstances special skills were demanded of their mounts, who were trained not merely to remain under control during action or immobile to escape detection; a horse also had to stand firm when required, for example if the rider needed to vault on to its back for a quick getaway. A time-honoured equitation manoeuvre was the command 'Stirrup!' to aid an unhorsed trooper in trouble by extending a leg for him to seize, clasp and be dragged to safety. The rider, his foot thrust hard forward in the stirrup, had to lean away vigorously to counter the weight of his comrade and trust his horse to brace against the sudden imbalanced load, while hoping to blazes his surcingle and girth would hold. It was a feat for which horse and rider had to train assiduously. Serving with Athol in 1906 was the gallant Captain Garnet Blamey, whose charger, Scott, had famously enabled just such a rescue: 'That we escaped unscathed,' Blamey declared, 'was entirely due to the extraordinary bond of mutual trust that Scott and I had in one another. I knew that he would respond instantly to any call I made upon his powers, and he trusted me to see him through.'[6] Experience of this kind of riding and training was invaluable to young D'Urban so that he already possessed the hands and instincts of a horseman. It was generally agreed that a gifted pilot could be recognized by his sensitive handling of controls and instinctive bodily response to the behaviour of his mount in any attitude and circumstance.

This belief still held when as late as September 1918 an article appeared in *The Lancet* attempting to summarize the innate qualities that made up a successful pilot.[7] It was based on a questionnaire which had been completed by young men in the flying service. Some of the conclusions were distinctly speculative, and *inter alia* the authors considered it 'very debatable' whether fighter pilots should possess (as the article put it) 'knowledge of mechanism and the whys and wherefores of flying'. This was reported in all seriousness by *Flight*, a magazine which for nine years had concerned itself with the development of aviation technology.[8] The *Lancet* article reported the authors' definite conviction that 'the less the fighting scout pilot knows about his machine from a mechanical point of view the better ... he must be prepared to throw the machine about and at times subject it to such strains that, did he realise how near he was to the breaking-point, his nerve would go very quickly.' However, they confessed that their survey (questionnaires had been returned by forty-seven pilots) did not yet provide them with 'a sufficient body of evidence in support of this statement'. By contrast, the survey revealed an undisputed conclusion that one of the most important characteristics of a successful aviator was 'hands' which the article described in terms of horsemanship: 'The horse-rider with good hands is able to sense the mentality of a horse by the feel of the reins and also to convey his desires accurately to his mount. ... In the same way the pilot with good hands senses unconsciously the various movements of the aeroplane and rectifies any unusual or abnormal evolutions almost before they occur.'

Not for nothing did the French borrow the word for equestrian stunt-riding – *voltige* – for aerobatic flying. The term had already been applied to experiments with aerobatic manoeuvres performed before the war by pioneer test pilots and exhibition teams, and in 1913 Blériot's test pilot Adolphe Pégoud had devised an especially adventurous series of flight tests involving loops, tail-slides and flying upside down. But this *voltige* consisted of experiments carefully prepared for, and performed in peacetime by men with finely honed skills. It was a different matter for a novice RFC pilot in an unsuitable aircraft with a mere handful of flying hours, and we can only echo Balfour's admiration of Armstrong's early confidence in the air.

The greatest peril in such evolutions was to fall into a spin, usually with fatal results. Although the naval pilot Lieutenant Wilfred Parke had gained fame by recovering from an inadvertent spin in 1912, for which his recovery method was recorded in *Flight* magazine (see image below), it was not an action that any early pilot wanted to practise on purpose, especially as airframes and engines were widely (and weirdly) varied. Not until mid-1914, disregarding dire warnings, did the brilliant Sopwith test pilot Harry Hawker *deliberately* experiment with spinning in a Tabloid and thereby learnt how to recover reliably.

Unfortunately this went unrecorded. Despite reporting 'Parke's Dive', the accidental spin of 1912, *Flight* magazine failed to record the reliable recovery technique scientifically tested by Hawker in 1914. Nor did the Sopwith factory itself. Consequently the spin remained widely feared; and for a long time, even after pilots in combat had devised for themselves a repertoire of dogfight manoeuvres which included the spinning escape, it was still considered so perilous that it was prohibited by Whitehall.[9]

No. 22 Squadron was forming up at Gosport while Armstrong was progressing to complete his next, more advanced stage of training. The aircraft

AUGUST 31, 1912.

FLIGHT

PARKE'S DIVE.

Salisbury Plain, Sunday, August 25th.

HERE is the true story of one of the worst experiences in mid-air from which any pilot has extricated his machine in absolute safety, and as the circumstances precisely represent the hypothesis of the most debated problem among pilots at the present time, the following particulars should be studied with the closest attention by all.

At four minutes past six this morning Lieut. Parke, R.N., accompanied by Lieut. Le Breton, R.F.C., as observers, started on the Avro biplane (60-h.p. Green engine) from Salisbury Plain for the three hours' qualifying flight in the Military Trials. At ten minutes past nine, having more than completed the required duration, he was returning from the direction of Upavon for the express purpose of alighting in front of the sheds.

The direction of flight was practically towards the south; the wind was blowing approximately from the south-west, with a tendency to back southwards. He was, therefore, flying virtually up wind. The speed of the wind was estimated about 10–15 m.p.h. by the pilot, and the maximum air speed of the machine with the present propeller is about 60 m.p.h., as tested over the measured distance yesterday. The engine was pulling well, and the machine in perfect trim. There was bright sunshine and some clouds.

Throughout the flight an altitude of between 600 and 700 ft. was maintained, and the pilot, observing that he was still at this height, decided that he had sufficient room for a spiral glide. At the point A, in the diagram, he closed the throttle without switching off (which kept the engine just turning) and immediately proceeded to glide round down wind. At the point B, having completed a half spiral, Parke thought the machine was in an unnecessarily steep attitude, and was insufficiently banked for the turn he was making. He therefore elevated, and believes that he may also have given a momentary touch to the warp, which two operations were for the purpose of reducing the steepness of the descent and increasing the bank respectively.

The machine at once started a spiral nose-dive.

At the point C, he drew the elevator lever hard back against his chest and put the rudder hard over to the left with his foot so as to turn the machine inwards, this latter being the principle of action that is accepted as proper in cases of incipient side-slip, and, therefore, naturally to be tried in an emergency such as this. The warp was normal, i.e., balanced with the control wheel neutral. These operations failed utterly to improve the conditions.

From C to D the machine was completely out of control, diving headlong at such a steep angle that all spectators described it as vertical and stood, horror stricken, waiting for the end. According to Parke, the angle was very steep, but certainly not vertical; he noticed no particular strain on his legs, with which he still kept the rudder about half over to the left (about as much as is ordinarily used for a turn), nor on his chest, across which he was strapped by a wide belt to his seat. His right hand he had already removed from the control wheel in order to steady himself by grasping the body strut forming an upright between the windows of the enclosed body. This he did, not for support against the steepness of the descent, but because he felt himself being thrown outwards by the spiral motion of the machine, which he describes as "violent." The absence of pressure on the legs and arms appears to me, however, to be evidence that the machine was falling as fast as the pilot, who was, therefore, unstable on his seat, and without a fulcrum until he fastened himself to the framework by the *prop* of his hand.

It was his recognition, through this forcible effect, of the predominating influence of the spiral motion, as distinct from the dive, that caused him to ease off the rudder and finally push it *hard over to the right* (i.e., to turn the machine outwards from the circle), as a last resource, when *about 50 feet from the ground.*

Instantly, but without any jerkiness, the machine straightened and flattened out—came at once under control and, without sinking appreciably, flew off in perfect attitude. Parke made a circuit of the sheds in order to get into position for landing in a good place up wind, and proceeded to alight in the usual way without the least mishap. Thus did he and his observer, who, having no belt and rather cramped accommodation, was thrown up against the front wall of the cabin, escape at the last moment from what looked like certain death and effect a perfect landing with the machine none the worse for its severe straining save for a slight stretching of some of the lift-wires under the main planes.

Like the majority, I was at breakfast when the dive occurred; for, having watched the Avro during the earlier part of its flight and up to the end of its second hour, its uniform behaviour inspired a confidence that one was not loathe to translate into an excuse for leave. Very soon afterwards, however, I saw Lieut. Parke on the field, and, together with G. de Havilland and F. Short, of the R.A.F., adjourned to the competitors' mess, where we held an informal, but extremely close, enquiry into the whole affair. It was so obvious to all that the problems of the accident were so near to having to be discussed under the shadow of the pilot's absence, that the opportunity of recording on the spot the essential facts and impressions as be understood them was not only unique, but of the utmost consequence to aviation. His own anxiety to facilitate this work for the benefit of others, and the fact that he retained his presence of mind from first to last in the emergency—although admittedly terribly alarmed—so that he was conscious of each operation and the effect produced serves to give to the aviation world at least one definite experience of an extreme character for its guidance.

The seriousness of the situation there is no denying. Parke himself stared death in the face; most of the spectators sickened for the crash, and among them were those who were also furious in the belief that he had attempted a "stunt" and failed. There was some reason for this belief, because the machine behaved throughout in a perfectly smooth, normal manner, despite its extremely exaggerated attitude, and when it flattened out so nicely at the last moment even those who had been convinced they were witnessing an accident were left in doubt, whether, after all, it had not been intentional.

If disaster had followed, all manner of "explanations" would have been forthcoming, and, among them, de Havilland would have given it as his opinion that the control had become jammed, having regard to the fact that there was no excuse otherwise for a pilot of such experience to get himself into that position. With this latter observation Parke himself heartily agrees; but it happened all the same. He was not tired after his flight, but he was keenly pleased at its successful termination after all the previous misfortunes that the Avro firm had borne in such good spirit, and had in mind merely the finishing of the flight safely, but in good style.

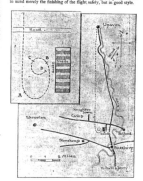

"Flight" Copyright.

Key map illustrating the flight of the Avro biplane which terminated in the spiral dive. Inset on a larger scale is a lettered diagram of the dive to which reference is made in the text.

787

32

were types such as Martinsyde Scouts, Bristol Scouts, Blériots and Moranes. Gosport acted as the forming-up base of many squadrons, and evidently DVA was to be deployed to No. 22 which had been assigned to the newly available Fort Rowner accommodation block. The station often continued to be referred to as Fort Grange and Fort Rowner: these had been the combined homes of the Royal Garrison Artillery before the Army base and drill ground became an RFC station and aerodrome. But flying was not all: he also had to undergo lectures and practical work in signalling including Morse code, in musketry, in squad drill, Lewis-gun instruction, engine instruction, map reading, reconnaissance, and all the other duties necessary to render him a useful member of his unit in the field.

Having completed a cross-country flight and passed an oral examination, he now became a fully-fledged RFC pilot sporting his first set of wings. In the portrait at Plate 2 these are displayed on the unique Army flying service uniform jacket known in cheery RFC slang as the maternity jacket. Although his log-book contained only thirteen hours solo, DVA had already shown himself a more than competent pilot and was scheduled to be sent for service in France with No. 22 Squadron upon its departure on 20 March 1916.

The machines allocated to this squadron were FE.2bs, another type on which he needed to familiarize himself. There is, alas, little positive to say about this Royal Aircraft Factory effort. It was an attempt at a fighter aircraft which resurrected the pusher design (FE signified 'Farman Experimental') owing to its one virtue, an unobstructed 180-degree field of fire for the gunner in front. Heavily armed and armoured, it was designed for large-scale wartime production with the purpose of such work as escorting unarmed reconnaissance patrols. However, the armour added weight to the drag already inherent in the pusher aircraft, and the machine-gun operator was highly exposed in the front seat, initially without even a seat belt. In later versions a second Lewis gun was added to compensate for the complete lack of rear defence, angled back over the top wing, ostensibly for the pilot to manipulate while holding the stick between his knees. (A front view of the FE.2d version can be seen on page 127.) The gunner could also fire this gun but only if he climbed up to stand precariously, at the mercy of anything that might throw him off balance. Some survived only by the quick thinking of their pilots who were able to catch their clothing and yank them back. The Fee was big, ungainly, and, by 1916, already outpaced by the more powerful German machines ranged against it. Its heroic crews achieved miracles in the face of such odds.

The impetus behind producing purely offensive fighter aeroplanes had been the introduction in 1915 of synchronization gear, developed to deadly effect by the Imperial German Flying Corps, a mechanism that permitted the bullets of forward-firing machine guns to pass unobstructed through the propeller arc. Thus the dedicated fighter became an inevitable final stage in a sequence which had begun with the use of warplanes as essential eyes in the sky, unprotected apart from the never-quite-satisfactory arming of observers, after which the next development had been armed escorts sent up as protection. With anti-aircraft batteries expending huge effort skyward for little result, in the end both sides had to strive for superior aerial firepower, developing better ways of harrying and attacking their opponents while airborne.

The era of the solo fighting scout, with the pilot using his machine as a flying gun-platform, was inaugurated in the summer of 1915 when aircraft designer Anthony Fokker is credited with the first successful installation of synchronization gear for the German *Fliegertruppe* in his Eindecker monoplane. Experiments with synchronization systems for firing bullets through the propeller had already been under way in Britain and Germany as well as in France, where the renowned French pioneer Roland Garros had been carrying out tests with a design patented by aircraft manufacturer Raymond Saulnier. Impatient with the lack of progress, Garros fitted an alternative arrangement to his Morane-Saulnier Type L (Parasol) in April 1915 whereby his machine gun fired forward through a propeller that was protected by angled armour plates fitted to deflect bullets at the point where they would meet the blades. His succession of victories created a short-lived sensation, earning him the title *as* (ace) from the French press. This was noted with alarm by the Germans until Garros was forced down and his aircraft captured, whereupon the urgent order went out to produce an improved version for the fatherland. Fokker developed his more efficient system by synchronizing the belt-fed German lMG 08 machine gun with the rotation of the propeller, making it possible for the hammer to strike only when there was no blade in the way. Thus resulted the 'Fokker Scourge' in which the Germans began to appear invincible – at least, as the Air Ministry fondly hoped, until outmatched by new British designs. Now there was a growing emphasis on sheer fighting aircraft in which the FE.2b, welcomed at first, was soon outclassed.

FE2b: on right is rear view of power plant.

Doubtless the newly-qualified Armstrong was as keen as any young man to get to the action as soon as possible, but fate intervened in the person of Captain J.G. (Jacob) Swart MC, a 22 Squadron flight commander. As noted in DVA's photo album (in which the above FE.2bs appear), 'I very nearly went out to France on these things early in 1916 but Capt Swart – a South African from Jo'burg – told me I hadn't sufficient experience and got me off'.

While based at Gosport, No. 22 Squadron had become the parent squadron from which a nucleus of pilots was drawn to form No. 45 Squadron. On 19 March, the day before 22 Squadron's departure, he was transferred to 45 Squadron which, to his pleasure, was starting to be worked up with scouts, Martinsydes and Bristols. This meant he continued at Gosport for some weeks while 45 Squadron waited endlessly to be deployed to France – but this was delayed until October when it was eventually sent out on Sopwith 1½-Strutters. Rather than being left to kick his heels, Armstrong was meanwhile transferred to another Gosport unit, No. 1 Reserve Squadron, based on the other side of the airfield at Fort Grange. Commanded by Captain Charles Gordon Bell, famed holder of RAeC ticket No. 100, this newly created squadron was to carry out systematic training on the full gamut of aircraft available at the station ranging from preliminary to advanced, all of which Armstrong was well acquainted with. The instructors were comprised of some pre-war RFC pilots and some returned from active service at the Front.

Having built up experience on the trickier scout machines, Armstrong was singled out for his piloting abilities and soon became gainfully employed assisting in the process of passing on skills to novice pilots who had fewer hours than himself. Such activities, training and encouraging others, would form a repeated pattern throughout his flying career. He certainly spent a great deal of time in the air around this time, in April/May 1916, and by his next posting he had perfected his skills while increasing his thirteen hours to ninety.

Pictured in his album from this period are several disastrous landings by friends, including one of Captain D.B. (David) Gray having landed a Martinsyde in the moat at Fort Rowner. A few Bristol Scouts are also photographed, including A4687 (80hp Gnome), 'Smith Barry's pet Bristol fitted with oxygen outfit', having been turned on its back by Second Lieutenant E.V. Smith. The officer who had modified this pet Bristol was the enterprising Captain R.R. (Robert) Smith Barry,[10] one of the instructors at Gosport, who was doubtless not best pleased. A very experienced pilot, he had been instructing there and at Netheravon after recovering from leg injuries in a crash in 1914 at the Front with No. 5 Squadron. Second Lieutenant Smith also appears with Armstrong and others in the following dozy group 'after a heavy lunch' relaxing in the Fort Rowner moat.

(Left to Right): Ashcroft, Smith, Holmes and DVA.

Armstrong's only photographically recorded mishap is a forced landing at Brooklands in what he describes as a 'clipt-wing Morane' on a flight from Hendon to Gosport in March 1916, of which the image is sadly indistinct; it has, however, been recaptured in the artist's impression below. It is recognizably a shoulder-wing Morane-Saulnier bearing RFC markings, and investigations into the pedigree of this machine have suggested that it was a Type H, serial 5705, one of a batch ordered on 25 March from the Grahame-White factory at Hendon. The wingspan of this H type was 9.12 metres instead of the 9.63 metres of the previous Type G, a reduction of about 20 inches, which seems to account for the reference to clipped wings. The serial marking is difficult to make out, but only two of the batch had numerals resembling those visible, and 5705 is the only one that fits the time frame, i.e. a ferry flight in late March ending in a forced landing, with the machine eventually delivered to Gosport on 10 April after the handful of days necessary to fix the problem. The destination of this machine ferried by Armstrong was to be No. 1 Reserve Squadron, so it is logical to assume that he had been transferred to this unit by late March.

In the course of these investigations the intriguing possibility arose, but was soon dismissed, that the machine ferried by DVA might have been a very interesting Morane once owned by the renowned exhibition and racing aviator Gustav Hamel. Impressed into the RFC from Hungerford at the outbreak of war, it was allocated the number 482 and given roundels on its wings. This was a modified Type G, on which the cabane had been increased in height for Hamel's daring displays of inverted flying. By the time it was impressed it had passed into the hands of a Mr Etches, who had retained Hamel's tall cabane,

The photograph of DVA's forced landing with Morane 5705 at Brooklands is here reconstructed by artist Leighton Alcock.

although we may safely assume this was restored to normal height by the time it was assigned to the Central Flying School (Upavon) in August 1914. After various moves to 7 Squadron, 1 Squadron and 12 Squadron, it too was later used by No. 1 Reserve Squadron at Gosport (from which No. 60 Squadron was formed), as recorded by various authorities including Jack Bruce, who states that 'as late as May 1916 it was lent to 60 Squadron shortly before that celebrated unit went to France'.[11] So although he didn't ferry Hamel's Morane, it is one that Armstrong would have flown in training. Harold Balfour, who like Armstrong was at Gosport being readied for No. 60 Squadron at this time, remembers this very machine in his memoir *An Airman Marches*: 'We were put on to Grahame-White Moranes,' he writes. 'Those which we had were the same as used for exhibition flights at Hendon before the War by Hamel and Hucks, in fact we had one of Hamel's old machines in the Squadron.'[12]

These nimble Moranes were the forerunner of the Type N Bullet on which Balfour and Armstrong would shortly find themselves at the Front in their first posting to France with the RFC. 'These were fairly tricky and difficult to pilot,' Balfour continued, 'but until he has flown an underpowered middle-wing monoplane such as these or a Blériot, no pilot has tasted the real sensation of flight ... tossed about the air like a leaf in the wind, with the white wings outstretched on either side, man comes nearest to feeling like a bird on the wing.'

Gustav Hamel's 80hp Morane-Saulnier Type G (later RFC serial 482) pictured at Cambridge in 1914: Hamel's exhibitions with this machine included inverted flight and loops, for which one of the most conspicuous alterations was that to the bracing pylons (cabanes) which were made taller to increase the angle of the bracing cables to the upper wing surfaces, thereby reducing the tension in the cables which enabled them to meet higher loads [Philip Jarrett].[13]

These must have ranked among the most carefree times of D'Urban Armstrong's teenaged years, when he was gaining a sense of that freedom of spirit to be found in the limitless ocean of the unconquered air. To mount up high through the uninviting grey layer that obscured all above from mortals below, until you burst through into dazzling sunshine, your wheels almost touching a vast white plateau that stretched in all directions. Or to play among the cloudbanks, perhaps in a tail-chase in and out of the mountainous peaks and summits that appeared so real yet became instantly formless should you venture inside their crags. And here you felt at home, privileged to inhabit a world that welcomed and embraced you as a lone winged visitor, enthralled by the contemplation of such immensity.

Being sent to the Front with only a dozen hours solo was not such an unusual occurrence, especially for a pilot who showed early promise. Cecil Lewis, who was to become a well-known writer and broadcaster, had joined the RFC straight from school and learnt on Shorthorns along with DVA. Lewis was with him at Gosport in No. 22 Squadron at the age of 17 and actually did find himself sent to France in March 1916 with just thirteen hours. His inexperience left him hopelessly ill-equipped, but fortunately for Lewis he was held back from the Front for some weeks, otherwise his brief flying career would probably have been cut short soon after it started. With the certainty of youth he was convinced he would come through it all, but the time was soon approaching when the average length of a novice pilot's life at the Front could be measured in weeks.

By the time of the battle of the Somme, which began in June, there was such a heavy toll of pilots bearing the brunt of the onslaught that replacements were being rushed out from England no matter what their state of preparation. Overstretched already, there was insufficient time or opportunity for the front-line squadron commanders to train them, and in the main they were left to fend for themselves as best they could. As the experienced pilots lost their comrades one by one, they took their pick of the better performing aeroplanes for themselves and left the unreliable, battle-worn machines for the newcomers. No deliberate callousness was intended, but there was always a degree of bitterness at the loss of fine fighting men and a feeling almost of resentment towards these callow, untrained youngsters whom War Office policy demanded to be sent as replacements for irreplaceable companions in arms.

Training for the newcomers often consisted of placing them at tail-end positions and instructing them not to stray, though simply keeping up with the rest was difficult enough when your machine was the runt of the pack. Most novice pilots also reported that in their early days they never caught sight of a single enemy aircraft, not even during engagements when shots were fired. As tail-enders they were liable to be known as 'rabbit pie', and it was reckoned that if a new pilot was not lost during his first few weeks at the Front he might by then have enough experience to survive an entire tour of duty. The enemy were aware of this, of course, and knew where the easy pickings lay. Later in the war, when the fashion for celebrating aces who racked up large numbers of victories reached its height, it was said that groups like that of Manfred Freiherr von Richthofen (ultimately credited with eighty victories) would isolate tail-enders and line them up to increase the tally for the famed Rittmeister, dubbed the 'Red Baron' in later years.

Cecil Lewis was lucky: on arrival in France he was kept back at No. 1 Aircraft Depot, St Omer, which was (until the end of March) the headquarters of the General Officer Commanding the RFC, Major General Sir Hugh 'Boom' Trenchard. St Omer was the main centre for aircraft testing and supply, where the ferry pilots were stationed. The role of test and ferry pilot was later to be one of Armstrong's jobs, working between St Omer and Farnborough for the first half of 1917, but this was not until after he had spent an arduous seven months at the Front with 60 Squadron.

Lewis's spell at St Omer did not last long, but he managed to gain a dozen more hours and a great deal more confidence, being encouraged to get into the air as much as possible. Whilst there he was introduced to two of the infamous rotary-engined Morane-Saulnier family of aircraft which were regarded by many, including himself, as among the most difficult of all

Morane Parasol high-wing monoplane training machine at Gosport.

the machines being flown at that time. He still had only twenty hours when at last his posting came to an active squadron – but not on the single-seater scouts he longed to fly. Instead he was sent to No. 9 Squadron flying BE.2cs. His flight commander, scandalized at his lack of experience, insisted that he take his machine up and fly it all day, map-reading and getting the lie of the land. Familiarization with the locality was standard practice for recent arrivals, but not all newcomers were afforded Lewis's ten hours of vital preparation, especially once the Somme offensive was under way.

Cecil Lewis's career in many ways paralleled that of D.V. Armstrong. Not always at the same time or in the same squadron, but Lewis and Armstrong served out their war as contemporaries in a sequence that involved them in similar duties at similar periods, initially even on similar machines. After training together, both men would go on to spend the latter half of 1916 at the Front on Morane-Saulnier monoplanes, going right through the Somme offensive – Armstrong with No. 60 Squadron, Lewis with No. 3 Squadron – followed by a period on testing and ferrying duties. In 1917 for a short time they were on active service together in No. 44 Squadron on Home Defence, flying Sopwith Camels, Lewis joining a little after Armstrong who was in at its formation. Both were outstanding pilots and seasoned fighters by then; and both were to end their war as exponents of the newly devised art of night-fighting.

Of DVA's own reminiscences we have only the very few notes that appear in the photograph album he kept; his war is reflected mainly in

Morane instructional Bullet monoplane (unarmed) used by 60 Squadron in France; the original 80hp Le Rhône 9C engine of Type N was later replaced by the 110hp 9J in Types I and V.

pictures which are reproduced throughout this book. With no first-hand memoirs to account for Armstrong's experiences we must rely on others to describe in their words the realities of wartime flying in those early days: the joys mingled with sorrows, the companionship mixed with loss, the moments of elation and seemingly endless spells of sheer dread, when even before facing the enemy you had to win victories over yourself. Certainly none apart from those who were there could speak of it with utter truth and poignancy, of a life that took one from youth to manhood in the space of a few short months. Cecil Lewis is just one of those from a century ago whose voices we shall hear, along with Oliver Stewart, Harold Balfour, Willie Fry, Clayton Knight, and many others who admired and served with our young adventurer as he made his way from apprenticeship to mastery of the dangerous skies over France.

Before all this, however, we must return to Gosport in the spring of 1916 when D'Urban Armstrong was readying himself for the British Expeditionary Force, having accumulated a respectable ninety hours in his log-book. Mounting expectations were met at long last by the news that he was destined for the Western Front in a new scout squadron, No. 60, formed of a nucleus flight from No. 1 Reserve Squadron as its parent unit, whose personnel were being gathered during April incorporating some of the finest pilots in the Corps. It was a sign of his proficiency that he was assigned to a flight operating the most challenging fighter of its day, the single-seat Morane-Saulnier Type N Bullet, in the only RFC squadron ever designated to have flights equipped with this machine. But Britain's General Trenchard, commander of the RFC in the field, had great misgivings about the design which Trenchard's assistant Maurice Baring described in his memoirs:[14]

> The General had ordered a squadron of these machines against his better judgement because the pilots had implored him to. He proved right and they proved wrong, because although the machine was a beautifully fast flying instrument, it suffered from the defect of all monoplanes: you could not see out of it except by banking, and a pilot cannot be banking the whole time. This machine proved to be the most expensive in pilots and cost us more in casualties than any other during the war. The squadron which had these machines was the only squadron which had to be taken out of the line for a prolonged period.

CHAPTER 3

60 SQUADRON, THE BATTLE OF THE SOMME

No. 60 Squadron, which earned itself an immortal reputation during the battle of the Somme, went on to become one of the foremost fighter squadrons on the Western Front by the end of the war. It was officially formed on 1 May 1916 when Major F.F. 'Ferdy' Waldron took command; he was a first-class pilot and ex-instructor with plenty of combat experience. Within less than a month the unit was sent across to France to prepare for the Somme offensive, and among its subalterns was one D.V. Armstrong with the rank of second lieutenant, General List (Flying Officer), effective from 15 May.

The Somme offensive, a joint French and British attack in the summer of 1916, had long been planned in the region of the river Somme, with the British expecting to achieve a rapid advance on the ground. However, they found themselves forced to relieve the pressure suffered by the French whose troops had been drained by four months of German onslaught at Verdun, for which reason the start of the offensive was brought forward from its planned date of August. But weapons, ammunition and equipment were inadequate to the combined task. A week-long preliminary artillery bombardment beginning on 24 June was intended to destroy the enemy's barbed-wire defences, but failed in this objective while alerting the Germans to the impending infantry attack which duly followed on Saturday 1 July. The enemy was not over-run as hoped, and on this day alone the British Army lost over 19,000 killed. The ensuing twenty weeks of the battle of the Somme became a byword for futility: a deadlocked and attritional battle of a million casualties.

For the first time in the history of warfare a deliberate air campaign was planned and executed to support ground operations. The strategy was to precede the battle with an aerial offensive, and for this a build-up of air power was needed. By the opening battle the RFC had twenty-seven squadrons with 421 aircraft plus a further 216 in depots. Each squadron comprised an A Flight,

B Flight and C Flight, each of four pilots, i.e. twelve pilots to a squadron not counting reserves. The various squadrons were equipped with a mixture of aircraft types and tasked with a variety of duties including reconnaissance, escort missions, balloon strafing and offensive patrols. But once the battle had commenced and become virtually immobile, the predominant business of the mainly young and inexperienced personnel of the British Army's flying service was twofold: to gain information about enemy dispositions behind the German lines by means of aerial observation, and to correct the fire of the artillery pieces in what was now a war of static lines.

To prevent hindrance by the enemy of this vital work the policy of General Trenchard, commander of the RFC in France, was to dominate the airspace by means of a constant offensive over German lines. This often inflexible policy resulted in heavy RFC casualties and is remembered for its watchword of 'no empty chairs', insisting that replacements must be sent out to the front-line squadrons no matter how insufficiently trained. But this insistence on control of the air, if not welcomed, was well understood by the men, and was also broadly successful in the context of the Somme. Senior commanders in the field had developed a firm appreciation of the RFC's Army cooperation activities and placed great reliance on them. It was now entirely accepted that the integration of air power was destined to play a vital part in winning battles.

Since No. 60 Squadron was destined to be equipped with aeroplanes manufactured in France by the Morane-Saulnier factory, most of its members crossed the Channel by sea instead of flying over. Armstrong's

album contains a few photographs taken aboard the HMT *Archimedes* (see image) commanded by Captain F.L.H.C. (Frederick) Clark, which landed on 26 May. The squadron's first flight commanders were all old Etonians: Captain Robert Smith Barry, A Flight, had done his first tour in France in 1914 and been rendered lame by his wounds; Captain A.S.M. (Alfred) Summers, B Flight, had transferred from the 19th (Queen Alexandra's Own Royal) Hussars as recently as December 1915 and accompanied DVA from No. 1 Reserve Squadron; and Captain H.C. 'Jimmy' Tower, C Flight, had been an instructor attached to the same reserve squadron, having lately returned from six months at the Front.

The above group from DVA's album is again on board the *Archimedes*, with CO Ferdy Waldron second from left. Robert Smith Barry (later lieutenant colonel) is on the far right, and next to him is Lieutenant N.A. (Norman) Browning-Paterson (later captain),[1] with Alfred Summers on the far left. The latter three would all die within months.

During a fortnight's training and familiarization at Boisdinghem, located between St Omer and Ypres, they were issued with some Morane Parasols for training purposes, but these were relinquished when the squadron moved south on 16 June to operate out of Le Vert Galant aerodrome – sometimes erroneously spelt 'Galand' – about twelve miles north of Amiens on the road to Doullens (see map page 52).

Also in DVA's album are fellow 60 Squadron pilots Lieutenant A.D. (Duncan) Bell-Irving, a Scots-Canadian who had transferred from the 3rd Battalion Gordon Highlanders and went on to enjoy a distinguished flying

A and C Flights of No 60 Squadron, Le Vert Galant.

Biplanes of B Flight, 60 Squadron, Le Vert Galant.

career (image left on page 46, having his propeller swung), and Lieutenant J.H. (John) Simpson of 5th Canadian Infantry Battalion (image right).

Other early pilots with DVA in the squadron included Harold Balfour, his co-pupil from Gosport, as well as Captain David Gray, Lieutenants C.F.A. 'Peter' Portal and L.E. (Lewis) Whitehead, and Second Lieutenants J.M. (John) Drysdale, C.A. (Claude) Ridley and G.D.F. (George) Keddie. Some of these, like George Keddie, appear in DVA's photograph album.

Above: *George Keddie's Morane Parasol after one of his numerous 'efforts' in RFC terminology.*

Right: *(L-R) L.L. (Lionel) Clark, J. (John) Laurie Reid, Captain Clark of the HMT* Archimedes, *Walter Bryant, H. (Herbert) Harris and observer H.J. (Henry) Newton.*

Others include W.E.G. (Walter) Bryant, seen in a group with the ship's captain during the Channel crossing, who joined the squadron as a second lieutenant observer and recording officer and eventually rose to the rank of air commodore.

Unfortunately the supply of aircraft failed to match the rapid build-up of the aerial fighter offensive for the Somme. The Morane Parasols issued for training purposes were soon returned to St Omer. DVA was a member of C Flight which, like A Flight, eventually settled down with Morane Bullets, and B Flight ended up equipped with the two-seater Morane Biplane together with a contingent of observers.

Familiarization with the new machines was essential for air and ground crews alike, and for pilots it meant practising skills like team flying and signalling. During machine-gun practice a number of snags had to be ironed out. The Moranes still employed deflector plates on the propellers, the pre-synchronization gear system that permitted firing through the propeller arc on the assumption that only some 4 per cent of bullets would be likely to come in contact with a blade. To prevent the lamentable eventuality of shooting off one's own propeller, steel deflectors were fitted to that part of the blade which came into the line of fire. The side effects were a loss of blade efficiency and an alarming vibration when bullet met steel, not to mention occasional split propellers, as were experienced during target practice with at least one Parasol and one Bullet.

On 26 June an unforeseen problem occurred when they were actually fired on by British anti-aircraft (AA) gunners who had mistaken their Bullets for the hated Fokker E.III monoplanes of almost identical profile. To aid recognition they started painting their spinners and cowls red, a colour scheme that later became applied also to the forward fuselage and undercarriage. The normal term for AA fire was 'Ack-Ack', using the phonetic alphabet code-word for the letter 'A', but the jocular slang term was 'Archie', already in RFC use as early as 1914, derived from a popular music-hall song with the title and refrain 'Archibald, Certainly Not!' – thereby greeting the enemy's efforts with derision as well as defiance.

Group Captain A.J.L. 'Jack' Scott, in his history of 60 Squadron, described the Bullet as less than successful, being too difficult to fly for the average pilot. Fortunately, 'several of our pilots, including Smith Barry, Gilchrist, Foot, Grenfell, Meintjes and Hill, and in particular D.V. Armstrong, were considerably above the average.'[2]

Having already seen service in France, Robert Smith Barry was convinced that RFC instructors needed to provide a thorough training, including aerobatics, a vital skill for all pilots in the aerial war. Although such risks during training were severely frowned on back home, nevertheless if a pilot was not master of his machine in every flight attitude, and confident enough to use the stall and the spin, still greatly feared, he was unlikely to last long in combat. Faced with life-or-death situations where extreme evolutions were required, he needed to be familiar not only with the skills involved but also the potential stresses on whatever machine was issued to him. As we have seen, dedicated fighter aircraft were a relatively recent development, conceived in response to the threat of fighters on the German side fitted with synchronization gear. Deadly aim combined with supreme flying skills had now became crucial to the fighter pilot in any encounter, especially when a dogfight developed. The watchword was 'stunt or die'.

By the time DVA joined 60 Squadron in May 1916 the German solo ace Max Immelmann had employed aerobatic skills to deadly effect with his forward-firing E.III. All Eindecker pilots were feared for their ability to lie in wait at altitude and come plunging down in a hawk-like dive upon slower-moving targets below. But Immelmann was particularly famed for inventing the Immelmann Turn, a hit-and-run style of attack which involved diving quickly then zooming up to fire at an enemy from underneath and completing the manoeuvre with a steeply banked turn, which achieved a reversal of direction allowing him to make his escape the way he had come. It was an impressive feat for the Eindecker with its outdated wing-warping lateral control. It was not, however, the figure known today as an Immelmann Turn, a distinction we will discuss later.

Wing-warping for lateral control was also still employed by the Moranes, but thankfully well-designed aileron systems were soon to arrive, allowing more lively manoeuvring. British aircraft design developed slowly, but French fighting machines available to the wartime Allies by the end of 1916 were much better, including the nifty little Nieuports and SPADs capable of hitherto impossibly agile performance: the Germans no longer had it all their own way. With more manoeuvrable aircraft the sideslip, stall turn and spin – vital for a quick getaway – became standard tactics. 'Dive and zoom!' was the advice when attacked, and every kind of vertical reverse was used including the lightning-fast half-flick and pull through, often described in memoirs as 'roll and dive'. The autorotative flick roll was then known by a variety of names including barrel roll, corkscrew or horizontal spin, and Captain R.M. (Roderic) Hill was one of those seen to demonstrate it to admiring onlookers after receiving his Nieuport in 60 Squadron. Maurice Baring observed the heartening effects of the 'fast fighting machines' now

coming on-stream, and while touring a handful of squadrons (including 60 Squadron) in early January he noted, 'One man on a Nieuport did a roll, that is to say he looped sideways.' Later the same month he saw a French star pilot, Fléchaire, doing stunts that included '*le tonneau*'. This word, meaning 'barrel', was and still is used in French to denote any 360-degree roll, which explains why the equivalent in translation – 'barrel roll' – was the most usual English term in the war for the only roll they knew – the flick.[3] [See explanatory diagram on page 129.]

To Smith Barry (above left), knowing the crucial need for such combat readiness, no longer was it acceptable that a pilot fresh out from Britain learnt such skills in the skies over France: he had to know his machine and how to handle it long before he arrived. Smith Barry had himself gained his wings at the Central Flying School at Upavon but was dissatisfied with the abysmal lack of systematic training methods. He had begun working out his own very individual ideas for the proper preparation of pilots to meet the demands of warfare, and was devising a course for the thorough training of instructors to teach them.[4] After long persistence he was eventually invited to set up the first dedicated wartime depot which standardized training for instructors, the famous Gosport School of Special Flying, but it became reality only in August 1917. To illustrate just how much this revolutionized flying instruction methods, Arthur Gould Lee wrote of his transfer at the end of 1918 to take the instructors' course at Shoreham, an offshoot of Gosport, after he had already been instructing for nearly six months:[5]

> After 700 hours flying as a pilot, I had thought when I arrived at Shoreham ... that this was where I came in. But as the course progressed I realised that I had been flying for nearly two and a half years without knowing how, for I had never formulated in my mind even the first elements of flying or of instruction. And the way in which everything was now explained and demonstrated, the detailed mechanics of piloting and aerobatics and instruction, all of this was to me a revelation.

Armstrong's friend in C Flight, H.G. 'Reggie' Smart (page 50, right) was another first-class pilot and later became a Gosport instructor. Smith Barry was their initial flight commander, and DVA clearly benefited from the wisdom of this dynamic Irishman who insisted on a complete mastery of flying technique, nothing less. It can be easily imagined how many long and animated hours were devoted to the topic of combat tactics, a subject that meant literally life and death. DVA was inseparable from Reggie Smart and Henry 'Duke' Meintjes in C Flight: the three were, in Armstrong's words, 'always together in France, we lived and worked together'. Meintjes had transferred from South Africa at the same time as DVA and would also perform to great effect in the war.

The squadron's immediate tasks at the start of the Somme battle were numerous: among them were twice-daily offensive patrols by Bullets, i.e. sweeping the lines for hostile machines and preventing the enemy's eyes-in-the-sky from observing and reporting Allied movements and troop build-ups. There were duties to provide fighter escorts for bombing raids by machines from other units. And there were armed observation sorties by their own reconnaissance Biplanes of B Flight sent out to locate enemy activity in 'Hunland', the offhanded term which recognized that the Germans were not, of course, operating out of bases in Germany; on the Western Front they were utilizing occupied territory in Belgium and France, with devastating results for the civilian population.

Things started well enough. On the first day of the infantry attack, 1 July, an LVG was forced to land by squadron CO Waldron, and the next day another LVG was driven down by the Biplane crew of Browning-Paterson and his observer Bryant. On the same day there was a victory for another Biplane team, Lewis Whitehead and Lionel Clark, who sent down

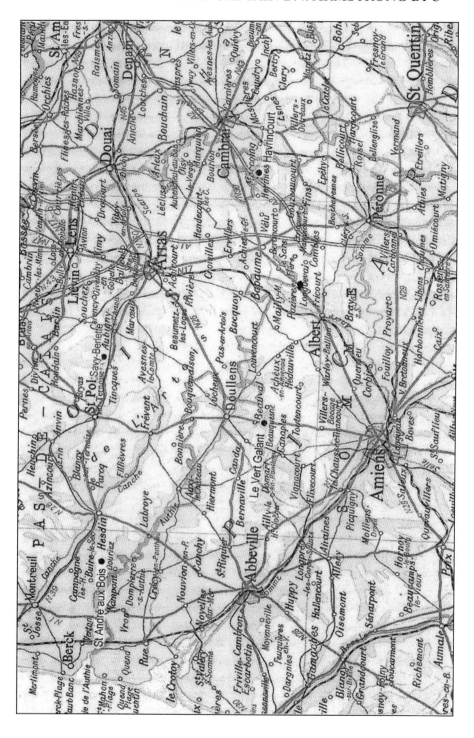

a Fokker E.III out of control, while an unidentified squadron member on offensive patrol was seen to engage another hostile and force it to land. These LVGs were *Luftverkehrsgesellschaft* aircraft, probably the two-seat reconnaissance C-series. The terms 'Forced to Land' and 'Driven Down' had specific meanings, the former signifying that the enemy aircraft (EA) was seen to land after a fight but not to crash, and the latter that it was forced to break off and flee from a fight, though without visibly being out of control.

The tide turned on 3 July when the squadron sustained a heavy loss in the person of Major Ferdy Waldron, one of the most popular officers in the Corps, who was killed on an early morning patrol over the lines which was designed to be a decoy while the town of St Quentin was being bombed. He was leading four other Bullets flown by Smith Barry, D'Urban Armstrong, John Simpson and Harold Balfour. As described by Balfour in the squadron's history,[6] 'Armstrong and Simpson had to fall out through engine trouble before we reached Arras. Armstrong landed by a kite balloon [tethered observation balloon] section and breakfasted with Radford' – Lieutenant B.H. Radford, the actor whose stage name was Basil Hallam. He was unaware of course that the squadron's CO had been fatally wounded in a fight with a swarm of Fokkers. Waldron was seen going down under control, an E.III on his tail, but although he landed safely he died of his wounds. There would be hushed voices at dinner in the mess that night.

Balfour later echoed DVA's experience on one of his own offensive patrols, when he too had a forced landing near the same balloon section and he too breakfasted with Basil Hallam, 'the darling of admiring audiences who used to sing "I'm Gilbert the Filbert" [in a popular revue in London] who was fated to be killed ... a very gallant officer'.[7]

Despite several more victories by 60 Squadron pilots, including Tower, Meintjes, Ridley and others, more losses were bound to follow, accompanied by the inevitable empty chairs. Smith Barry replaced Waldron as squadron commanding officer; as commander of A Flight he was succeeded by Browning-Paterson, who on 21 July was flying Morane Bullet serial A128 when he was shot down by a Fokker Monoplane. Armstrong's photo album records the bitter story in few words: 'I saw him shot down in flames near Pozières by a Fokker.' He was replaced as A Flight commander by John Simpson, pictured on page 46, and on the same day the flight was joined by Second Lieutenant Euan Gilchrist who had transferred from the 7th Hussars to the RFC in May. Responsibility came rapidly in the RFC under pressure of war, and Gilchrist would soon be promoted to captain and would

later himself lead A Flight. His name will be recognized as a distinguished CO of No. 56 Squadron in 1918.

A more rewarding result was achieved by Summers who successfully attacked an enemy kite balloon with Le Prieur rockets on 21 July, and on the 27th three LVGs fell victim: one was crashed very satisfactorily by Second Lieutenant S.F. (Stanley) Vincent, newly arrived to join A Flight, with two others driven down by Reggie Smart and Second Lieutenant B.M. (Melvyn) Wainwright, another newcomer.

A poignant photograph (above), captioned in Armstrong's handwriting, depicts a 60 Squadron group of whom two would soon meet a sad fate. On 30 July four of the squadron's Morane Biplanes were attacked by LVGs in the St Quentin area and two were forced to land. Lieutenant Williams, observer, seen in the back row at the far right, was instantly killed and his pilot, Captain Charles, died in captivity. Whitehead and Bryant were wounded.

Three days later, on 2 August, 60 Squadron was officially due to be relieved of patrol duties after its ten-week tour in France. On this day Armstrong described the last of the squadron's Morane Biplane outings: 'Meintjes and I on our Monoplanes were escorting four Biplanes on a Photographic Reconnaissance over St Quentin when two of them obtained direct hits within a couple of minutes.' As Balfour wrote in his memoir, 'one second flying with us: the next just blown to atoms'. Second Lieutenant Henry Newton, observer [photographed above, next to Williams] was reported missing, later confirmed killed. DVA wrote: 'I saw Newton who was an Observer in one of our Morane Biplanes get a direct hit on his machine from a Hun anti-aircraft gun at 12,000 feet over St Quentin.' Newton's pilot, the Canadian Lieutenant J.A.N. Ormsby, who had joined 60 Squadron twelve days earlier, died of his wounds.

On the very same day, 2 August, they also lost another squadron member pictured in DVA's album – this was observer Lionel Clark, photographed with Henry Newton on page 47 above. Armstrong continued: 'I saw Clark fall out of a Morane Biplane on the same job as Newton was killed on. He obtained a direct hit from Archie on his tail plane which was knocked clean off. This caused the machine to drop vertically and the force of the gale hurled him out.' His pilot, newly arrived Sergeant Pilot Walker, was killed with him. For those flying escort the feelings of frustration were unbearable. Scout pilots could take aggressive action to protect their vulnerable comrades from machine-gun attacks by enemy aircraft, but a hit from the ground by anti-aircraft fire simply blew its target to fragments while they could do nothing but watch helplessly.

Morane-Saulnier Type BB Biplane.

Though it has been said many times before, it is always worth remembering that for these men of the flying services every day meant pioneering an entirely new kind of warfare: one in which a wholly volunteer cadre of officers were given unprecedented tasks to perform, at altitudes never before conquered, in aeroplanes whose designs constantly lagged behind the needs and challenges ranged against them. Equally, their life at the Front somehow represented a reversal of the normal military order, with largely inexperienced young officers daily facing the wrath of the enemy, while supporting them in the comparative safety of their base station were teams of skilled men trained to maintain machines combat-ready in conditions the like of which five years earlier would have kept all aeroplanes firmly on the ground.

Those who flew were themselves keenly aware of the contrast with warfare on the battlefields below, and counted themselves lucky to have living conditions of relative comfort, eating decently and tended by batmen ... apart, that is, from those airborne hours of freezing temperatures with every sense and sinew strained, their courage and staying power tested to the limit. Vision was damaged, nerves were shattered, skin was frostbitten, guns were guaranteed to jam, engines guaranteed to fail. Yet they met the punishing stress with their own kind of airy cheerfulness and studied understatement. With fear came excitement and a close companionship with fellow-airmen in their own unique world.

To set the seal on 60 Squadron's gallant service during this first phase of the offensive, on 3 August Claude Ridley was sent on a mission to drop a French spy behind enemy lines. He suffered engine failure in the Parasol provided, A143, and had a forced landing near Douai which left the machine on its back in a cornfield. 'His adventures were remarkable,' to quote the squadron's official history:

> His spy got out, told Ridley to hide for a little, and presently, returning with civilian clothes and some money, told him he must now shift for himself. Ridley did so with such address that he eluded capture for three months on the German side of the line and eventually worked his way via Brussels to the Dutch frontier and escaped. This was a good performance, none the worse because he could speak neither French nor German. The method he adopted was a simple one – he would go up to some likely-looking civilian and say, "I am a British officer trying to escape: will you help me?" They always did.

He had many interesting adventures. For example, he lay up near the Douai aerodrome and watched the young Huns learning to fly and crashing on the aerodrome; here he saw one of our BEs brought down, and the pilot and observer marched past him into captivity. Later the conductor of a tram in the environs of Brussels suspected him, but, knocking the man down, he jumped into a field of standing corn and contrived to elude pursuit.

In recent years parts of the above account have been investigated and recorded more accurately, including recognition of how he was aided by the Resistance in Belgium.[8] A fuller version, with more entertaining details, is to be found in Harold Balfour's memoir. Ridley had found, at the last moment before departing for Hunland, that he had no money on him, so he hastily pocketed the remaining balance from the flight mess of a few hundred francs; he had, of course, expected to return that night. As it turned out he was wise to take this precaution because it helped him make his way through occupied France and Belgium. The story ends with his finally reaching England on 12 October bearing valuable military intelligence and being awarded the DSO for his exploits. It was not until he was sent back to report to the Intelligence Branch in France that Ridley was at last able to return to 60 Squadron and repay the mess funds! Stanley Vincent later recalled that 'on learning how useful it had been in bribes during the escape, all was forgiven'.[9]

Barred from serving again in France, Ridley was posted to Home Defence in 1917 to lead B Flight, No. 37 Squadron, becoming CO (at the age of just 20) of their base at Stow Maries aerodrome on the Essex coast where he is still commemorated today. Here he was reunited with another former member of 60 Squadron, George Keddie. On 7 July Ridley in a Sopwith Pup did his best to attack a group of German Gothas on their return from bombing London. Then, on 22 July, he led a 37 Squadron formation against another Gotha raid but to his disgust his Pup sustained damage under shellfire from local AA batteries and he was forced to land. He went on to command other squadrons and distinguished himself as CO of No. 28 Squadron on the Italian Front.

A few words should be devoted here to the early French Morane-Saulnier family of aircraft which comprised two two-seaters, the Biplane and the high-wing Parasol, plus a much faster single-seat shoulder-wing Monoplane nicknamed the Bullet (the Parasol also came in a single-seat version).

Claude Ridley in Instructional Bullet.

They relied on that wing-warping system mentioned previously, with wires that twisted the outer trailing edges, demanding considerable muscle power for lateral control which obviously inhibited any deft manoeuvring. High wing-loading and flimsy construction meant that spinning and steep dives were avoided like the plague in the Morane: the structural integrity was just not trusted. Its maximum speed at sea level was a decidedly un-bulletlike 89mph, its endurance was an hour and twenty minutes, and it was armed with a single Lewis gun.

Cecil Lewis described the Bullet as 'a devil to fly (it landed at about seventy)'. He himself flew the more amenable Parasol, which by then had the enormous advantage of ailerons, but even it was regarded, like the rest of the Morane family, as a death-trap: 'thoroughly dangerous, needing the greatest care and skill, the lightest hands, and the most accurate judgement to land. Subsequently I flew every machine used by the Air Force during the war. They were all child's play after the Morane.'[10] Yet, in the hands of an expert pilot with a perfect understanding of its tricky characteristics, it could be a handy and responsive mount.

Death-traps they may have been, but clearly if you survived flying Moranes you ended up with superbly honed handling skills. However, the machines under-performed against the enemy and too few of 60 Squadron did survive.

Individual Moranes were routinely shared between members of 60 Squadron but some have been positively identified as flown by Armstrong, including Type N serial 5197, Type I serial A198, and Type V serial A204, the latter being a version of the Bullet fitted with long-range fuel tanks.

This Morane Bullet photo in DVA's album has no caption which suggests it may have been his machine at the time; note wing-warping wires.

A204 was issued to the squadron on 12 August and was also flown by Captain H.C. 'Jimmy' Tower, who later became his commander in C Flight.

But before these new versions came on-stream, the near obliteration of 60 Squadron, having suffered an appalling rate of casualties throughout the Somme offensive, forced its withdrawal on 3 August 1916. It was moved farther north to St André aux Bois, near Hesdin [see map p. 52] to recover and refit. After deaths, injuries and other losses just four of its pilots were left. DVA was the only one remaining from his flight. In recognition of its outstanding services, the French government expressed the wish to decorate 60 Squadron with the *Croix de Guerre*.

Hugh Trenchard, commander of the RFC, had by now determined to cease mixed-purpose groups and instead concentrate single-seat fighters into 'all-scout squadrons'. No. 60 would become an early example, to be provided with Nieuports and augmented by an influx of leading pilots from Nos 1, 3 and 11 Squadrons. But first a week's rest was prescribed, followed by intensive retraining overseen by Smith Barry. DVA's service card omits any detail of this, but we are fortunate in learning from another source that he and Duncan Bell-Irving were posted to machine-gun school for a week. This took place at the gunnery school of the Machine Gun Corps at Camiers, a few miles north of Étaples, on the coast in the Pas-de-Calais department of northern France. Sun and sea were available to enjoy, while the extensive training facilities at the depot included a couple of machine-gun ranges, the Lewis Gun school being at Le Touquet to the west of Étaples.

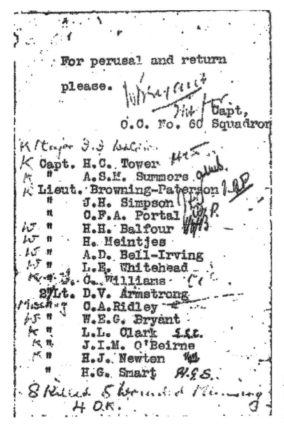

For perusal and return
please.

O.C. No. 60 Squadron

Capt. H.C. Tower
A.S.M. Summers
Lieut. Browning-Paterson
J.H. Simpson
O.P.A. Portal
H.H. Balfour
H. Meintjes
A.D. Bell-Irving
L.E. Whitehead
C. Williams
2/Lt. D.V. Armstrong
O.A. Ridley
W.E.G. Bryant
L.L. Clark
J.I.M. O'Beirne
H.J. Newton
H.G. Smart

8 Killed 5 Wounded 1 Missing
4 O.K.

No 60 Squadron personnel:
'8 Killed 5 Wounded
1 Missing 4 OK'.

In DVA's album can be found photographs of a variety of people he encountered in his RFC days, and among them is a young officer listed as 'Baby' Denne who wears the insignia of an observer – pictured opposite. This is Lieutenant R.A. (Robin Alured) Denne from Sittingbourne in Kent, whose birth date of 16 March 1898 would make him 18 years of age in late 1916. The nickname 'Baby' is easy to understand.

Denne had transferred from the Wiltshire Regiment (Duke of Edinburgh's) and taken his aviator's ticket at Brooklands as recently as 5 May, had been wounded as an observer, and had been flying Sopwith 1½-Strutters during the Somme offensive with C Flight of No. 70 Squadron. Known in the family as Alured, he attained the rank of captain and survived the war. Denne kept a diary which by good fortune is the source of this information thanks to his son, Thomas, who has kindly shared the entry in which his father reported how he met DVA when he, too, was sent to Étaples for a week's special machine-gun course. 'This was a real holiday,' he wrote. 'We stayed in a large house overlooking the sea with many RFC people from other units. I shared a room with Duncan Bell-Irving and Armstrong, both pilots in the brilliant No. 60 Squadron, which was equipped with Morane Bullets. We returned to our squadrons much refreshed after six very happy days, bathing, working and playing.'[11]

Back in harness, the 60 Squadron survivors underwent intensive retraining together with their new personnel. Among the newcomers was young Lieutenant Albert Ball – later to become one of the RFC's immortal heroes and earn the Victoria Cross – who had already begun to make his name with 11 Squadron and would do famous work with No. 60. Pilots coming from squadrons already equipped with Nieuports, like Ball, brought their own machines with them, but the arrival of Trenchard's envisaged Nieuports for the others was slow and sporadic. DVA's C Flight would be the last to receive them, having soldiered on into October with Morane Bullets, which had meanwhile been re-engined, their 80hp Le Rhône 9Cs replaced by 110hp 9Js, which served only to aggravate their already detestable handling characteristics.

Returned to the Front on 23 August, by the end of that month the pilots of 60 Squadron had achieved a series of eighteen new victories. In the

records pieced together since 1916, those who continued flying Moranes contributed five: Jimmy Tower, Reggie Smart and Melvyn Wainwright accounted for three on 25 August, Duncan Bell-Irving and Alfred Summers one each on the 28th and 31st.

On 1 September they moved to the squadron's latest home, Savy-Berlette near Arras, only to be grounded for a week by low cloud and mist. On 15 September began the final stage of the battle of the Somme, when tanks were to be used for the first time. To prevent observation of Allied troop movements the renewed aerial offensive began with attacks on German balloons.

The first of these was despatched on the evening of the 14th, set alight by rockets fired by Duncan Bell-Irving, whose current work and previous achievements earned him the Military Cross. Alfred Summers destroyed another on 15 September but lost his life in the process, being shot down in flames by the defending anti-aircraft batteries. The available reports indicate large-scale German retaliation, e.g. on 19 September an onslaught by twenty fighters over Bapaume during which Captain Jimmy Tower was shot down by the widely respected Oswald Boelcke (Morane A204 was lost with him). Within the space of that week in mid-September the squadron had lost the commanders of all three flights – A Flight's Frank Goodrich, B Flight's Alfred Summers and C Flight's Jimmy Tower.

Albert Ball, now promoted to captain, became commander of A Flight on his return from leave in mid-September, and continued to wreak devastation on enemy aircraft and balloons, three times achieving three victories in a single day. Eventually the intense pressure forced him to seek leave again; he continued to the end of the month and left for home on 3 October.

On arrival the 20-year-old Nottingham lad was the first British air service pilot to be idolized by the public. This was a phenomenon existing in France and Germany, but under Trenchard's advice to Field Marshal Haig the British adopted the contrary view, believing that credit should adhere to the air service rather than the individual. Fighting achievements were reported in the press but the names of pilots were rigorously suppressed except in the case of gallantry awards. Albert Ball's status as a national hero in 1916 was an exception in that it predated the official tributes later recorded upon the award of his VC. Eventually the War Office recognized the demands of the British press and public who were constantly hearing stories of foreign pilots whose exploits their own, apparently, could not match. Yielding to pressure they allowed articles to be written, especially when it became politically vital to counteract the news of terrible casualties emerging from battles like the Somme. By then, however, the aces of other nationalities had been elevated to heights of worldwide glory unattainable by most of the RFC's leading stars. Despite similar or greater achievements, to this day few resonate down the decades as household names.

While Ball was leading A Flight, Captain E.O. (Eustace) Grenfell was posted to take over as commander of Armstrong's C Flight, whose personnel included Meintjes and Smart. They were housed in huts on Savy airfield, as the *Sixty Squadron* history recounts, 'to deal quickly with any Huns who were bold enough to cross the line, [while] the remainder of the squadron were billeted in the Mayor's château in the village itself, some half a mile away'.

Albert Ball with Nieuport 16 A134 in No. 11 Squadron, July 1916.

Willie Fry, whom we met earlier (writing in *Air of Battle* about the docile BE.2c), was one of the new pilots sent to join them; he had already been sent to St Omer to familiarize himself on Moranes, but clearly found them intimidating. Let us allow Fry to resume the story on reporting to the CO, Major Robert Smith Barry, and, in particular, give the reader an idea of what it was like for a newly trained pilot to come to the Morane Bullet, the monoplane which Cecil Lewis described as a devil to fly.[12]

> For a young officer the first meeting with Smith Barry as a CO was an alarming experience. He fixed you with a glassy stare, almost a glare, accentuated by the fact that his eyes did not seem an exact match. He spoke in abrupt sentences and then, just as you were beginning to get alarmed, a smile or grin would suddenly come over his face. Far from finding yourself in the trouble you anticipated you found instead a fellow conspirator – the more so if the interview had anything to do with higher authority. Everyone in the squadron loved him. Many of his actions became legendary in the RFC and RAF.
>
> The squadron now had two flights of early-type Nieuport Scouts and one flight of 110hp Morane Bullets ... The CO told

me that as I had come as a qualified Morane pilot, I was to go to C Flight and report to the flight commander. This flight, in order to be more readily available to take off on enemy interception duties, was detached from the rest of the squadron and lived a separate existence with its own Mess and living quarters in two Nissen huts on the edge of the aerodrome, close to the canvas Bessonneau hangars. The pilots of the flight were a happy, wild lot and one sensed this immediately on entering the little Mess. Very much apart from the rest of the squadron, even the CO rarely interfered with us.

The flight commander, Captain Eustace Grenfell, black-haired and glowering, had done a long tour in France with No. 1 Squadron, going out with it from England and winning an MC and bar. ... After luncheon Grenfell had a Bullet wheeled out and ordered me to take it up, fly round for a time and make three landings, adding, 'And I hope you break your bloody neck'. As I soon learnt, he meant no harm by this; it was just his way of being casual, although disconcerting to a terrified young pilot.

Morane Bullets were very small ... so light – they could not have weighed more than 10 cwt, engine and all – that one man could lift one up by the tail skid and wheel it in or out of the hangar. It had a round fuselage with a large spinner, painted red, on the nose, attached to the propeller boss and the propeller. The spinners had a splendid streamlining effect and

Morane-Saulnier Type N Bullet fitted with 110hp Le Rhône engine.

made the machine look exactly like an unlit cigar with two small wings attached, but the effect of the spinner was that only the cylinder heads of the engine received a direct stream of air for cooling ... There also existed a theory that the spinners made the machine even more unstable laterally ... They had a balanced elevator and warped banking control, both worked off the joystick, which made control of the machine very light fore and aft and correspondingly stiff and heavy laterally, as one had to warp both wings by brute force to bank at all. They did not have a fixed tailplane with trailing elevator such as we were used to ... It would have been easy to pull the stick back till the tailplane was nearly at right angles to the line of flight and thus break the flimsy tail off. Anyhow, we had a flight of four of them in the squadron, the only ones used operationally in France in the RFC, and here I was having to fly them.

I was numbed and almost speechless with fear at having to take the machine into the air but I wasn't going to show it. ... My only consideration was how to manage to keep in flight and in the air. After a few minutes I began a very gentle wide turn to the left, not from choice, but because I was afraid of losing the aerodrome if I kept flying on a straight course much longer. I succeeded in coming round eventually, picked up the main road again, flew back past the aerodrome and turned again somehow to approach into the wind, throttled down and glided in, too fast of course.

However I landed safely, which was almost miraculous as I had been so frightened that my mind and wits had scarcely been functioning at all. Some of the spectators anticipating a crash began to disperse ... After that I was relieved to go back to the Mess – but no less scared of the Morane. I see from my log-book that the next day I was sent up twice to look for hostile aircraft which had been reported on the Front, so it was not long before one became operational.

Willie Fry was fortunate, for the squadron was already starting to receive its fast French Nieuport 16 biplanes, designed as dedicated single-seat fighters and among the best fighting machines of the Somme. DVA's measured opinion was that they were 'infinitely better machines and very much easier to fly'.

Nieuport 16 (110hp Le Rhône) as used in 60 Squadron. [Mike O'Connor]

Like the Bullets, the Nieuport 16s had been given the doubtful benefits of having the more powerful 110hp Le Rhône strapped on to an airframe – in this case the Nieuport 11 Bébé – originally designed for the 80hp version. The heavier engine and concomitant reinforcement made it nose-heavy, and it was less agile due to the increased wing loading. However, the Nieuports easily outpaced and outperformed their predecessors, and the sesquiplane design (with narrower lower wing) offered strength while reducing drag, and gave the pilot a great field of vision.

No. 60 was the first RFC squadron to be fully equipped – eventually – with the popular and manoeuvrable Nieuport 16 and 17 fighters, which enabled them to produce more successful results that autumn with fewer losses, and for a while the Nieuports helped redress the aerial balance against the Germans. Again the aircraft were shared among the various individuals, but Armstrong certainly flew Nieuport 16 A211, and by the time of his last few weeks with the squadron he had acquired one of the improved Nieuport 17s, serial A306, which with their redeveloped airframe afforded a powerful rate of climb. Their drawbacks included a certain proclivity to flutter in the pull-out after a prolonged dive. But to Armstrong and his unit the performance of the little French fighters with the recognizable V-struts must have been transformational and any defects would have been of small account to a group which had spent nearly half a year on Moranes.

Acknowledgements are due to Alex Revell's Osprey publication *No. 60 Squadron RFC/RAF* and in particular to the exhaustive research into 60 Squadron carried out by Squadron Leader D.W. 'Joe' Warne and published in *Cross & Cockade International*, the journal of the First World War Aviation Historical Society.[13] To continue with Willie Fry's narrative:

> I, for one, was only too glad to see the end of the Bullets. The reason we did not have more casualties with them in the flight was, I feel sure, because we had some of the finest pilots in the RFC at the time as a nucleus, which included Eustace Grenfell, Armstrong, Reggie Smart, Stanley Vincent, Meintjes and Pidcock. It is the only type of plane I have ever flown which made you certain it was doing its best to kill you.
>
> When I joined C Flight ... Meintjes, Armstrong and Smart had all three come out from England with the squadron, and ... Weedon and Joyce had been members of the flight for a month or so. Meintjes was a South African who came to England to

Willie Fry [via Alex Revell].

join the RFC after having first served as an infantry officer in the South African Forces through the German South West Africa campaign. He later became our flight commander when Grenfell was wounded, and we all loved him. Armstrong was another South African, strong and fearless. Later, after he had returned to England and was flying in a Home Defence squadron, he was generally reputed to be about the best pilot in the RFC. Yet as far as I can remember, he showed no exceptional flying skills while in 60, but then no one tried to shine on Morane Bullets ...

Life was boisterous in our little Mess, with a lot of ragging and horseplay, and I, being the youngest, was often at the receiving end. Armstrong in particular was full of high spirits and very strong, as were Eustace Grenfell and, later, [Captain Alan] Binnie. It was no good going to bed if you did not feel like any more of the hilarity, because during a pause someone would be sure to say, 'Where is so and so? Let's get him out.' The whole flight would then crowd into his small room and throw themselves on his bed. It was a frightening experience in the dark.

One night they were all on top of me on my bed making a frightful racket and refusing to go away. I got rather desperate and picked up my oil lamp, which had the usual glass container for the paraffin, and hit Eustace Grenfell over the head with it, shattering the glass container. He hardly noticed the blow. ... We sorted ourselves out, someone fetched a torch and we discovered that Grenfell was bleeding from a deep cut on his head and forehead where I had broken the glass lamp on him ... He appeared the next day with his head wrapped in bandages. I had visions of trouble for striking my senior officer, but all was smiles, right up to the CO. I think I had established myself by standing up for myself in that rowdy C Flight.

Harold Balfour and DVA, friends from Gosport days, served together only until the beginning of August. In his memoir Balfour wrote candidly about suffering from feelings of self-doubt and loss of nerve during his first time at the Front, and when he accidentally crushed the fingertips of both hands in a deckchair and had to be hospitalized, Smith Barry 'without any fuss or bother arranged that I should go back to England. There was no question of being sent home in official disgrace, but purely that at that time I was of no real use to the unit and therefore was better off out of the way. ... Within 48 hours I was a member of the Test Flight at Upavon.' He returned to the Front with No. 43 Squadron in 1917 and acquitted himself admirably, being awarded the MC.

Balfour and DVA had been acknowledged as two of the squadron's top pilots, and Jack Scott, in his book *Sixty Squadron*, described Armstrong as 'perhaps the finest pilot the Flying Corps ever produced'. In fact, all those who commented on DVA's career soon rated his skills head and shoulders above the rest. In recollections by contemporaries writing later in the journals of *Cross & Cockade* published on both sides of the Atlantic, Armstrong was always described as a great aerobatic flier and a superb Morane pilot.[14]

By then the Royal Flying Corps had a reputation for fighting hard and playing hard: to fly was to be daring, a risk-taker, and it attracted the young bloods whose distinctive uniform and insignia singled them out. Nerves that were daily strung taut to breaking point had to be relieved somehow, and hilarity and horseplay in the mess were the counterpart to the strain of duty on the front line.

Above left and right: *July 1916: Harold Balfour (on left) with DVA; note that it was acceptable for trousers and shoes to be worn with SD jacket during informal periods on an airfield. [Right-hand photo courtesy of Trevor Henshaw.]*

Despite the esteem in which he was held, there was until recently no verified victory by Armstrong recorded with 60 Squadron. Substantiating any claims relating to this squadron in 1916 is problematic because precious records were destroyed by a fire in mid-November that year. Even a number of known squadron victories are unable to be attributed with confidence to named individuals. Jack Scott, who wrote the squadron's history in 1920, joined the unit only in April 1917 so was unable to account for the previous year from personal knowledge. As Joe Warne wrote in his Appendix III to Scott's *Sixty Squadron*:

> Errors and Omissions in the Officers Record Books (which were recommenced late in November 1916 after the fire in the Squadron Office) do not match with the log-books of individual pilots contacted, or with consolidated returns/summaries by successive Squadron Commanders and those in higher posts when recommendations for awards were written.

Equally disconcerting is Warne's comment that records in the Public Record Office (now the National Archives) 'between them do not include a complete set of all submitted, serially-numbered combat claims'. In the course of enquiries other researchers have confirmed that combat report files at the National Archives are in some disorder and have even suffered from theft. German records are also patchy and not always reliable.

It must be assumed, in consequence, that where official records are missing, any claims relating to this unit may be open to question until corroborated in other sources, some perhaps less formal than one would wish. Presumably this uncertainty prevailed from the moment of the fire and for many years thereafter, especially in regard to any actions by a lowly second lieutenant from a foreign background like Armstrong, who would scarcely have merited the assiduous searches needed to verify them.

That said, investigations by more recent historians of the period have identified and corroborated several previously unverified engagements by members of 60 Squadron. It is significant how very few of those modified Moranes feature in the lists, and when they do, how often they are accompanied by the demise of their pilots. Willie Fry – who, thankfully, survived – participated in the squadron's last Morane sortie on 17 October when no enemy aircraft were sighted and nothing useful accomplished but, alas, his companion, Lieutenant N.McL. Robertson, posted to the unit the previous day, misjudged his landing and became the hated machine's last victim.

Fully equipped with Nieuports by 19 October, C Flight took part in a major engagement on 9 November 1916 in which some forty aircraft participated.[15] The day started at 08.00 with six Nieuports from 60 Squadron escorting eight FE.2ds from 11 Squadron performing photo-reconnaissance.

An hour later twelve 60 Squadron Nieuports joined sixteen other aircraft to fly an escort for bombers of Nos 12 and 13 Squadrons. Their target was the German HQ and ammunition dump at Vaulx-Vraucourt which proved heavily defended: a large formation of enemy fighters attacked the bomber/escort detachment and, during the fray, Duncan Bell-Irving drove down a Halberstadt but was wounded and had to crash-land. Fortunately he survived the crash and was sent back to England to be hospitalized. He was awarded a Bar to his MC, joined Smith Barry's Gosport School and became its commander.

As the bombers returned home a force of six Nieuports took off, led by Captain J.D. (Douglas) Latta and including Second Lieutenant D.V. Armstrong (presumably those pilots who had been on the 08.00 sortie) to escort the bombers home. At 10.00 Latta engaged with enemy aircraft and had his machine badly damaged. In the same scrap we find the encounter which has recently been recorded as an Armstrong victory.

But the day's work had not yet ended for C Flight. At 15.00 they took off again, with DVA leading Weedon, Meintjes, Smart and Fry, providing renewed escort duties for the reconnaissance FE.2ds of No. 11 Squadron, during which Meintjes brought down an LVG 'Forced to Land'.

Returning to Armstrong's victory at 10.00 that morning, the little we know is that it occurred over Bois d'Havrincourt, during which his Nieuport 16, serial A211, was damaged in combat. Usually such events as driving down an enemy are described as a claim, but in this case the standard term cannot be used in view of the loss of documentation: we do not know whether DVA made such a claim. Unfortunately his log-books seem to be lost, and his photograph album reveals nothing of his personal combat exploits. It is therefore incumbent on this biography to seek credible corroboration.

DVA with 60 Sqdn [Alex Revell].

Warne's Appendix III to Scott's *Sixty Squadron* (published 1990) lists Armstrong's enemy aircraft driven down on 9 November as a Roland D.I.[16] 'Driven down', it will be recalled, signifies that the enemy aircraft has been forced to break off and flee, though not confirmed as out of control. Warne, who was scrupulous in weeding out 'vague claims of enemy aircraft driven down', referred to supporting evidence which had come to his notice. Clearly he had been trawling exhaustively through non-official records.

Also published in 1990 was the book *Above the Trenches: A Complete Record of the Fighter Aces and Units of the British Empire Air Forces 1915–1920,*[17] which is considered authoritative in this area. It gives the same details of this engagement (time, date, etc.) but the enemy aeroplane is more credibly identified as an Albatros D.I, listed as 'Destroyed'. Added to four other recorded victories, this makes a total of five which thereby qualifies DVA for a place in its pages. Further background to the engagement is supplied, indicating that Squadrons No. 60 and No. 11, and some BE.2s, were involved in this fight in which at least three 'Destroyed' claims were given. 'It is believed all three were given to 60, as 11 Squadron records indicate they got none and the BE.2s got one Out of Control.' Norman Franks, one of that book's co-authors, acknowledges that discrepancies exist, but has confirmed that Armstrong's victory was supported by squadron combat reports.[18]

'Nieuport11', a member of the online Great War Forum, has commented that Armstrong's victory on 9 November is also 'noted in both the *Cross & Cockade* Nieuport Monograph and in the serial listings assembled by Mike O'Connor and Mick Davis – both top experts about the service of the Nieuports in the RFC and RNAS'.[19] He adds that the military historian Ray Sturtivant also had the engagement listed in his notes but cited it as a Roland D.I driven down (which suggests the same source as Warne's).

We should not leave this subject without mentioning that, in his reflections on DVA's war service, Air Vice Marshal Sir Leslie Brown KCB CBE DSO AFC noted that he was credited with the destruction of six machines and a balloon during operations with No. 60 Squadron. Once again caution must prevail but, on the other hand, in the whole of Sir Leslie's valedictory recital of Armstrong's achievements, the full record cited is in every other respect accurate (see Appendix III). Indeed it contains service details that are unlikely to have come to his attention except through personal enquiry. An Old Hiltonian himself, it is possible that Brown took an interest in young Armstrong's progress and made occasional enquiries of his commanding officers, especially once his name became a byword for accomplishment as a pilot. Perhaps he was told that DVA participated in engagements that produced

Nieuports of No. 60 Squadron lined up prior to Offensive Patrol.

shared victories. With our present state of knowledge we cannot substantiate Sir Leslie Brown's claims; but they are also hard to dismiss out of hand.

When considering the difficulties of verification it is worth reflecting that pilots of the Allied forces in France had to contend with persistently prevailing westerly winds at operational height. This led the Germans to adopt the policy that, although they patrolled the lines, their fighters seldom came much distance over the Allied side. Breaking off early allowed them to regain safety with the aid of a helpful tailwind, at the same time drawing pursuit over their own territory; this put their opponents at a significant disadvantage, exacerbated by the peril of a forced landing among the enemy. Consequently, should a German machine be apparently (but not certainly) destroyed or driven down, it was acutely hazardous for the pursuer to sacrifice time and altitude attempting to ascertain the real outcome visually. His first concern had to be preserving height and fuel to fight his way back to base, while battling a headwind that could slow him to the status of a sitting duck for AA gunners.

It goes without saying that Armstrong, like his fellow pilots, would often have been forced to break off owing to a variety of problems and malfunctions including gun stoppage or lack of fuel or ammunition, or through damage or engine trouble, or to avoid collision, or to prevent the certain destruction of his own or a companion's machine. In those aeroplanes, and under such conditions, it would be a miracle if all combat reports by First World War pilots were 100 per cent accurate, especially for actions occurring behind enemy lines.

As already mentioned, it was at about this time that those wishing to bolster morale at home in Britain began to adopt the accolade of 'ace', following the example of France and Germany, which led to the publicizing of comparative scoring tables; however, this was considered by some an encouragement to competitive headhunting, exerting extra pressure on those few who were selected to be lionized as leaders of the field. To a serving airman, far more important than an individual's total of victories was the skill, determination and fighting spirit of the man himself: the best comrade was the team player who set aside personal gain for the good of his companions in arms; and the best flight commander was one like James McCudden VC, who was more proud of the low casualty rate of his flight than of anything else he achieved.[20]

Whether this was a topic of argument at squadron level is extremely doubtful. For anyone who slogged through years of carnage such a title probably meant very little. Indeed, it had not initially been thought necessary always to accord every victory to every individual concerned, and some were simply listed under OP (Offensive Patrol). Joe Warne, in his series of articles on 60 Squadron for *Cross & Cockade International*, commented that 'some pilots did not enter victory claims in their log-books'.[21]

The situation was very different in September 1918 when Duncan Grinnell-Milne joined No. 56 Squadron at the Front on SE.5as, to be met with the proud claim that the squadron had brought down more German machines than any other in France – they were keeping a tally of their 'total bag'. In this climate Grinnell-Milne found that *confirmation* was the watchword: a young pilot would return from some furious fight, jump out and report enthusiastically that he'd 'Got two Huns down in flames' – to which would come the chilling reply, 'Can you get confirmation of that?' The pilot himself needed no such endorsement, Grinnell-Milne remarked, 'but the authorities had to be considered'.[22]

In the search for information about DVA's final weeks with 60 Squadron there is little of use in his further service record. It states that he had a short taste of leave from 27 September to 4 October, but these few days obviously afforded no opportunity to see his family back home – though he may have visited his sister in England. On 16 November he was again withdrawn from the Front, with a posting to Paris on twenty-four hours unspecified temporary duty. Nothing more is known about this, although his flying career was often punctuated by assignments that involved giving flying demonstrations and providing instruction or support to other units (as in 1918 when he was attached to the French Aviation Corps). Alternatively,

More Nieuports of 60 Squadron.

and probably more likely, this may have been the welcome task of collecting a replacement Nieuport from Paris: 'the chance of a trip to fly one back was eagerly looked forward to by every pilot,' says Jack Scott in his *Sixty Squadron* history.

On 30 November, aged 19, he was promoted to lieutenant. Next, according to his service record, from 1 to 8 December Armstrong was reported as assigned to 'Machine Gun School' for a week. Was this a return visit to the gunnery school at Camiers? Or was it a date erroneously assigned to that training already undertaken in August? We are given no clue in his photograph album.

The remainder of his service with 60 Squadron, flying those much more efficient Nieuports, apparently passed without significant incident so far as Armstrong was affected. Actions soon wound down as the year came to an end with long periods of bitterly cold and unflyable weather, but not without more casualties. In December Eustace Grenfell, commander of C Flight since September, broke his ankle in a crash-landing and Duke Meintjes replaced him. Scott described Meintjes as 'one of the best pilots and almost the most popular officer 60 ever had'.

At the end of the month DVA's 1916 tour on the Western Front finally ended and he was posted to Home Establishment just in time for Christmas.

CHAPTER 4

PART 1: BLOODY APRIL

Over the 1916/17 winter when D'Urban Armstrong was withdrawn after seven months at the Front, there was much reorganization and reallocation of personnel. New faces in 60 Squadron (now moved farther north to Filescamp Farm), joined those from the autumn intake who continued their tour of duty dealing face to face with the enemy, though the prolonged hard weather greatly reduced opportunities to be airborne.

Of the three others who had survived along with DVA in August 1916, Reggie Smart had left at the same time in December to become a test pilot and flying instructor; John Simpson had already departed in August and would eventually attain the rank of air commodore; and Charles 'Peter' Portal, who also left in August, went on to enjoy a glittering career in the service to become Marshal of the Royal Air Force in 1944, later being raised to the peerage. Of those who had been wounded, Duke Meintjes returned to see further action with 60 Squadron, but not Duncan Bell-Irving or Walter Bryant, although they continued their flying careers. Meintjes did excellent service for the squadron until February 1917, then returned again to France in April as a flight commander in No. 56 Squadron flying SE.5as. On 7 May he was shot down during Albert Ball's final dogfight and wounded in the wrist. Awarded the MC and AFC, back in South Africa he served in the SA Air Force and rose to the rank of major.

Meanwhile more members of ground- and air-crew were brought in to serve at the Front. Over the long winter months both sides were readying themselves for what everyone knew was a build-up to a new push in the spring of 1917. On the German side, early versions of the *Albatros Flugzeugwerke* D-series Albatros had appeared sporadically from the autumn of 1916, although rarely encountered at that time in 60 Squadron's area of operation. Against them the French-built 110hp Nieuport 17s with single Vickers gun could just about hold their own, despite the German pilots' 160hp Mercedes engines and twin machine guns. As Jack Scott remarked in the squadron's history, 'The Silver Nieuport was a good machine to fight in, but a bad one either for running away or catching a faint-hearted enemy, as its best airspeed, even near the ground, rarely exceeded 96 or 97 miles per hour.'

However, the Army authorities at home wanted British-built machines so at the turn of the year there appeared the Sopwith Pup, the British response to the enemy's high-performance Albatri ('Albatri' being the RFC's whimsical quasi-Latin solution to the awkward plural). Delightful though it was, the Pup was powered by a Le Rhône engine of 80hp, and for armament had only the standard solitary Vickers gun. It had first been introduced for RNAS service twelve months earlier, and in truth the era had now been missed when the Pup might have turned the aerial war in favour of the Allies.

Not only had the Germans produced technologically superior aeroplanes, they had also devised radically new tactics which they employed at the same time over the Western Front. Special new 'hunting squadrons' – *Jagdstaffeln* – were formed, manned by élite handpicked teams of leading fighter pilots, the first of which, *Jasta 2*, was led by the greatest of them all, Oswald Boelcke. One of its recruits was Manfred von Richthofen, who would go on to become the leader of *Jasta 11*. As established by Boelcke, their operational ethos was to maintain tightly disciplined groups flying

This iconic shot taken by a German official photographer shows Albatros D.IIIs of Jagdstaffeln 11 and 4 at historic La Brayelle aerodrome, Douai (France) in the spring of 1917. Manfred von Richthofen's red-painted aircraft is second from front (with boarding stepladder in place).

in protective close formation, a tactic so effective that it would remain the guiding principle for future aerial combat. The leader was always in charge, it was he who decided which target to dive upon, and only when the attack was launched were individuals free to break out and pursue their own prey. Boelcke taught his pilots well and, with the advantage of power, speed and armament, they were opponents to be reckoned with. His doctrine was maintained even after his death, which occurred in a collision at the end of October. Meanwhile on the 8th of that month the German *Fliegertruppen* had gained a degree of independence and become the *Luftstreitkräfte*, due in great part to Boelcke's charismatic influence.

In January 1917, with a growing tally of victories, Manfred von Richthofen was awarded the *Pour le Mérite* (the Blue Max), and took over the mantle of national hero. In command of *Jasta 11* he continued Boelcke's policy of handpicking the best pilots available. He also demanded a more agile aircraft, settling on the Albatros D.III as his preferred machine, which was subsequently produced in large numbers and brought forward in readiness for the impending battle of Arras. For him its importance lay in being able to manoeuvre into the optimum position to aim at his target: the D.III copied the Nieuport V-struts and, more importantly, its sesquiplane design, thereby profiting from the excellent field of vision this provided. Shooting such animals as wild boar had been his preferred recreation in civilian times, and his cool marksmanship was the principal asset that assured him his high degree of success. By contrast with German fighter training which advocated aiming for the aeroplane rather than the man, von Richthofen stipulated 'Aim for the man and don't miss.'

It was while he was with *Jasta 11* that he famously chose an all-red livery for his machine, and encouraged the rest of his unit to adopt conspicuous colour schemes to aid identification. Later the German air service organized *Jagdgeschwader* – groups of *Jastas* forming the equivalent of a wing – which developed a tactic of extreme mobility so they could be moved quickly to any base in order to strike wherever on the lines they were needed. With cheerful RFC irreverence they became known as Flying Circuses. The most notorious of these was von Richthofen's *Jagdgeschwader 1*, with its clutch of first-rate pilots flying brightly-coloured aeroplanes.

These, then, were the German aircraft and airmen ranged against the RFC at the outset of the battle of Arras. By the end of 1916 the unresolved conflicts of Verdun and the Somme had ground to a halt with a total of some 500 RFC aircrew lost; but hopes were pinned on a spring offensive for which forces were replenished by hundreds of fresh pilots sent out to take their place, though many were sadly ill-prepared. The squadrons were needed at full strength to ensure the performance of essential Army cooperation work in the assault that began on 9 April 1917, when once again the British found themselves called upon to launch a combined attack which included support for a major French offensive taking place elsewhere, fifty miles to the south on the river Aisne. Thanks to outstanding work by the Canadian Corps the opening battle of Vimy achieved a notable territorial gain, and the battle of the river Scarpe was also prosecuted with success by the British. But again the casualties were heavy and the French Aisne offensive failed to achieve a breakthrough, triggering mutiny in the French Army. The Allied casualties amounted to a quarter of a million, the Germans even more. Unknown to the Allies, the resolve of the German troops was also gradually weakening as they saw hopes of their great victory receding.

The Allied losses in the air were uniquely punishing, so much so that for the RFC it became known as Bloody April, the most disastrous period in its history. German pilots shot down Allied aircraft in a ratio of four to one. But despite inflicting such terrible losses they failed to prevent the RFC's most crucial work: the flow of reconnaissance information and photography from the air which assisted the British Army's decisions on the ground, plus their valuable support of Army action by means of artillery spotting and bombing raids.

No. 60 Squadron continued bravely at the Front but lost its CO, Major Evelyn Graves in March. He was succeeded that same month by Major Jack Scott who would be faced with the prospect of leading the squadron in the aerial offensive which started on 4 April to precede the forthcoming battle, with aims including the disabling of enemy observation balloons. At this time the squadron was joined by Lieutenant W.A. 'Billy' Bishop who became one of Canada's great heroes and, like Ball, would later be awarded the VC. Within two weeks Bishop had been given command of C Flight and within a month was promoted to captain. Like Manfred von Richthofen he had a predilection for the hunt; blessed with phenomenal eyesight, he made his watchword accurate shooting which he practised assiduously. This impelled him to go out on multiple patrols seeking the enemy, often unaccompanied, and his successes in these lone-wolf actions were not always verifiable. But his aggressive fighting spirit was a tonic at this critical time, and his rapidly mounting tally made him a feared adversary.

Meanwhile the importance of reconnaissance work was highlighted by an unexpected move on the part of the enemy, unnoticed during a spell of unflyable weather, which was reported when patrols resumed:[1]

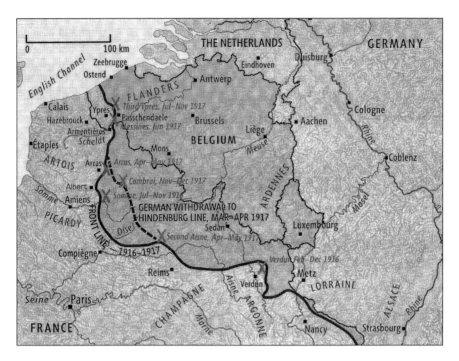

On March 30 the first patrol to land reported 30 or 40 fires in the tract of country east of the Arras-Albert sector [see map above]. Every village for ten or fifteen miles back was alight. ... The German retreat of March 14 came, therefore, as a complete surprise to us.

Over the ensuing days, in spite of stormy weather, the squadron continually sent out aerial patrols to ascertain the depth of the withdrawal and locate the new German positions. For miles around they saw the entire countryside of occupied France reduced to a battle-scarred wasteland of rubble and water-filled shell holes. Every village was flattened, every farm and building systematically destroyed, along with every tree, animal or other sign of life. Columns of retreating men were making their way east, demolishing roads and bridges behind them. The scenes of wholesale devastation, described by Maurice Baring as 'past belief', received a horrified reaction in unengaged countries around the world.

The Germans, with their forces facing pressure on all fronts, had planned this retreat for months, constructing their rearward *Siegfriedstellung* defence, known to the Allies as the Hindenburg Line, much of it with forced labour by Russian prisoners of war. It provided a heavily-protected fallback

PART 1: BLOODY APRIL

Razed to the ground: the village of Monchy-au-Bois, near the Bois d'Adinfer, the nearest point of the old Front Line that members of 60 Squadron were able to reach to inspect the destruction.

position which made it possible to retire from the deadlocked Somme while they prepared their new offensives.

While the RFC endured Bloody April, awaiting the provision of aircraft capable of matching the modern fighters of their enemies, the German *Jastas* benefited from the overarching policy that had consistently kept them on their own side of the lines. Such a policy allowed them to strike and retire to safety, time and again, their return usually aided by a following wind, while luring their opponents to the perils of dogfights and forced landings in occupied territory. An extract from the history of 60 Squadron gives a graphic picture of what Bloody April meant for just one unit facing the daily onslaught:

> From the last week in March to the last week in May our losses were very severe; in fact, counting those who went sick and those injured in crashes on our side of the line, we lost 35 officers during those eight weeks, almost twice the strength of the squadron, which consisted of 18 pilots and the squadron commander. One weekend in April, the 14th, 15th and 16th, was especially unlucky. On Saturday A Flight went out six machines strong (full strength) and only one returned. ... On the next day, Sunday, B Flight (five strong) lost

Abandoned in the retreat: German ferro-concrete blockhouse with gun embrasures.

> two pilots. ... On Monday C Flight (Bishop's) went out without
> the flight commander and only one returned. ... In three days
> ten out of eighteen pilots were lost, and had to be replaced
> from England by officers who had never flown a Nieuport.

The carnage in the air would eventually diminish with the arrival of a
new generation of British fighting aircraft to exert increased pressure on
the overworked *Jastas*. Within months machines like the Sopwith Camel,
SE.5a and SPAD S.XIII entered service with the result that German losses
rose, putting an end to their period of greatest air superiority. RFC training,
incorporating Smith Barry's visionary ideas, became more professional.
And the outcome all along the Western Front for those hard-pressed Allied
ground forces, as they laboured to make a breakthrough, was the advantage
of consistent aerial intelligence thanks to efficient fighter protection.

CHAPTER 4

PART 2: FERRYING & FLIGHT TESTING

To return to D'Urban Armstrong's role in the great scheme of things, we left him posted to Home Establishment on 20 December 1916 after a seven-month tour at the Front. The following day he transferred to Farnborough as a test and ferry pilot with the Southern Aircraft Repair Depot (SAD). With the build-up and launch of the spring offensive his duties constantly sent him between England, Scotland and France on a non-stop variety of missions: testing new and reconditioned aeroplanes, collecting and delivering all manner of machines, taking them for service at home and abroad, and occasionally being called upon to fly personnel about, including top brass. As an aside, it's possible that while there he met Malcolm Campbell, later Sir Malcolm, of land speed record fame, who was also based at SAD from early April 1917.

In France the ferry pilots were stationed at No. 1 Aircraft Depot, St Omer. This was where machines had to be delivered for deployment in conflict and from where many were also brought back. Armstrong would make so many trips to St Omer that it would become a second home. Flying some of the aircraft from as far afield as Glasgow to the Channel ports and then over to France, he would return sometimes by air, sometimes by sea. On these duties he crossed the Channel eighty-eight times. Calculated as an average figure, this would equate to one Channel crossing for every two days of his six-month tour.

Below is a page from his album showing rare photographs of Armstrong about to take off in the first Bristol M.1B Monoplane to go to France, A5139 (110hp Clerget 9Z). George Turner, shortly to be promoted to captain, shown speaking to him, was Officer i/c Ferry Pilots, Central Aircraft Repair Depot, Aircraft Park Lympne.[2] It is known that DVA test-flew the Monoplane upon its arrival at No. 1 Aircraft Depot St Omer, but until these snaps were discovered it was not generally known that he also made the delivery for assessment. Records show that on 23 January 1917 the test pilots were

CAMEL PILOT SUPREME CAPTAIN D.V. ARMSTRONG DFC

Lieutenant D.V. Armstrong, Captain Allan Maxwell Lowery and Captain (later Air Chief Marshal) Roderic Maxwell Hill. The latter two more senior officers handed in official reports which were negative, and the Bristol

Another snap of DVA with Bristol Monoplane A5139. [Trevor Henshaw]

Monoplane was never adopted by the RFC. The contents of Armstrong's test report are not known, but subsequent assessments suggested that the Monoplane would have been a very useful addition to the war effort. Maybe DVA's report was suppressed because it failed to support the official view.

No. 1 Aircraft Depot at St Omer, feeding the northern armies, was one of the two large stationary RFC depots in France where stores were kept and aircraft repaired and replaced (No. 2 at Candas fed the southern armies). Here all machines had to pass on their way to and from the Front; the squadrons proceeding overseas landed there from England and then went on to their allotted aerodromes, as did new and reconstructed aircraft and those sent across in parts to be erected at their destination. The essential task of salvage was carried out to reclaim as much as possible from aircraft damaged beyond repair, and a pool held spare machines to replace those lost in action. Engines were overhauled, guns tested, compasses swung, component parts sent out to the squadrons, and when enemy aircraft were captured intact they were always sent up to the depots to be flown. Armstrong was among the pilots who tested these and also new and modified types produced by the Allied manufacturers.

In the next series of photographs, DVA can be seen ferrying Sopwith Pups to France. At the turn of the year the favoured British scout machine was still the French-built 110hp Nieuport 17, though some examples that began to arrive were subject to structural failures due to declining production standards. New designs were needed, especially when the Germans started equipping their scouts with 160hp Mercedes engines. The pusher-type 100hp Airco DH.2 had reached the end of its usefulness when synchronization gear permitted the faster tractor types to fire forward, using the aircraft itself as a gun platform. And although some early RFC squadrons went to France equipped with the new Royal Aircraft Factory SE.5s, there were persistent problems with the 150hp Hispano-Suiza V-8 engine that powered them.

The latest British-built contribution sent over in quantities was the 80hp Le Rhône Sopwith Pup which, although clearly underpowered, enjoyed a remarkable agility; best of all, it could turn inside any German machine. The knowledge that they were outclassed seemed to engender a fierce loyalty to the Pup by pilots of the Corps, and some of the most riveting accounts of Pup versus Hun may be found in *Sopwith Scout 7309*, the memoir of Gordon 'Bill' Taylor of No. 66 Squadron, who arrived at the Front in March 1917. On first impression he thought the machine an ugly little craft, squat and top-heavy looking, 'but she was undeniably nimble and seemed to welcome whatever aerobatics I chose to put her through'.

Close-up of Sopwith Pup 'Phyllis' flown by Jimmy Meredith Davies with 112 Squadron.

On better acquaintance this 'great little aircraft' had a tight, well-balanced feel and could climb 20,000 feet with its tiny 80hp engine. And so the loyalty grew 'into a protective instinct that would tolerate no outside criticism of the machine at all'. However, there were early teething troubles with the engines and at the outset it was rare for all six aircraft of his flight to be serviceable, or to complete a patrol without an engine failure or forced landing. Eventually the mechanics became familiar with the Le Rhônes and the pilots learnt to use them properly, even though they often had to be revved unmercifully to get the best performance. 'Ballraces went; cylinders; pistons; tappet rods fell out. On one patrol a cylinder began to miss, making the engine vibrate so violently that I could not keep up with the flight; I gradually lost height, keeping under the shelter of the formation – expecting to be picked off by a Hun Albatros at any minute – till I finally made it back to the lines and was able to go shuddering on down to a landing.'

Fighting on such unequal terms, 'I felt very naked behind the little rotary engine as I looked into the smoking face of the Albatros, with six feet of Mercedes to shield the pilot from my fire.' Confronting such an adversary demanded a well-thought-out strategy. The Pup could turn inside the Albatros, but the Albatros could easily outclimb the Pup at 14,000 feet. Its speed was also greater, so it could leave the Pup standing in a dive. 'These factors made surprise attack absolutely essential, going in from above without being seen, using the height to overcome the deficiency in level speed, then trying to lure the heavy Albatros into a close duel.' Withdrawal was hardly possible: once involved he had no chance to fly out again ... although fortunately the German pilots often showed a disinclination for close manoeuvres. Despite outclassing the Pup in power, speed, rate of climb and armament (their Albatri carried twin Spandaus against the Pup's single Vickers), they would frequently break off and head east aided by the following wind. Not so, however, the brightly-coloured von Richthofen *Jastas*. Taking full advantage of the performance of their D.IIIs, they formed the policy of climbing to great altitude above their home bases, which were around Douai at the time, and simply waiting there for the inevitable opportunity to dive upon RFC machines on their thrice-daily forays into Hunland. These élite *Jastas*, when encountered, were more than willing to dogfight. 'Whatever I did the Huns just soared above me. ... I couldn't reach them to attack, and couldn't climb away to escape.' Again, it was the Pup's speed of manoeuvrability that allowed its pilots their best means of survival. 'Every combat with the Albatros was a flashing series of crises, each of which had to be analysed and dealt with within fractions of a second.'

Only a first-hand account like Bill Taylor's can portray how a front-line fighter squadron faced the days, weeks and months of constant encounters with the enemy:[3]

> The flight was fused into a team, in a united squadron. ... Perhaps I should be able to tell stories of broken, disillusioned pilots drinking desperately in the bar, of emotional outbursts, fear, triumph, hatred, dramatic re-creations in the Mess of the day's fighting. But none of that sort of thing happened. There was drama all right, but it was kept carefully out of our life on the ground.
>
> The bar was a place to lean on quietly with a drink, a centre where we met, and chatted, and enjoyed relaxing much as we might have done in any English pub. Sometimes the gaiety at the bar might have been slightly forced, when a well-established or particularly popular pilot was killed or thought to have been.
>
> But the disquiet passed, like everything else, and soon became unreal and distant. We had looked upon the threshold of death – but it was gone now, and we were back within our own limitations which, mercifully, were not visible to us; and the world was the war and the sky and the Huns and the Mess and ourselves.

The service life for an aeroplane in regular combat was no more than a hundred hours, whereupon it was returned to the Aircraft Depot at St Omer

DVA taking off in Sopwith Pup.

to be rebuilt or sent back to England as a training machine. So for Armstrong the great Arras offensive in early 1917 meant that a large amount of his work involved incessantly ferrying Sopwith Pups.

Pictured above in the cockpit DVA describes himself as 'dressed up for the Channel', and indeed he needed serious protection, for the 1916/17 winter was long and bitterly cold: a challenging prospect for an open-cockpit pilot, and a reminder of the contrast in weather compared with his native sub-tropical Natal, which at that time of year would be enjoying its highest midsummer temperatures.

The caption to the photograph below states that it was taken while the aircraft was just a few feet above the photographer.

The second photograph below is of another Sopwith Pup with 1st AM Blow – probably Air Mechanic 1st Class Corporal John C. Blow of Lympne. DVA would have known him as a vital member of the service employed in handling all manner of aircraft from a wide variety of manufacturers and ensuring their airworthiness.

Next in his album is the SPAD pictured above, a successful design in both French and British hands. His caption says nothing; but in the hallowed tradition of those who love to fly he was already amassing a good collection of aircraft types for his log-book, and we may safely assume he lost no time adding the SPAD to his list. By the end of the war he was officially credited with having flown forty-seven different types – doubtless unofficially the total was much greater.

Pictured opposite is a particularly interesting aircraft he encountered at this time: Sopwith Triplane N533, one of the two early Sopwith Triplanes delivered to the RFC, which he flew from the RNAS (Royal Naval Air Service) station at Cranwell, Lincolnshire, to Farnborough. He is seen climbing into the cockpit prior to leaving. The Triplane, known familiarly as the Tripe or Tripehound, was originally ordered by the Admiralty, whose air service and its equipment were separate from the Army's flying service, and who had their own contract with Sopwith Aviation. They first took delivery of Triplanes in December 1916, after which the type was used extensively by the RNAS and saw significant naval action from February and throughout the spring of 1917.

On its first appearance this grand Sopwith invention immediately created something of a sensation for its performance and combat prowess –

it could out-climb and out-turn the Albatros D III, which was so outclassed by the Tripehound that the Germans hastened to copy it. They produced numbers of different prototypes of their own, of which the most successful was the Fokker Dr.I, later made eye-catchingly famous by the Manfred von Richthofen Circus. Fewer than 150 Sopwith Triplanes were built, but they flew impressively and fought with distinction. Apart from some structural flaws their main drawback was the time it took for repairs, with many key installations like the fuel tank being inaccessible without disassembly. Triplane production lost favour in the latter part of 1917 when spares became hard to get, especially after the Camels came on-stream and immediately gained preference. But the adventurous three-plane design retains a unique place in aviation history and is much favoured by builders of models and replicas to this day.

The prospect of crossing twenty miles of sea from Dover to Calais, especially in an unfamiliar aircraft, was not one to be tackled lightly. Harold Balfour learnt a salutary lesson during his time with 60 Squadron when it was the practice that an extra twenty-four hours' leave was offered to any pilot who would bring an aeroplane back from the English supply base to France on his return. Having volunteered to do so, he was detailed to fetch a DH.2 pusher scout with 100hp Gnome Monosoupape rotary engine. Balfour had 'never flown a pusher scout nor operated a Mono type of Gnome', but

Another snap from his ferrying days is this Naval Bristol Scout at Chingford RNAS aerodrome, just north of London.

he proceeded to Farnborough and took it up for an exploratory circuit and landing, equipped with a few words about the throttle settings for take-off and cruise.[4]

> Receiving nothing concerning the petrol pressure system, I, with the carelessness of all young people, did not take the trouble to enquire into it before taking off. The memory of that journey to France is still clear, for I had scarcely left Farnborough, avoiding low clouds over some of the Surrey hills, than I was completely lost. I flew in the direction where I thought the South Coast should be and was so indicated by a somewhat inaccurate compass.
>
> The first place I struck was Ramsgate RNAS Aerodrome. It was comparatively easy to make Folkestone, where I planned to fill up with petrol preparatory to crossing the Channel. Between Ramsgate and Folkestone the engine cut out twice, but by extremely good fortune on each occasion there was a good landing ground below me. I succeeded in pumping up sufficient pressure to feed the engine both times, and also trained the local inhabitants sufficiently to get them to start the engine.

When I arrived over Folkestone the same thing happened again. I telephoned for mechanics and eventually got the DH.2 there by two p.m. The Channel was misty and the sky interlaced with intermittent rain squalls [this was July 1916]. I therefore decided not to attempt to cross that day, but only to carry out a test-flight in order to check the compass ready for the next day. The method of doing this was to fly between two concrete bases on the top of the cliff. By flying direct from one to the other the pilot was straight in the correct direction for the Channel crossing [to Calais]. As the pilot got on to this course he could check the reading of his compass, and so allow for any errors.

At about three o'clock I started off to do this, flew the course and took my compass reading, then commenced to work out the correction. By the time I had completed this I looked round and to my consternation found that I was right over the Channel, that the land had been completely blotted out by the mist, and that below me was nothing but a grey sea, empty of all ships. I was scared of turning for fear my compass would not steady up sufficiently to allow me to make the English Coast, so decided the only thing to do was to carry on, keep strictly to my compass course, and hope to hit the French side at some point. I was alternately just above the waves or enveloped in the clouds as I held the stick for what seemed the longest flight of my life. I knew at any moment the pressure system might play me the same trick as it had already done three times that morning. ... [After about 30 minutes] I saw ahead the blessed sight of land. I had struck the coast north of Calais. ... Fortunately the engine did, yet once more, and for the fourth time, its now celebrated trick of stopping, and made imperative a descent into a field below.

The reason it was fortunate for Balfour was that he then learnt he had been contour-flying along the wrong road. Back in the air, with the weather even worse, he found himself down at about 200 feet when the engine spluttered and cut out for the fifth time – over a forest. 'By the grace of God I had just passed over a small clearing,' he wrote; and turning into wind he floated down just missing the treetops. 'The clearing was so small that there was only one thing to be done, which was to send a lorry to dismantle the machine and tow it to St Omer. I count this as one of the very lucky escapes of my flying career where I was saved from the results of my ignorance by sheer providence.'

It is worth noting that the standard method of navigation at the time, whether over land or sea, consisted of reading maps and following visible features; for directional aid there was a whisky compass of wandering habits,[5] which gave readings of such inconsistency that it took great skill and concentration to maintain a heading within anything like five degrees of accuracy. Arthur Gould Lee, flying with No. 46 Squadron in 1917, described the compass as a joke: '... the slightest jerk of the rudder sets it spinning, and it needs a longish spell of smooth straight flying to settle down again.'[6]

The other instruments available to the pilot, aside from those associated with the fuel/engine installation, consisted of a simple airspeed indicator using a pitot-tube system (this can be seen on the front starboard interplane strut in Plate 4); a rudimentary slip-bubble like a builder's spirit level to gauge lateral inclination; and a less-than-reliable altimeter.

To aid the pilot Britain and France had extensive and reliable maps together with quite sophisticated meteorological services at this time, and for airfields in regular use the height above sea level would be known. However, this could not be accurately set on the altimeter on take-off because the instrument's calibration was not fine enough: it could only register thousands of feet in 200-feet gradations. The best the pilot could do was simply to set the zero on the dial opposite the point where the needle rested at ground level. Essentially an aneroid barometer, the altimeter worked on sensitivity to barometric pressure and indeed the current and trending range of local barometric pressures would be available on the ground. But because he had no in-flight radio, the pilot could not be made aware of whatever changes in surface pressure were taking place while he was aloft, changes that could mean his altimeter was no longer reading accurately when he needed it most, i.e. on coming in to make what could be an emergency landing. Plus there were other problems. The needle could easily be affected to the extent of plus or minus 200 feet by the vibration of the engine. And there was always altimeter lag, which made readings generally too low during ascent and too high during descent (in 1922 it was discovered that solder was largely to blame).[7] For these reasons the advice from the Air Board Technical Department in a July 1917 booklet on instruments was that pilots should rely on the Mark 1 eyeball, not the altimeter, at heights less than 1,000 feet and when landing.[8]

A pilot like Armstrong ferrying between depots in England and France would have easy access to current and forecast weather and barometric pressure, but since the decision to fly depended normally on adequate visibility (unless you were Harold Balfour), and since there were no high terrain features or hazards you needed to avoid on this route, it's doubtful whether such aids were actually useful for the job in hand. It would be a different matter if you needed to make a forced landing when lost in dire visibility, or over the Front at night in the kinds of operations DVA would pioneer in 1918.

For a ferry pilot, there was always the added pitfall of operating a foreign machine with altitude and airspeed calibrated in metric units (metres/kilometres) rather than imperial (feet/mph).

Cork lifebelts were provided for sea crossings, but not parachutes. The absence of parachutes for pilots and observers is well recorded, and in later life Air Vice Marshal Arthur Gould Lee, who lamented this lack of provision while serving as a Pup pilot in 1917, investigated the records but failed to find whether the roots of the omission lay in a particular reason or policy. Certainly the practical hurdles had been overcome even before the war by the invention of a compact, quickly-deployed parachute suitable for use in flight, developed by the British railway engineer Everard Calthrop. Had it been adopted and improved by systematic trialling, aeroplane manufacturers could have developed designs to accommodate parachutes. But in October 1915 the Superintendent of the Royal Aircraft Factory was refused when he tried requesting a modest expenditure on tests. A year later another request was turned down.

However, in January 1917 General Trenchard heard that Calthrop's invention was being tested successfully by enterprising pilots at the Orfordness Experimental Station, and suggested such tests be continued in France (they were not). Meanwhile he ordered twenty black parachutes to be used for dropping agents behind enemy lines by night (they were). Lee concluded that most of the blame lay with 'the collective official mind', the evident ignorance of aviation and the failure to grasp the realities of combat flying on the part of members of the Air Board and Directorate of Military Aeronautics. After more attempts, and more rebuffs, a Parachute Committee was eventually set up; they were still deliberating when, in mid-1918, parachutes suddenly became news as the Germans started issuing them to their pilots. Whitehall at last placed a substantial order, too late for use before the Armistice.

In his search for a policy decision, Arthur Gould Lee seems not to have found a certain report of the Air Board which has since come to light: 'It is the opinion of the Board that the presence of such an apparatus might impair the fighting spirit of pilots and cause them to abandon machines which might otherwise be capable of returning to base for repair.'[9] Not only was such a sentiment demeaning of a cadre of men who had voluntarily come forward to fight in the air, it also deprived the aviation industry of vital feedback from pilots who could have survived to report experiences in the field, thereby identifying the many design and construction flaws that led to crashes.

Also in his book *No Parachute*, Lee gave a clear-eyed summary of the shortcomings of RFC machines: 'the aeroplanes of the day not only lacked brakes, but had an open cockpit, no heater, no oxygen, no parachute, no radio link with air or ground, and no compass worth the name. These deficiencies were in keeping with the construction, wooden frames braced together by wires and covered with highly inflammable doped fabric.'[10]

Their young pilots nevertheless – including Lee himself – savoured the sheer adventure of taking to the air, accepting the deadly hazard offered by war among the clouds but seldom reflecting upon it. They lived for the day, for the hour, for the excitement of fighting in the skies. 'Only when you are young,' said Lee, 'can you relish to the full the exhilarating sensations of mortal danger.'

CHAPTER 5

HOME DEFENCE, FORMING UP WITH 39 SQUADRON

In May 1917 the German High Command launched mass daytime bombing attacks on London and south-east England, using Gotha G.IV heavy bombers based in occupied Belgium. It was part of an overall plan which included unrestricted submarine attacks on all Allied and neutral shipping. The main aim of the aerial attacks, as General Erich Ludendorff wrote, was the moral intimidation of the British nation and the crippling of their will to fight, in the hope that the civilian population would overthrow the government and demand an end to the war. This grandiose scheme had very limited success, but there were several direct hits scored, and the public became incensed at incursions over Britain and angry at civilian casualties; plus the frequent alarms had the effect of interrupting munitions and other production. In response the British government determined on urgent reinforcement and restructuring of the London air defence organization, and new Home Defence squadrons were formed.

Lieutenant D.V. Armstrong's next three postings were all to Home Defence, beginning with No. 39 Squadron, one of the first HD squadrons to have been formed (in April 1916 at Hounslow), and which had performed signally in defence of London against raids by Zeppelin airships that year. Indeed, the early HD squadrons were so successful against Zeppelins that the German airship service never recovered after October 1916 when Heinrich Mathy, their premier airship commander, had died in his flaming L.31 over Potters Bar after bombing Cheshunt. That victory was achieved by Second Lieutenant W.J. (Wulstan) Tempest of No. 39 Squadron, who was awarded the DSO.

No. 39 Squadron had three flights each operating from a different base in Essex: A Flight at North Weald Bassett in Epping Forest, B Flight at Sutton's Farm, Rainham, south-east of Romford (later RAF Hornchurch),

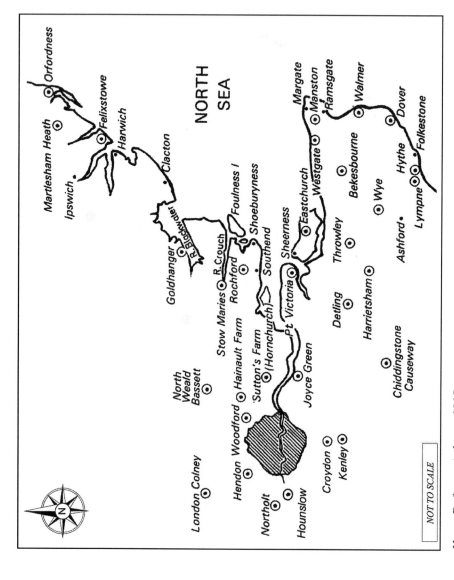

Home Defence air bases 1917.

NOT TO SCALE

and C Flight at Hainault Farm in the Ilford area, north-west of Romford (Second World War RAF Fairlop was later established nearby).

In reality each hadn't more than about a dozen machines on strength, being obsolescent types such as the BE.2c, BE.12 (a single-seat version of the BE.2c) and FE.2b. No modern fighters had ever been allocated to Home Defence on a permanent basis as their one job had been to shoot down the slow-moving conventional airships.

On 25 May 1917, the date of the first mass Gotha raid, the peace of small-town English life was shattered at about five o'clock on a Friday afternoon as people in the south-east prepared for their Whitsun holiday. There had been no air-raid warning. No. 39 Squadron had eleven of these low-performance machines to send up, alongside eight from 37 Squadron and thirteen from 50 Squadron, although the better equipped RNAS coastal bases were airborne ahead of them with their Sopwith Pups and Triplanes. But no home-based air defence aircraft managed to attack the Gothas until their deadly business was done, and in the space of about ninety minutes the German bombs killed ninety-five and seriously injured another 192.

While the War Office hastily tried to re-establish the Home Defence Group, now largely depleted after the Zeppelin threat had been seen off, the Gothas continued with waves of attacks throughout the summer. The second took place on 5 June, ironically enough immediately following a practice alert by squadrons of the Southern (HD) Wing which had sent up about thirty aircraft at 15.00 with instructions to patrol for about two hours. The first sighting of the bombers was at 17.40, when the squadrons on patrol had returned to refuel. Nevertheless, about the same number of machines managed a quick turnaround to get airborne again, the first being from 50 Squadron at a few minutes after 18.00, swiftly followed by flights from 37, 39 and 78 Squadrons; some twenty-two machines of the RNAS soon joined them. Among the forty-four RFC aircraft that rose in hopes of intercepting the enemy that evening were nine assorted types that were scrambled from the aircraft parks at Hendon and Lympne; and one of their pilots was D.V. Armstrong, who availed himself of Sopwith Pup B1731 which was due to join 66 Squadron in France the following day. He just happened to be on the ground at No. 8 Aircraft Park, Lympne, which had already suffered as a target in the first raid on 25 May when Gothas of *Kagohl 3* were prevented from attacking London due to the weather and chose Lympne as a secondary target. Without a system of speedy coordination with ground observers, the pilots themselves had very little hope of even sighting their adversaries, and on this date only five of the aircraft, all RNAS, proved to have been able to make any kind of contact.

No. 39 Squadron continued to field their handful of BE.12s until August, but in July they enjoyed the significant addition of six of the superior fast new SE.5s that were delivered to their Sutton's Farm base, where a group of experienced pilots were being concentrated to fly them. They included Lieutenant E.S. (Edward) Moulton-Barrett and Captains G.W. (Gilbert) Murlis Green, W.H. (Bill) Haynes, J.I. (James) MacKay, and J.H.T. (Tryggve) Gran. Gran had personally been involved in overseeing the provision of the SE.5s.

With more intensive Gotha bombing raids through June and into early July, the public outcry hastened the development of dedicated new

The photos above and below from DVA's album show an SE.5a fitted with 200hp Hispano-Suiza engine (mid-1917, replacing the SE.5's original 150hp HS8A) complete with pictures of him flying it; the 2-blade propeller suggests this could have been a 39 Squadron machine.

fighter detachments supported by early-warning systems. No. 39's group of experienced SE.5 pilots from Sutton's Farm would form the nucleus of a new 44 Squadron, while a new No. 61 was projected as an offshoot of 37 Squadron, and a new No. 112 as an offshoot of 50 Squadron.

On Sunday 8 July the pilots of No. 46 Squadron at the Western Front received orders with bewildering suddenness to fly over to Sutton's Farm in England where they would commence Home Defence operations against the Gotha threat. On the same day No. 39 Squadron's B Flight at Sutton's Farm, including the anti-bomber combat detachment, received equally sudden orders to pack up and move north to Hainault Farm. On Monday 9 July, in conditions of pouring rain, they arrived to settle in with the squadron's C Flight already based there, which included Captain O.V. (Owen) Thomas and Lieutenant G.T. (Gerald) Stoneham, to form up the new No. 44 HD fighter squadron to be established later in the month.

Machines employed hitherto on Home Defence had not operated in formation, under a group leader, as had become usual on the Western Front in the face of the German *Jastas*. All this would change once the bombing raids on England began. Since the huge Gothas worked in formations bristling with armament, HD squadrons had to adopt new tactics against them. While practising how to get off the ground as fast as possible, their key task was to develop the art of concentrated full-squadron formation attacks upon powerfully armed groups of bombers, with the aim of repelling or at least deterring their incursions inland.

An indication of how critical it was to develop this key skill is given in the following comments by former USAF F-4 Phantom pilot Jonathan A. Hayes (holder of 5 DFCs [one with Valor Clasp] and 22 Air Medals).

> It can be thought of as the aerial extension of marching in formation – the military purpose of both is the same. Beyond fundamental stick and rudder flying skills, formation flying boils down to two things basic to all military operations: teamwork and discipline. Teamwork is the meshing and co-ordinating of individual efforts to achieve a group result. It is one of the most simple and most complex things imaginable, involving everything from ground crews right through to operational scheduling. The organization of British air defences in 1917/18 provided the basis of the air defence structure that was so successful in the Battle of Britain, 1940.[1]

The new unit at Hainault Farm was initially equipped, for the purpose of expediting training in formation flying, with the already outdated two-seat Sopwith 1½-Strutters, these to be replaced by Sopwith Camels as soon as the new fighters became available. And so formation practice became the order of the day as the embryo fighter squadron later to be No. 44 began to take shape.

At the same time an efficient early-warning system was developed to give the alert of an incoming raid. Arthur Gould Lee, for whose squadron (No. 46) the 39 Squadron pilots had vacated Sutton's Farm, was undergoing precisely the same HD training process on Sopwith Pups:

> With every alarm, practice or in earnest, the squadron became more and more adept at speeding the take-off. As soon as the warning *Readiness* came on the phone to the squadron office, and the klaxon shrilled, the whole camp leapt to action. Every man dropped whatever he was doing and ran to the hangars, the mechanics had to haul the Pups to the tarmac and start them, the pilots to throw on their flying kit and clamber into their planes. Within ninety seconds the eighteen pilots could be seated in their cockpits, taxiing out by flights to predetermined positions on the aerodrome. If the order to patrol had already come, flights took off at once and assembled in the air. Barely two minutes would have elapsed.[2]

At Hainault Farm the unit that would become No. 44 Squadron was rapidly dubbed 'the Circus' by the thousands of onlookers who came to watch the practice flying and stunting during the long summer evenings.

There is little information in official records about DVA's spell with No. 39 Squadron, but it was in mid-July 1917 (officially 15 July) that he joined them on an interim basis – it is believed he flew No. 2 in his flight – in anticipation of the move to No. 44. By 21 July, as well as 1½-Strutters the parent unit already had at least ten of the latest Camel fighters on its strength; and on 24 July 1917 the new No. 44 Home Defence Squadron came into being. After this the remainder of No. 39 reverted to operating with BE.12s based at North Weald Bassett as a safeguard against any further Zeppelin attacks.

Among the interesting personnel who coincided with DVA whilst in 39 Squadron was the remarkable Sergeant Major Albert Hutton, much respected for inventing the illuminated Vickers gunsight named after him (see opposite).

This relaxed group snapped in a lull between training flights at Hainault Farm depicts (L-R): Geoffrey Buck, T.J.C. (Thomas) Martyn (of 101 Night Bomber Squadron), DVA, and Tryggve Gran. Martyn later became a journalist and founded the US magazine Newsweek.

Here Albert Hutton is seen inspecting the SE.5a's Lewis gun on the centre section; it was also armed with a single Vickers, with synchronization gear to fire through the propeller, mounted on the fuselage forward of the pilot.

A group from No. 39 Squadron taken at North Weald, with Tryggve Gran second from left seated. [G.T. Stoneham]

Even more remarkable was the intrepid Norwegian pre-war aviator and member of Scott's Antarctic expedition named Tryggve Gran, inevitably known as 'Trigger'. He was brought into the squadron while acting as a military attaché for his government, having been passed off as Canadian and given the unlikely alias 'Captain Teddy Grant'.

The factory Camels initially received had 130hp Clerget 9B rotary engines with the Lang LP2850 propeller, recognizable by its fabric-covered tips, but there were continued experiments with the configuration as deliveries came to Martlesham Heath that summer. Modifications had already been applied to the Sopwith 1½-Strutter, improving the field of vision by converting it to house the pilot in the rear cockpit; then Lewis guns were added on the upper wings as seen on the SE.5a on the previous page. These and other ideas were tested and the results were known with typical irreverence as Comics. Similar airframe and armament modifications were now applied to some of the new Camels, which in their turn acquired the same nickname of Comics.

Moving the Camel's single cockpit one bay farther aft was not difficult and simply required the fuel tank to be moved forward. Meanwhile the 110hp Le Rhône 9J engine became preferred to the Clerget, delivering

Sopwith F.1 Camel E.5165 gives a clear indication of the Comic configuration: it was issued to No. 151 Squadron in September 1918 having special camouflage for night operations. [Colin Owers]

better performance despite its lower hp rating; and this was significantly improved when the squared-tip Lang propeller was replaced by the coarser-pitch AD644; this configuration soon became standard. It was a while before the full Comic modification came into use for the Camel, but it proved excellent for the night-fighter role and conversion kits began to be supplied at the beginning of 1918. It was not adopted by Armstrong.

CHAPTER 6

44 SQUADRON: ARMSTRONG MEETS CAMEL!

No. 44 Home Defence Squadron was officially formed on 24 July 1917 under Major T.O'B. Hubbard MC at the 100-acre Hainault Farm Aerodrome, its base throughout the war. Although the Camel was delivered in quantities to the RNAS, No. 44 was described by DVA as 'the first Sopwith Camel Squadron with the RFC', which we may take to mean that it was the first to be wholly Camel-equipped. For the record, No. 70 Squadron in France received a very early delivery on 29 June, but their remaining machines arrived only at the end of July.

Designed to replace its predecessor the Pup, whose single Vickers machine gun was susceptible to freezing up at high altitudes, the Camel

DVA is here pictured in probably the earliest photograph of B3826 with 130hp Clerget and Lang LP2850 propeller, taken at North Weald Bassett Aerodrome in summer/ autumn 1917; his wardrobe includes a thigh-length shearling-lined leather coat with fleece collar.

acquired its typically frivolous nickname because of the metal fairing that protected its gun-breeches against this problem, producing a hump in front of the cockpit. The Camel's double armament, fitted as standard, was one of its major developments: it was the first British fighter to mount the classic installation of a side-by-side pair of synchronized Vickers guns firing through the airscrew. The belt-fed Vickers was preferable to the Lewis gun used on other British aircraft because it had a higher rate of fire than the Lewis, which required a magazine change every ninety-seven rounds. The Vickers also used a closed-bolt mechanism which was more reliable with synchronization gear.

By the time 44 Squadron's brand-new Camels began arriving on 21 July there had been nearly three months of Gotha bombing raids while the RFC soldiered on with their 1½-Strutters plus an additional complement of BE.2cs and Avro 504s. During this time Home Defence had remained entrusted to a handful of courageous units using these types of underpowered and under-gunned machines.

Armstrong's first Camel was B3826, equipped with 130hp Clerget 9B rotary, and it quickly became the machine on which reports of his astonishing prowess spread throughout the Corps. The date he took delivery is unknown, but it was built by the Sopwith factory at Kingston-upon-Thames and received by his flight by at least 12 August, the day when one of his first defence flights took place against a force of thirteen Gothas targeting Chatham docks. Some 139 defensive sorties were recorded that day, but few made contact with the enemy. Within weeks No. 44 Squadron, now under the command of Captain Gilbert Murlis Green, was fully equipped with Camels – some with Clerget engines and some with Le Rhônes. Soon the intensive German bomber offensive was being successfully counteracted by effective early-warning systems of telecommunications which alerted the cordon of waiting Home Defence squadrons to incoming Gothas. The following photo is hugely reminiscent of Battle of Britain pilots awaiting similar warnings to scramble.

By these means the daylight bombing raids of 1917 were effectively brought to an end as the summer months drew to a close; but there was no respite for the HD squadrons. From September they would have to contend with a new and daunting prospect: Gotha bomber raids at night.

Thus in 44 Squadron began DVA's partnership with the Sopwith Camel, an aircraft with which his name is forever associated. A tremendously challenging machine, it concentrated the masses of armament, engine, pilot and fuel within an overall length of about seven feet. Its notorious sensitivity

Waiting for orders: (R-L) Brand, Adams, unknown, Craig, unknown (possibly Gran), Banks, Lomas, Cecil Lewis lying with back to the camera, possibly DVA lying in foreground with face hidden. [Trevor Henshaw]

on the controls was coupled with a powerful gyroscopic effect from the rotary engine that produced a natural torque which, once mastered, assisted in fast and responsive manoeuvring. J.M. Bruce, writing in *Flight* magazine, confirmed that it owed its success to its phenomenal manoeuvrability. 'The elevator was extremely powerful and the ailerons sensitive, but it was the Camel's startlingly quick reaction to coarse handling that was the undoing of so many of the pilots who attempted to fly it. At full throttle it was markedly tail-heavy, and the absence of an adjustable tailplane made it tiring to fly.'[1] Others might disagree about those ailerons: in fact their performance was, to put it kindly, disappointing and occasioned significant adverse yaw; while the poor directional stability of the undersized vertical surfaces made the machine skittish when using the rudder.

The Camel's *métier* was the dogfight, in which it excelled: it could turn in an astonishingly small radius thanks to its short fuselage and the concentration of weights. The torque effect from its rotary engine caused it to turn with greater alacrity to the right than the left, and its ultra-fast right-hand turn was its great advantage although the 90-degree precession induced the nose to pitch down, and once this happened the inadequate top (left) rudder could not bring the nose up again. So in the instant of turning right the pilot learnt to prevent the nose dropping by pre-emptively applying left rudder, which would feel decidedly odd. To make a fast right-hand turn without losing height he had to push on full rudder before full bank. This was far from intuitive and would have caused no end of heartache, ending in many inadvertent spins. Plus it would quickly spin if a turn were tightened too much. But once a Camel pilot had become accustomed to his sensitive mount and understood its idiosyncrasies he found it an ideal fighting aeroplane. H.F. King, also writing in *Flight*, observed that with the right hand on the stick it was the deadliest fighting machine in existence. Even its tricks and vices could be transformed into virtues.[2]

If anyone may be said to have had the right hands for a Camel, that person was D'Urban Armstrong. He was, of course, well used to the behaviour of French rotary engines, having flown them throughout his entire tour at the Front in 1916. The Clerget presented no more problems than the Le Rhône and, compared to pilots who were accustomed to stationary engines, he would have found the transition straightforward.

RNAS pilot W.G. (William) Moore, one of the Camel's famous exponents, declared it was like having a pair of wings strapped to your shoulder-blades:[3]

> Once you knew them, you could do anything you liked with them and turn their peculiarities to advantage. They were wonderful in a dogfight because they could make the quickest change of direction of any machine that flew in that war. Its peculiarities made it the most manoeuvrable fighter ever built and the best all-round performer.

Inevitably, stunting quickly became a favourite sport with the agile and responsive machine, and this was where DVA's prowess began to earn him a fast-growing reputation. Colonel Stanley Walters, a fellow South African who became a close friend of the Armstrong family after the war, vividly remembered what an impact he made as 'unquestionably a brilliant pilot'.

> The Camel was a completely unstable aircraft which could be likened to sitting it out when taming a wild horse. ... A right-hand turn was made with almost complete application of left rudder and bank, carefully coordinated, while the pilot had constantly to monitor the carburettor mixture adjustable from the cockpit for the Clerget engine. The Camel became a

DVA's album describes this as B3826, although the markings are difficult to reconcile; it is equipped with 130hp Clerget rotary/Lang LP2850 propeller, and is modified to provide exit ports for cartridge cases and spent links.

magnificent fighting machine in France; for to get a sighting on an aircraft with such behaviour and unpredictable performance in an adversary became its defence.

The death-roll in the Training Schools to qualify on the Camel in England was worrying and morale was understandably at a low ebb. Yet the Camel was a remarkable success in France. In order to restore confidence D'Urban Armstrong, whose magnificent flying of the Camel had become legendary, was withdrawn from his squadron and he was sent round the Schools to demonstrate and to describe how the machine could be mastered. His efforts bore fruit and the flow of trained Camel pilots was restored. Armstrong's ability in stunting, now termed aerobatics, was truly wonderful to watch.[4]

Cecil Lewis added his voice to the growing admiration: many times he saw DVA go straight into his loop on take-off, a favourite trick that never ceased to amaze. 'Everyone who saw him would agree that Armstrong was the finest pilot in the Force,' he averred. 'He was a past master at that most dangerous and spectacular business of stunting near the ground.'[5]

In case it should be supposed that the difficulty of flying the Sopwith Camel was exaggerated, the following is extracted from the well-known diary attributed to Lieutenant John McGavock Grider, an American awaiting his commission in the RFC in March 1918 after the Sopwith Camel had been in service with the Corps for a good nine months.

His unit was at the School of Aerial Fighting in Ayr, Scotland, when six American naval pilots arrived to take the course on Camels, thinking they were as easy to handle as the Hanriots they'd been flying in France. Three of them were killed. Then an American instructor who had 300 hours on Curtisses in the USA spun a Camel into the ground and killed himself. The next day another man died the same way, and before he could be buried two English pilots also killed themselves, all in Camels and all doing right-hand spins.[6] The attrition rate during pilot training described by Grider was truly horrifying.

This high rate of casualties to Camel trainees was common to all training schools, so the average young student was well aware of its reputation and approached it with fear. It has been estimated the Camel killed some 350 trainees,[7] but official figures for this are lacking. In a snapshot survey of home-based (i.e. non-combat) Camel casualties, whether in training or otherwise, out of the 516 crashes surveyed nearly 50 per cent (229) were attributed to spinning, of which 167 resulted in death.[8]

This sombre reality prompted the urgent need to demonstrate to trainee and transitioning pilots the true nature of the Camel and encourage them to embrace its potential, whilst instilling due respect for its unforgiving propensities if mishandled. Smith Barry's innovative school at Gosport was designed to produce instructors properly trained in stunting, but it was not until quite late in the war that they started coming through and then not in sufficient numbers to provide widespread training on advanced machines. And meanwhile the need for men skilled enough to handle them in combat was relentless. So demonstrations by someone like DVA were crucial in spreading confidence and fostering the belief that the Camel could be a responsive, rewarding mount and a deadly effective gun-platform.

Unfortunately, despite its many advances over previous machines and its delightful agility once mastered, there were hidden design flaws in the Camel which were never fully appreciated until its service life was over. As pointed out by Wing Commander Norman Macmillan OBE MC AFC DL, in his book *Great Aircraft*, 'There was something about a Camel which could elude even the greatest experts among pilots. ... Time after time the Camel would perform manoeuvres with identical results; but on the tenth or

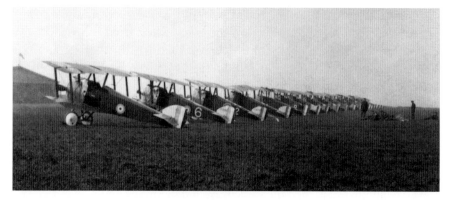

DVA's B3826 is seen 3rd from the front in this line-up of 44 Squadron Camels, with several of A Flight closest to camera: his now familiar squadron marking of number '2' can be seen on fuselage and turtle-deck. A few in the line have adopted the Comic configuration with Lewis guns above their centre-sections.

twentieth or perhaps the fiftieth time it would behave differently.' Macmillan was well acquainted with the aircraft, having been a flight commander and flying instructor in the First World War. In another book, *Into the Blue*, he proposed a simple reason which could have accounted for many Camel crashes, and we will return to discuss this in Chapter 9.

DVA had been posted to join A Flight which was led by his fellow-South African Captain C.J.Q. (Quintin) Brand, later Air Vice Marshal Sir Christopher Brand KBE DSO MC DFC. Armstrong flew No. 2 in this flight on Camel B3826, with Lieutenant C.A. (Cecil) Lewis recorded as flying at No. 3; Lieutenant C. (Cyril) Patteson, who had been with DVA in 60 Squadron, flew at No. 4.[9] However, within a couple of months Lewis fell out of favour with the CO and was posted to No. 61 Squadron on his preferred SE.5s which were powered by stationary rather than rotary engines.

B Flight was led by Captain James MacKay and its known members included Captain Tryggve Gran at No. 2, Lieutenant Edward Moulton-Barrett at No. 3 – the only SE.5 pilot of 39 Squadron to have engaged the Gothas during the 1917 daylight raids – together with Captain G.A.H. (Geoffrey) Pidcock (later Air Vice Marshal) and, all too briefly, Lieutenant G.R. (George) Craig MC, who died in the squadron's first flying accident on 19 August. George Craig had transferred to the RFC in 1916 and had joined No. 44 Squadron via HD units No. 33 and No. 39. He had earned his MC for conspicuous gallantry while serving with the Lancashire Fusiliers on the Western Front.

C Flight was initially led by Captain Gilbert Murlis Green, who was moved away in August to replace Hubbard as squadron commander. No. 2 was Captain Bill Haynes, and at No. 3 Captain G.A. (George) Hackwill MC, with Lieutenant L.F. (Lionel) Lomas and Sergeant S.W. Smith at 4 and 5. Hackwill was later appointed C Flight Commander and flew one of the early night-flying modified Camels known as Comics. Another in C Flight was Lieutenant R.G.H. (Ronald) Adams.

Further squadron members included Lieutenants C.C. (Charlie) Banks MC, R.S. Bozman, J.T. (John) Collier, G.W. (Gerald) Gathergood, E. 'Pat' Gribben, E.M. (Ernest) Gilbert MC, C.R.W. (Clayton) Knight, C.J. 'Chaps' Marchant, W.E. (William) Nicholson, T.M. 'Dubs' O'Neill, A.H. (Augustus) Orlebar, G.T. (Gerald) Stoneham, E. (Edward) Travers-Smith and W.B. 'Bert' Wood, plus Second Lieutenant R.M. (later Air Vice Marshal Sir Robert) Foster.

Many members of 44 Squadron went on to illustrious careers, and some were immortalized in print. Several of them recorded vivid memories of having known DVA, including Ronald Adams and Clayton Knight of whom more later.

Lieutenant G.S. (Geoffrey) Buck is also pictured in a couple of DVA's album photographs together with Armstrong and other members of HD squadrons, almost always with the ubiquitous Quintin 'Flossie' Brand.

A rather poor quality photo from DVA's album taken at Hainault Farm showing (Left to Right) Dubs O'Neill, Ernest Gilbert, Pat Gribben, DVA and Quintin Brand.

A fine display of Camels in formation – except that this photo is faked! DVA's album reveals that it was taken by a naval photographer at Fairlop, an RNAS training unit which was situated virtually just across the road from Hainault Farm. Airborne R–L are DVA, 2/Lt David Greswolde Lewis, and Capt. William Haynes. The two machines to the left are faked. Rhodesian D.G. Lewis, the 'Baby' of the squadron, was to be von Richthofen's last victim, brought down on 20 April 1918 and survived.

Buck may have served in No. 39 and/or No. 44. He had distinguished himself in his former squadron (No. 19) being Mentioned in Despatches, and was awarded the MC in August 1917 when he was promoted to captain and flight commander.

Cecil Lewis's memoir described how he and Bill Haynes, with Armstrong making a third, 'used to see how close we *could* fly in formation. Happy in the skill of being able to keep our machines in perfect control, we used to float over the surrounding country: the two pairs of wing-tips either side of the leader's, sandwiched in between his mainplanes and tail, within four feet of his body ... taking such risks was, in those days, part of the fun.'[10]

The name of A Flight commander Quintin Brand cannot be allowed to pass without reference to the nickname 'Flossie' he acquired during his time in the RFC. Being stationed at Hainault Farm, just beyond Ilford in Essex, meant that London's West End, home of all the fashionable theatres and night-spots, was within easy reach. Many hilarious evenings were spent in town at the theatre and at parties afterwards, often joined by girls from the shows.

As recounted by Clayton Knight, Brand was regarded as a very upright gentleman and quite strait-laced. Since the others in the squadron had girlfriends and he didn't, they decided to invent for him a secret passion and came up with a number of stories about his clandestine meetings with showgirls. DVA's album lists a variety of names they invented, including Hilda, Chloë, and Sophie, but 'Flossie Highkick' was the favourite. The stories didn't last long, but the nickname 'Flossie' did.

A related story was told by C.J. 'Chaps' Marchant (of 46 Squadron fame) and passed on to this writer by Frank Cheesman.[11] Sometimes the different officers' messes would host various performers from the shows to tea parties or dinners on their days off, at which someone, usually DVA, would be asked to give one of his displays. On one occasion when some celebration was called for – it may have been Flossie's birthday – the event was marked by a mass visit by '44' to the theatre followed by dinner. The leading lady of the show happened to be Beatrice Lillie, who was well known to them all and always game for a giggle. She was playing a lively wife bored with her husband and carrying on an outrageous affair with her lover, a veritable stud. The ringleaders cooked up a jape with Bea Lillie so that throughout the play that night, every time her lover appeared she called him 'Flossie'! – much to the delight of all present – and much to Brand's

shock as you couldn't imagine a greater contrast with this stud character than Flossie who was very quiet and proper.

All this while, the Germans pursued their deadly aim of demoralizing British civilians with waves of night bombing raids on south-east England. Early attempts at interception in the usual sedate, low-powered aircraft had been woefully inadequate, and clearly the only solution was a dedicated night-fighter defence force. Nevertheless there was a general reluctance to deploy the ferociously tricky Sopwith Camels after dark, the Top Brass in their wisdom having failed to appreciate that those fighting skills honed over the summer's daytime engagements

DVA with Quintin Brand, 44 Squadron. [Clayton Knight via Peter Kilduff]

had developed in their pilots a complete mastery which produced an ideal fighting combination. The authoritative description of how night-fighting was introduced can be found in *The Air Defence of Britain 1914-1918*[12] and is worth quoting in detail here.

> There was no suggestion that day-fighter squadrons, least of all No. 44 flying the unstable Sopwith Camel, with its reputation as a 'hot' aeroplane, should operate at night. ... [But] on the night of 3-4 September, when [Hauptmann R.] Kleine's Gothas were making their first night raid on England, official policy was calmly overturned and the stability myth buried forever by what [was] later described as 'perhaps the most important event in the history of air defence'. The spontaneous decision by No. 44 Squadron's commanding officer that Camels could be flown at night is the more remarkable since 22-year-old Capt. Gilbert Ware Murlis Green, C Flight commander, had been acting squadron commander for less than a week. ...
>
> With enemy bombers spotted over the North Foreland, the idea of sitting idly on the ground at Hainault Farm was anathema to Murlis Green, so he telephoned Home Defence Brigade and extracted permission to take off. Whether he mentioned that neither he nor the other two pilots prepared to go with him had previously flown a Camel at night is doubtful. [These were Quintin 'Flossie' Brand and Charlie Banks.]
>
> The three took off from an improvised flarepath without difficulty and patrolled the Thames estuary for more than an hour, then returned to encounter none of those gloomily prognosticated perils on landing. Despite having seen nothing – perhaps not surprising in the circumstances – they came back in a state bordering on euphoria. Their first experience of that special magic surrounding night flying was sharpened by the satisfaction of having demonstrated that the redoubtable Camel was not a creature to be handled with kid gloves in daylight only ... it could be flown with complete safety by night. Records show that in the course of more than 200 subsequent operational night patrols by home-defence Camels there was not one fatal accident.[13]

With German night bombing causing even greater disruption and unrest among the civilian population, the authorities were forced to revise their thinking. Needing proper aerial protection for the home front and its production of vital war supplies, they made night patrols a priority. Home Defence units swiftly stepped up to the new skills and equipment involved. Cecil Lewis said learning to fly at night was almost like going back to his first solo.

Curiously, the Camel proved well adapted to night operations. Its forebear, the Pup, usually considered tamer and friendlier, had similarly sacrificed stability for agility: both presented difficulties which were magnified when it came to night flying. Of the Pup, even an experienced RNAS pilot like Flight Lieutenant Egbert Cadbury said 'it was pretty rotten flying an unstable fast machine in the dark.' But the Camel offered significant advantages over the Pup, including a rather greater wing loading, so that it could be flown firmly down to the flarepath where it stayed put: Group Captain Gilbert Insall said it could be landed in fifty yards without undue difficulty, a feature that had an important bearing on night-fighting morale.

DVA engaged in night sorties continuously from September to December 1917 but, like so many of his companions, he failed to make contact with the

Hainault Farm, mid 1917: (L-R) Geoffrey Buck, DVA, Lionel Lomas, Owen Thomas, Thomas Martyn, Quintin Brand; this is an early occasion on which we see the extra-length maternity-style RFC jacket which DVA often favours.

117

DVA photographed in B3826 over Fairlop by a naval photographer.

enemy. Visually scouring the dark night sky at maybe 10,000 to 15,000 feet, without radio or any other aid, it was a matter of sheer luck whether you sighted hostile aircraft let alone managed to aim at them. Nevertheless the value – and deterrent effect – of activities by RFC and RNAS squadrons was recognized, and No. 44 Squadron was one that received a high-level visit from Field Marshal Lord French, Commander-in-Chief of Home Forces, together with T.C.R. Higgins, Brigadier General Commanding Home Defence Brigade, with Lieutenant General Sir Francis Lloyd and other Top Brass. In his album there is a long-distance photo of DVA being presented to Viscount French, 'having amused him in the air' with one of his trademark Camel displays; unfortunately the group of figures silhouetted against the horizon can barely be made out.

In this new operational area the combat techniques and equipment for night-fighting had to be rapidly developed, and the RFC's Orfordness experimental station listed the following as prerequisites: the night-fighter must have superior performance; gun flash to be dampened down; non-tracer ammunition used; 45-degree upward-angled guns to be installed; and exhaust flames must be reduced. In these and a myriad of other ways the Camel became modified and equipped for night flying, an art in which DVA was to excel and was extensively called upon to give instruction.

By this stage of the war it had long been vital for pilots flying patrols at great height to take precautions against the freezing temperatures and, to combat frostbite, many slathered their faces with whale grease. The choice of clothing consisted mainly of leather greatcoats lined with fur

Members of 44 Squadron in 1917: Bill Haynes is second from right linking arms with DVA who is third from right; Lt A.E. 'Steve' Godfrey MC is at DVA's feet in front row (courtesy of Peter and Mathew Craig).

and/or sheepskin, along with fur gloves and enormous thigh-high fur boots of fleece-lined suede. Even so they still felt the cold bitterly, which was exacerbated by flying at night, until in late 1917 the Sidcot suit came into service which DVA can be seen wearing in the above photograph. It was invented by the Australian aviator Sidney Cotton, who discovered that his old grease-soaked overalls resisted the cold far better than all those combinations of bulky fur and leather. His experiments produced an all-in-one flying suit which had three layers: a thin lining of fur, a layer of airproof silk, and an outside layer of light Burberry material. Its protection was greatly valued by pilots who had to fly in piercing arctic cold.

Armstrong's B3826 underwent a few modifications over his time with 44 Squadron, including some obvious changes of propeller/boss/spinner as can be seen in photographs in this chapter. It came to be regarded as his own personal hack, and there seems a tone of regret where he writes in his photo album that he 'had to leave it' on his next posting at the end of 1917.

Just before departing 44 Squadron he captions a group of three photographs as 'my first Le Rhône Camel in 44'. Trenchard had issued advice on 9 December for all Camels across the Corps to be equipped

Above: *DVA's Camel with Le Rhône engine, in A Flight No. 2 livery, running up the motor in the snow; fuel pressure pump is visible on rear starboard centre-section strut.*

Below: *DVA in the same machine coming out of a loop.*

Durban,
Natal

26 July 1897.

2nd Lieut:
D'urban Victor Armstrong. R.F.C.

2461.

12 Feb. 1916

Plate 1. Second Lieutenant D.V. Armstrong passed the Royal Aero Club aviation tests to gain his 'ticket' number 2461 on 12 February 1916. He is seen here still wearing service dress uniform from his original unit, the South African Aviation Corps, but fitted with RFC badges and buttons. (© *The Royal Aero Club Trust*)

Plate 2. Second Lieutenant D.V. Armstrong in March 1916 with wings displayed on his new plastron-style uniform jacket. The RFC had developed its drab khaki version of the Lancer plastron, but devoid of buttons and flaps for eminently practical reasons, avoiding items that could get snagged on the multiple tensioning wires of their aircraft. It is just possible to make out his second lieutenant's single star ('pip') at the end of his shoulder strap – the only place where rank was displayed on this style of uniform. The RFC also adopted its own drab khaki field service cap in place of the Army's dark blue. (© *RNF courtesy of Hilton College*)

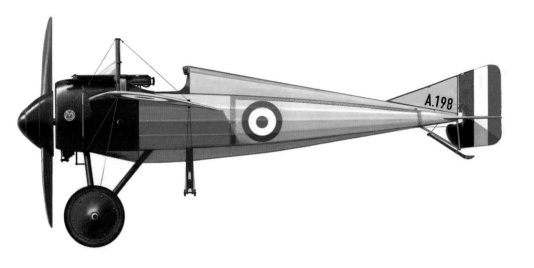

Plate 3. Two aircraft flown by Second Lieutenant D.V. Armstrong in No. 60 Squadron. (*Leighton Alcock*)

Top: Morane-Saulnier Bullet Type I serial A198 (110hp Le Rhône 9J) flown by Armstrong in September 1916; the Type I was armed with one Vickers gun with synchronization gear (offset to port side). A198 had been rebuilt and reissued after forced-landing by John Simpson in August.

Bottom: Nieuport 16c-1 serial A211 flown by Armstrong from 18 October 1916, in which he was credited with a victory on 9 November 1916, shortly before being promoted to lieutenant on 30 November. It was eventually wrecked in a landing crash by W. P. Garnett in March 1917.

Plate 4. A portrait of Sopwith F.1 Camel B3826 (130hp Clerget 9B / AD644 propeller) with DVA at the controls, pictured in early summer 1917 visiting RNAS station Fairlop, near Hainault Farm. Leader's streamers are visible on rear struts, which means that he was deputizing in his commander's absence. His caption draws attention to the pitot tube of the airspeed indicator on the machine's RH front strut and the twin Vickers guns under the centre section. Some Curtiss machines can be seen in the background. 'I had this Camel all the time I was in 44,' he adds, 'and I did 123 hours flying on it without straining a wire.' (© AJC)

Plate 5. Now with No. 44 HD Squadron, Lieutenant D.V. Armstrong is here seen in his British Warm greatcoat on a chilly day in 1917, perhaps on the same occasion as when he was snapped by his friend Clayton Knight (see page 134), about to visit his dentist in London. (*Courtesy of National Museum of the Royal Navy*)

Plate 6. Armstrong in Camel B3826, on a visit to Sutton's Farm, spies a line of parked Camels with one machine missing. With wheels brushing the grass he performs a loop through the gap … (© AJC/Lynn Williams)

Plate 7. … He completes the loop taking his 28ft wingspan Camel for a second time through the 39ft gap with wheels skimming the ground again. (© *AJC/Lynn Williams*)

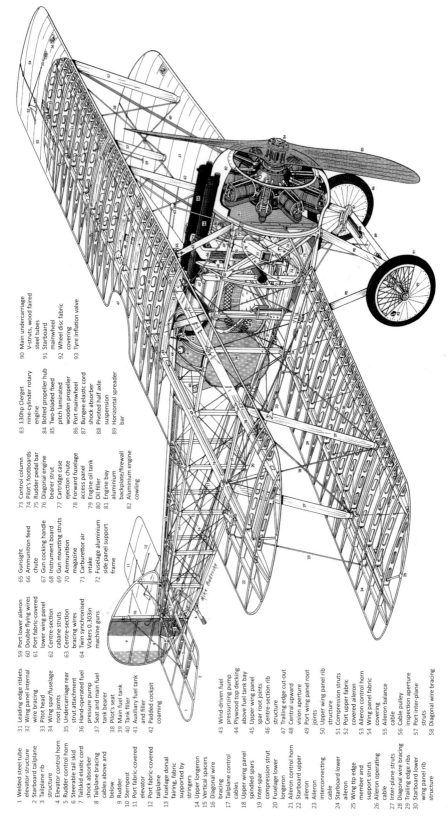

Plate 8. Sopwith F.1 Camel anatomy created for Haynes Sopwith Camel Manual. (© *Mike Badrocke courtesy of Haynes Publishing*)

1 Welded steel tube elevator structure
2 Starboard tailplane rib
3 Tailplane rib structure
4 Elevator control horn
5 Rudder control horn
6 Steerable tail skid
7 Tailskid elastic cord shock absorber
8 Tailplane bracing cables above and below
9 Rudder
10 Sternpost
11 Port fabric-covered elevator
12 Port fabric-covered tailplane
13 Fuselage dorsal fairing, fabric supported by stringers
14 Upper longeron
15 Vertical spacers
16 Diagonal wire bracing
17 Tailplane control cables
18 Upper wing panel spindled spars
19 Inter-spar compression strut
20 Fuselage lower longeron
21 Aileron control horn
22 Starboard upper aileron
23 Aileron interconnecting cable
24 Starboard lower aileron
25 Wing tip edge member and support struts
26 Aileron operating cable
27 Inter-plane cable
28 Diagonal wire bracing
29 Trailing edge ribs
30 Starboard lower wing panel rib structure

31 Leading edge riblets
32 Wing panel internal wire bracing
33 Pitot head
34 Wing spar/fuselage root joints
35 Undercarriage rear strut attachment
36 Hand-operated fuel pressure pump
37 Seat and main fuel tank bearer
38 Pilot's seat
39 Main fuel tank
40 Tank filler
41 Auxiliary fuel tank and filler
42 Padded cockpit coaming
43 Wind-driven fuel pressurizing pump
44 Plywood top decking above fuel tank bay
45 Upper wing panel spar root joints
46 Centre-section rib structure
47 Trailing edge cut-out
48 Central upward vision aperture
49 Port wing panel root joints
50 Upper wing panel rib structure
51 Compression struts
52 Port upper fabric covered aileron
53 Aileron control horn
54 Wing panel fabric covering
55 Aileron balance cable
56 Cable pulley
57 Port inter-plane struts
58 Diagonal wire bracing

59 Port lower aileron
60 Double flying wires
61 Port fabric-covered lower wing panel
62 Centre-section cabane struts
63 Centre-section bracing wires
64 Twin synchronised Vickers 0.303in machine guns
65 Gunsight
66 Ammunition feed chute
67 Gun cocking handle
68 Instrument board
69 Gun mounting struts
70 Ammunition magazine
71 Carburettor air intake
72 Fuselage aluminium side panel support frame
73 Control column
74 Pilot's footboards
75 Rudder pedal bar
76 Diagonal engine bearer strut
77 Cartridge case ejection chute
78 Forward fuselage access panel
79 Engine oil tank
80 Oil filler
81 Engine bay aluminium backplate/firewall
82 Aluminium engine cowling

83 130hp Clerget nine-cylinder rotary engine
84 Bolted propeller hub
85 Two-bladed fixed pitch laminated wooden propeller
86 Port mainwheel
87 Bungee elastic cord shock absorber
88 Pivoted half axle suspension
89 Horizontal spreader bar
90 Main undercarriage V-struts, wood faired steel tubes
91 Starboard mainwheel
92 Wheel disc fabric covering
93 Tyre inflation valve

Plate 9a. Clerget 9B rotary, 130hp. (*httpscreativecommons.orglicensesby2.0 via Wikimedia Commons*)

Plate 9b. Le Rhône 9J rotary, 110hp. (*http://www.gnu.org/copyleft/fdl.html via Wikimedia Commons*)

Plate 9c. Sopwith F.1 Camel cockpit: Shuttleworth Collection replica photographed by Chief Pilot Dodge Bailey. The hand air pump is evident at the lower RH side of the pilot's seat. Only the slip indicator (inclinometer) is modern.

Plate 10. On 14 January 1918 Hubert Broad flew Sopwith Triplane N5351 from Fairlop over to 78 Squadron at Sutton's Farm where he noted in his log-book 'Scrap with Armstrong in Camel'. After the mock dog-fight Armstrong put Broad's Tripehound through its paces, then re-mounted Camel C6713 to give one of his inimitable displays of stunting which concluded by 'chasing everyone off the tarmac'. (© AJC/Lynn Williams)

Plate 11a. Early portrait of C6713 and her team in No. 78 HD Squadron, L–R fitter Evans, rigger Fowle and pilot Armstrong (who is still wearing RFC uniform); it has been commented that the body-language between the three speaks of an easy and congenial relationship. (© *AJC*)

Plate 11b. Line-up of Armstrong's A Flight of Sopwith Camels, No. 78 HD Squadron at Sutton's Farm, Spring 1918. (© *AJC*)

Plate 14. 'He led his flight down the Thames and they flew under all the bridges' probably starting with these bridges at Richmond. (© AJC/Lynn Williams)

Plate 15a. 'This photo was taken [early 1918] on an occasion when I went across to Hainault for a War Office cinematograph show. It was taken by a professional photographer – the weather, however, was extraordinarily bad and dull, which probably accounts for the photograph's being so bad. My Camel *Doris* in foreground having new tail-skid fitted.' (L-R) John Summers, Chaps Marchant, John Wingate, John Collier, DVA, Charlie ('Sandy') Banks. (© *AJC*)

Plate 15b, 15c. Two mementos of Doris. (© *RNF courtesy of Hilton College*)
On the right is her red tail fin with serial number painted exactly as seen in the photograph above. On the left is an unusual metal ID plate, about 270 x 95mm, with brass characters carefully fashioned utilizing copper rivets and set against a dark blue painted background. Attached to a piece of greenish-brown aluminium, it could have been cut from the centre of her lower cowling. This attractive plate may have been created by ground crew after her red livery was camouflaged – perhaps as an aid to identify machine No. 1 of A Flight in the dark, or perhaps simply for the pleasure of making it.

Totsiens … Hamba kahle … Go well …

Plate 16. Visualization by Lynn Williams of bronze created in 1920 by renowned British sculptor and war artist John Tweed (1869–1933), by kind permission of R.N. Fletcher and Hilton College. Known particularly for military portraiture, and having close connections with South Africa, John Tweed was engaged by that country's government to go to the battlefields of France and produce life drawings and models for a planned war memorial. (© *AJC/Lynn Williams*)

with the 110hp Le Rhône 9J, which then became the standard power plant at this time, with numbers of machines being converted at unit level. It appears from these photographs that this particular machine's cowling was not factory-produced for the Le Rhône 9J, and in the port side view there appears to be a Sopwith Company serial box visible between the legs of the airman at the tail. So although the number is not visible, this may well have been B3826 re-fitted. A useful clue as to date is provided by the snow. Flying would have continued throughout a fairly mild and dry November-December in the south east, with periods of light snowfall in the third week of December; only in the first two weeks of January 1918 was there a wintry spell with heavy snow which would have kept most aircraft hangared.

From our point of view, in an age of in-line and occasionally radial engines in light aircraft, the rotary is a rare and exotic bird: it may not be immediately apparent, therefore, what the pilot of a rotary engine had to contend with.

Rotaries, being air-cooled, were initially very widely favoured when weight-saving was a major element of aircraft design, and the French were very good at them. Both the Clerget and Le Rhône as used in Armstrong's Sopwith Camels were 9-cylinder rotaries; when the 110hp Le Rhône 9J came to be preferred it was a number of reasons. Briefly stated, despite its more complex valve arrangement the Le Rhône was considered to be

Another view of DVA's 'first Le Rhône Camel in 44'.

better engineered. Another advantage was that the guns could be equipped with the hydraulic Constantinesco-Colley synchronizing gear. This, when developed for the twin Vickers, gave better and more reliable performance than the Clerget's mechanical Sopwith-Kauper, notably in the freezing air at altitude when the latter's mechanical system was prone to shrinkage.

With the partnership between engine and propeller being critical to the aeroplane's performance, the Clerget also left something to be desired with its initial Lang LP2850 propeller (recognizable by its fabric covered squared-off tips). It was better when paired with the coarser-pitch AD644 propeller (with its more curvilinear profile), but when the AD644 was then paired with the 110hp Le Rhône the result was noticeably superior, enabling a greater top speed, improved rate of climb and higher ceiling.

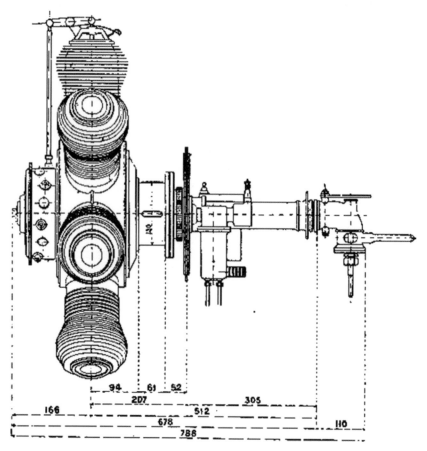

The 50hp Gnome Omega, the first rotary aero engine to be produced in quantity. [public domain via Wikimedia Commons]

The rotary engine and propeller were in effect one big piece of machinery rotating clockwise as viewed from the rear, making a massive gyro with a large radius of gyration, which was mounted on a light stick-and-rag framework. The key to understanding the Camel was its combination of instability and precession, which aided its lightning-fast right-hand turn as described earlier. Test pilot and aerobatic specialist Neil Williams agreed with many others when he described the Camel as 'a gyroscope with wings'.

One of the salient distinguishing features of the rotary engine was its spectacular appetite for castor oil. It relied on a total loss oil system because the whirling engine, and the centrifugal force it produced, prevented any lubricant being recirculated. Castor oil was a superb lubricant and would be burnt in the cylinders with the fuel/air mixture. But there was no means of capturing the exhausted fuel/oil in an exhaust pipe, so the exhaust gases were intended to escape as each cylinder neared the bottom of the cowling. Depending on the engine type and ignition timing, various cut-outs were provided in the lower part of the cowling with the aim that most of the fumes passed along the underside of the fuselage and into the wide blue yonder.

At the same time every pilot sitting behind a rotary was constantly showered with castor oil that escaped the engine to be blown back over the front fuselage and cockpit.[14] The silk scarf traditionally associated with early pilots was not only to ease the chafing from constantly skewing his neck to scan the sky, and for protection against sunburn and frostbite, but also for the vital function of wiping the accumulation of castor oil that clouded his goggles.

Generally speaking both the Clerget and Le Rhône were controlled by throttle and mixture devices, simple carburettors that combined a petrol jet and flap valve for throttling the air supply (not automatic carburettors as we understand them). In practice the pilot would set the throttle – usually near fully open – then adjust the mixture to suit. Experienced pilots would 'feel' the fuel lever at frequent intervals to make sure the mixture had not become too rich. It was better to run the engine slightly on the lean side, so that when a situation demanded full power you only had to increase the fuel supply. By contrast, over-rich running could cause sparking plugs to soot up and cylinders to cut out. The large crankcase volume meant that if the mixture was badly over-rich (and if raw petrol was present) it could result in several long seconds without power, i.e. a worrying silence followed by coughing and rough-running as the engine tried to clean itself.

Rotaries had a blip switch, producing that characteristic sound indelibly associated with a rotary engine in the circuit. This switch would cut off the

ignition supply to the cylinders, and it came into its own for power control on landing. The aim was that, in case of problems, power was 'instantly' available without any of that fiddling with air and mixture. So you approach by throttling back to about 50 per cent power and then use the blip switch to reduce power further as you complete the approach and landing. If you need to go around you release the blip switch, and the power previously set will be enough to stop the descent; you can then open the throttle some more and climb away.[15]

Most of the time the Camel cockpit could be described as quite a busy place for its occupant: periodically adjusting mixture, watching or pumping up fuel tank air pressure, coping with freezing slipstream of around 100mph, keeping well strapped in while peering about for other aircraft trying to kill you, and listening to that all-important engine note for any signs of roughness that might signal problems. In an aeroplane without built-in stability, your hands and feet were meanwhile constantly jockeying with stick and rudder. Your attempt to hold the aircraft in balance entailed a strong but continually variable stick force (remembering the centre of gravity moved forward as fuel was consumed), which was tricky to maintain while all the time inputting small, delicate adjustments for turbulence, etc., but then you had to change hands when you needed to pump fuel pressure which meant that you lost the muscle-memory of your right hand on the stick. And this is without mentioning the important matter of aerial gunnery.

Eventually B3826 passed into the capable hands of red-haired Charlie Banks, inevitably known as Sandy, whose 'trick flying' was rated by Cecil Lewis alongside DVA's as the best ever seen during the war. Banks was one of a 44 Squadron group who one day, after a well-oiled lunch, voted that DVA should lead them in an aerial tail-chase over the English countryside. Lewis described them as taking off in all directions, a hair-raising sight: 'Machines staggered into the air at stalling speed, missed each other by inches, turned vertically within a foot of the ground, invited every kind of accident; ... at last we managed to get into a line – a long snake of eighteen machines ... and set off contour-chasing all over Essex.'[16]

This hedgehopping game of follow-my-leader continued for half an hour and came to an end only when Armstrong, spying a flock of ducks, sped off over the Thames marshes in pursuit. Whereupon his followers, losing interest at last, watched him disappear into the distance while they quietly made their way back to base.

A comrade in No. 44 Squadron was Lieutenant Ronald Adams (later to be known in the Second World War as Wing Commander Ronald Adam OBE,

44 Squadron members L-R: Bert Wood MC and Bar (had an impressive 13 victories); Geoffrey Pidcock; DVA; Quintin Brand; Robert Foster.

having dropped the 's' from his surname during his inter-war theatre and film career). In an interview for *Cross & Cockade USA* he recalled that DVA's staggering flick rolls and loops were the talk of the tarmac and mess, and gained for him a famous reputation.[17]

'On one occasion, when a heavy fog hung over Netheravon and the fellows were lounging around the sheds talking, out of the low cloud came a Sopwith Camel: it skimmed by the long row of vapour-shrouded sheds and – flick! – a quick roll and it was gone.'

Netheravon, Kenley, Waddon, Chingford, all were DVA's ports of call: for he was often sent on confidence-boosting duties around air bases.[18] Decades afterwards many who saw him talked of Armstrong's performances, most of which were so low as to seem suicidal. At Kenley, it was rumoured, there were threats of a court-martial!

Another onlooker, aero engineer Frank Kappey, wrote in *Flight* magazine: 'The first time I saw Armstrong loop straight off the grass at Fairlop [Hainault Farm] and flick roll between the Bessonneau hangars I was horrified and incredulous; but on seeing these and other equally frightening exploits repeated with exactitude left only respect and admiration for his complete mastery.'

A unique anecdote was related by Ronald Adams who remembered an incident when DVA 'outfought the celebrated French ace, Captain René Fonck, in a mock dogfight. Fonck landed nearly in tears at his inability to get on Armstrong's tail.'

For Adams, DVA as a person remained somewhat of a mystery. However, as described by John Barfoot of the First World War Aviation Historical Society: 'DVA was without exception described by fellow pilots as a charming and congenial chap. The word "lovable" has been used several times: rather an unusual tribute, I thought.'[19]

This is not the place for a treatise on aerobatics, but it should be observed that (to state the obvious) the art is extremely difficult to execute with precision. It also requires total control which in turn demands total concentration. Lieutenant (later Major) Oliver Stewart, who became an acclaimed exponent, described in *Words and Music for a Mechanical Man* the procedures he followed in order to achieve a mastery of aerobatics. Stewart had gained his pilot's certificate a month after Armstrong and went on to serve with No. 22 and No. 54 Squadrons, but was fortunate enough to be withdrawn from combat duties at the end of 1917 ('granted a reprieve', as he put it) and re-assigned to the RFC's experimental station at Orfordness which was linked with the Aeroplane and Armament Experimental

Snap of FE.2d (250hp Rolls Royce Eagle); the group of three at right are L-R 'Dubs' O'Neill and DVA (back to the camera) talking to Quintin Brand.

Establishment at Martlesham Heath. His period as a fighting pilot, he wrote, had been limited to a single year, yet left him permanently marked.

Such a reprieve was rarely available. When DVA was using his hard-won skills to assist pilots converting to the Camel, and at the same time grappling with the enemy while developing the new techniques of night combat, Stewart was occupied with test-flying aircraft and simultaneously spending every minute of spare time teaching himself a complete aerobatics repertoire: perhaps the first pilot who had the leisure to do this combined with free access to a suitably responsive aeroplane. He would climb well away from the airfield, he reported, and practise until he was sick. Like DVA, Stewart's preferred personal mount was a 110hp Le Rhône Camel. His aim was to perform not just a loop but a perfectly geometric loop, with constant radius and wings level throughout. For such a goal the Camel was not always cooperative. Among its bad habits it had a tendency to yaw at the top of a loop and fall out sideways. Or on completing a flick roll, Stewart found, having insufficient thrust, the Camel would sink.

Stewart then wanted to perform these manoeuvres close to the ground, but in this there was always the fear of an engine cut. The margin between flying and stalling being small, any sudden withdrawal of thrust could entail a disastrous stall going into an incipient spin too low to allow time for extrication. So he proceeded to devise methods of recovery without too much height loss. One of these, if a loop came to grief on its upward path, was to convert it to what he called an Immelmann Turn. This was an early example of mis-characterizing Max Immelmann's combat turn, overlooking how dramatically aeroplanes had developed in the interim. Given that Stewart wanted to preserve height when near the ground, Immelmann's actual manoeuvre would certainly not have assisted since, even with a fully-functioning engine, the German ace's wing-warping Eindecker could not have sustained any of the height he initially gained.

Stewart, unable to complete his half-loop, probably substituted a simple wing-over or chandelle style of steep turn, converting his upward trajectory into a sideways displacement and levelling his wings in the process, a simple manoeuvre involving minimal loss of altitude with the benefit of the Camel's biplane wing surfaces. We can, by the way, categorically rule out Stewart using the very different modern-day figure known familiarly as a 'Roll-off-the-Top' which is also too often anachronistically called an Immelmann Turn. This figure requires the aircraft not only to reach the inverted stage at the top of the loop, but also to summon up enough thrust at that point to make a half-roll from inverted to erect. It was certainly not Stewart's escape manoeuvre from a loss of power in a pull-up.

All the rolls and half-rolls executed by Stewart were flick rolls, known today in the USA as snap rolls, which employed gyroscopic forces as when entering a spin. Such gyroscopic forces came in abundance with the rotary engines in use at that time, therefore any rolls used in combat in the First World War can also be assumed to have been flick rolls: indeed, only lightning-fast manoeuvres made any sense in a dogfight.

RNAS pilot W.G. Moore, quoted earlier, commented that many pilots had their own different control inputs for what he called 'the horizontal spin', which could be quite a dangerous manoeuvre as momentarily you were really out of control. 'It is very impressive done low down – in a Camel you could roll three times in about as many seconds. ... My method was to get into a very shallow dive, pull the nose up about twenty degrees above horizontal flight – rightly or wrongly that gave me the impression the whole mass of the machine was hurtling through the air slightly upwards rather than downwards and that gave me confidence. Within a second of pulling up the nose I would cut the engine on the blip switch, put ailerons hard over to the left, full left stick and joy-stick into my tummy. This was the only time I ever used that very sensitive elevator control harshly.'

In the later agile machines like triplanes, even the coordinated turn was often sacrificed in favour of a flat skidding turn or slip-turn made solely with rudder, generally known as 'viffing' and credited to Werner Voss.

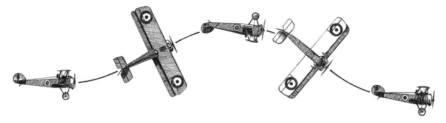

The flick roll.

The stall turn (hammerhead in US terminology) had long been in common use after zooming under an enemy's tail to attack, then ruddering into a sideways dive at the apex when all forward speed was lost.[20] Essentially a large repertoire of unpredictable control inputs was the key to keeping your opponent guessing, and units practised dogfighting and 'split-arse stunting' to hone their combat skills. However, this kind of impromptu trick-flying was the very antithesis of the careful and precise aerobatic manoeuvres that Stewart and Armstrong aimed for; it was the choreography of their aerial displays – and in Armstrong's case, the added element of drama – that won them such admiration.

Notably, Oliver Stewart confessed in his book that he never learnt to perform the slow roll (or aileron roll). For a pilot flying the Sopwith Camel, acquiring the technique of rolling straight and level by means of ailerons would have required long and careful study, which is worth mentioning *because Armstrong*

Oliver Stewart pictured with monogrammed Sopwith Pup, 1917.

did master the technique of the slow roll, an achievement described by one of his comrades in a 1962 article which will be quoted in our next chapter. Meanwhile this digression serves to show that even Oliver Stewart, with his abundant spare time and plentiful facilities, and operating far from enemy encounters, still failed to approach D'Urban Armstrong's accomplishments.

In another book, *The Clouds Remember*, he wrote at some length about the Camel being the chosen instrument of the greatest aerobatic pilots such as DVA: it responded to a touch and could be 'thought' round turns. 'From level flight it could be stood up on end so suddenly, by a mere easing of pressure on the control stick, that it would stall.' This super-sensitiveness 'enabled loops to be made from a relatively low speed with the aeroplane under full control all the way round. It also enabled flick rolls to be performed without loss of height, and it gave the machine good powers of manoeuvre when it was being flown upside down. ... Captain Armstrong, an almost legendary figure, was perhaps the supreme exponent of low aerobatics. He was stationed with a night flying squadron at an aerodrome east of London and here he frequently gave exhibitions of aerobatics which were perhaps the most remarkable ever done. He specialized in loops done from a relatively low speed from ground level. His flick rolls were started at less than the height of the sheds, and it is recorded that on one occasion a wingtip brushed the grass as the aeroplane went round.' Stewart agreed with Moore that the flick roll could be dangerous because the aeroplane was autorotating, 'consequently the pilot abandons control for a moment, to regain it as the full turn is completed. Armstrong succeeded in doing these flick rolls without losing height by starting them at about 80mph and bringing the engine in fully as the machine went over. There was just enough thrust to hold the machine up as it came out in a stalled condition and at a big angle of incidence [i.e. angle of attack].'

Air historian J.M. Bruce was another admirer of Armstrong's astonishing prowess; he echoed Stewart's description that he would loop from ground level to ground level, and that he specialized in flick rolls which he performed at about fifteen feet. He, too, had heard it said that one of his wingtips had been seen to brush the grass while flick-rolling. When the RAF Museum was opened in London in the early 1970s Bruce enquired after the possibility of exhibiting memorabilia of DVA and his Camel:

> To anyone who knows anything at all about military aviation of the First World War, the name of Captain Armstrong is synonymous with the most extraordinary and outstanding aerobatic flying

ever done anywhere in the world during that strenuous period of conflict. ... Those who were fortunate enough to witness it indicate that he was a pastmaster in the handling of that remarkably temperamental aircraft, notably at very low altitudes.

Throughout Oliver Stewart's leading involvement in post-war aviation, whenever he wrote of aerobatics he seldom missed an opportunity to express his admiration for Armstrong's mastery of the formidable Sopwith Camel ('the very term "Camel pilot" held a special meaning', he said, 'and was in itself regarded as a sort of commendation'). He was clear that Armstrong was no mere gadfly out to impress, but had studied the science of his aerial manoeuvres to the same extent as had Stewart himself. Although it might seem that he had no possibility of escaping if the engine failed or faltered, he had discussed this with Stewart and held that he had means of sideslipping out safely.

The following is an account of one of the younger man's Camel displays which Stewart prefaced with the title 'Artistry in the Air':[21]

Imagine a small aerodrome to the east of London. A few hangars of the old type flank one side; on another side there are some trees. A narrow strip of tarmac extends in front of the hangars. There are low clouds and a slight, fitful wind.

A Camel is wheeled out of its shed ... other pilots gather on the tarmac ... a mechanic swings the airscrew ... the pilot tries his controls. The engine roars and fades, a hand waves from the narrow cockpit, the chocks are jerked from the wheels, the pilot turns his head quickly to right and left, the engine roars again and, simultaneously, before the machine has started to gather way, the tail lifts.

Now watch closely. The machine jumps forward, heeling on to the left wing. The left wing tip is brushing the grass as the machine rises. The machine rises as if it were being lifted from the ground and a surprisingly large expanse of top plane exposes itself flat to the view of the spectators on the tarmac. The machine has turned vertically across wind as it is taking off.

It flattens out and vanishes round the corner of the farthest hangar like an express train into a tunnel. The sound of its engine dies for a second then shrieks as the machine reappears two feet above the sheds. It comes down steeply towards the tarmac, turning slightly, and then, as its wheels skim the grass, it points its nose slowly upward. At that height and in that position it seems that the only possible manoeuvre open to the pilot is a zoom.

But watch!

Over!

The machine goes on slowly turning its nose upwards until it is standing on its tail. Then the nose comes over on top and the large expanse of that top plane again appears horribly close to the spectators below. It seems impossible that the machine should have room to flatten out before hitting the ground. One watches it almost panic stricken. But it continues – without a falter or the slightest unevenness – to curve round. It curves round and its nose rushes straight for the tarmac; its engine roars louder and louder. So close is it that the machine seems to have grown in size out of proportion to its surroundings. It curves round and with a *fortissimo* crash of its engine right in the spectators' ears, it passes along over the tarmac having completed a perfect loop at slow speed, right down on the ground.

No pilot could watch one of those low, slow loops without being dumbfounded with admiration and astonishment. But more extraordinary manoeuvres are in store. The Camel zooms after its loop, then falls towards the ground in a vertical sideslip, flattens out, turns and comes across the aerodrome parallel with the tarmac, its wing tip about over the edge of the tarmac and some ten feet up.

Opposite the central hanger it lunges up and round in a quick twist. The huge expanse of top plane again flashes into view to be succeeded by a close view of the lower plane and the undercarriage wheels. The machine wriggles, as it were, turns clean over and is again flying level about ten feet up. The pilot has performed a flick roll starting and ending it some ten feet from the ground.

The whole display might last five minutes but they were minutes so closely packed with the superfine execution of difficult aerobatics that the whole technique of flying seemed to be compressed into them. And finally the machine would settle on the edge of the tarmac, placed there precisely as a man might place a piece on a chess board.

I had the pleasure of meeting the pilot who used to give these displays. The impression that they were the reckless work of a madman was soon dispelled when one heard his theories. Every detail of every manoeuvre had been worked out and practised with almost inconceivable care at a safe height. And then the separate manoeuvres had been put together to form a carefully constructed whole ... which for sheer spectacular effect exceeded any other flying exhibition.

These were aerobatic displays which outdistanced the greatest subsequent marvels of fact or film and which, had they been staged in peace time, would have drawn all London. This pilot set a standard in aerobatics which in artistry and spectacular effect has never since been surpassed.

Many pilots had cause to be grateful to DVA for technical advice he freely shared. In an article published in *Cross & Cockade International* in 1993, Tryggve Gran described some of his own aerial antics, including an incident when he and Armstrong flew over to the coast at Southend for some practice flying and pretended to collide in mid-air. They were together in 44 Squadron during its first two months, and Gran described how in August 1917 he had the notion one day to put his machine into a rolling spin over the aerodrome at Hainault Farm. 'Downwards it went with lightning speed and very soon the earth was no more than 1,000 feet under me. Now, I said to myself, neutralize the rudder and put the elevator control stick forward as far as it will go. But no, round and round went my bus and I thought I was a gonner. Then I remembered Lt Armstrong's words: "As a last way out of it I bust the motor". I put my throttle full on and to my delight the aeroplane came under control again. However the earth was already there and the next moment I heard a bang, saw stars and went out in the land of dreams. When I woke up all the boys were standing round me: "You had the luck of the devil," they said.'[22]

Courtesy of Trevor Henshaw.

Squadron duties also entailed training up new pilots, and a group of cadets were attached to No. 44 Squadron from the United States Air Service which was the only way they could get practical experience. One of them was the American Clayton Knight whose reminiscences were given to *Cross & Cockade USA* in 1972 and retold in a later article in *Cross & Cockade International*, 2010. They were billeted in pairs around Ilford, while the 44 Squadron pilots including DVA (whom he considered the best pilot in the RFC) lived in the farmhouse at Hainault, an empty and sparsely furnished gloomy brick building across the road from the aircraft hangars.

Knight recalled that, while at Hainault Farm, 'the squadron was often asked to perform exhibition flights over London in support of war bond sales. ... [But] the people of London missed some of the really fine performances by the young stunt pilots. When they came back over Hainault and broke formation to land, Armstrong put on a hair-raising exhibition,

'Dressed up for London: dentist!' says DVA's album caption for this shot of him in No. 44 Squadron wearing his British Warm greatcoat. Original photo kindly supplied by Peter Kilduff who credits it to 'Armstrong's admirer Clayton Knight', his companion in 44 Squadron.

diving toward the hangars and then rolling his wheels gently on each of the saw-toothed hangar roofs. He would top this off with a loop off the ground, followed by a half-roll out of the top of the loop.'[23] We shall meet another American in Chapter 8 who declared this half-loop-half-roll should be named the 'Armstrong Turn'.

Knight's most vivid recollection was his very first flight with DVA in 44 Squadron on 8 December 1917 aboard BE.2e A8646 – a version of the very stable BE.2c with greatly extended upper wings – which was recently back from night light bombing duty with 100 Squadron in France:[24]

> He was an outstanding stunt flier who was fascinated with looping the BE.2c [*sic*]. The total flight lasted about 20 minutes and consisted of a series of vertical banks and loops. For the latter Armstrong was roundly told off by Captain Quintin Brand, who was his Flight Commander. ... Armstrong grinned at Captain Brand and commented, 'Well, I didn't take the top wing extensions off the old BE.' And, sure enough, when they were checked on the ground they were not even strained.[25]

A8646 is here photographed at CFS Upavon after returning from France. The BE.2e was a redesign featuring entirely new wings that were braced each side by a single pair of interplane struts; seeking even greater stability with increased wing area, it had long extensions to the upper wings overhanging the lower wing panels of shorter span. [Mick Davis]

Knowing this biography was in preparation, the renowned aviation historian Frank Cheesman contributed a story to include (illustrated in plates 6 and 7) that he regarded as unique among the welter of apocryphal tales about DVA, coming as it did from an impeccable source. His informant was a pilot of great experience as a fighter pilot in the First World War, both day and night, who was later involved in test flying, in airline operations and in aircraft construction. This pilot was also a very close personal friend of DVA in late 1917 and early 1918 when they served in the same and later in adjacent Home Defence squadrons. He wrote as follows:

> One day in late 1917 [with 78 Sqdn] I received a message at Sutton's Farm from Armstrong at Hainault Farm [home of 44 Sqdn] that he would be coming over to see me. His normal method of arrival was always spectacular, but this one beat all.
>
> Parked out at right-angles to the hangars was a row of some half-dozen Camels in the middle of which was a gap left by the removal of one. As he approached, Armstrong noticed this gap, put his nose right down and went through it at some 150mph with his wheels nearly on the ground. He then pulled up into a loop which he completed by passing through the gap again and equally close to the ground.
>
> This was a deadly accurate piece of flying done on the spur of the moment and terrifying to watch. I was standing near enough at the time to be able to see the large amount of left rudder he applied progressively as he went up into his loop. After reproving him for scaring me to death *I had the gap measured* and found that in the course of his remarkable performance he had taken a 28ft wing-span Camel twice though a 39ft gap.[26]

CHAPTER 7

78 SQUADRON: BY DAY AND BY NIGHT

D'Urban Armstrong's last recorded sortie with No. 44 Squadron was with B3826 on the night of 22/23 December 1917, repelling bombers over south-east coastal towns. The following month, on 28/29 January 1918, the Germans launched a major night raid targeting London with Gotha and Giant bombers. For no known reason operational reports covering this raid are missing, so although numerous sorties were flown that night by both No. 44 and No. 78, we lack full records of their pilots' names.

However, for the following night of 29/30 January DVA is recorded for the first time flying his new Camel, serial number C6713, on two sorties with No. 78 Squadron from Sutton's Farm: evidently he had moved to his new squadron at the start of the new year, his third posting on Home Defence. A few weeks later, on 1 March 1918, DVA was promoted to captain and flight commander, 6 Brigade.

Originally formed in November 1916, No. 78 Squadron had for its initial CO the celebrated South African pilot Major Pierre van Ryneveld who later pursued a prominent post-war career in aviation. As part of the HD reorganizations of September 1917, No. 78 had been moved to various bases in south-east England including Sutton's Farm (on Sopwith 1½-Strutters) where they settled under the command of Major C.R. 'Toby' Rowden MC, who would die in a flying accident in April 1918 aged just 21. The squadron's next CO during DVA's service was Major Gerald Allen who had joined the RFC from the Connaught Rangers in 1914 after being wounded. Married as recently as March, he had been an instructor at the Central Flying School and would later command No. 46 Squadron in France.

DVA was commander of A Flight which was billeted in the farmhouse of the Crawford family who owned the land. In his album he draws attention to this photograph of a crashed aircraft with a caption ruefully pointing out that it had ended up in one of Mr Crawford's trees!

Sutton's Farm gained fame as a prominent Home Defence aerodrome in both world wars, being directly on the usual aerial route for attacks on London. It was reacquired in 1928 to become RAF Hornchurch. During the Battle of Britain it became a home once more for fighter pilots defending London and the South-East, this time flying Spitfires. The aerodrome has since been demolished, but memories of its brave past are still preserved. A memorial stands in the grounds of R.J. Mitchell School nearby, named in honour of the Spitfire's renowned designer.

In No. 78 Squadron DVA flew his most famous aircraft, Sopwith Camel No. C6713, equipped with the latest 110hp Le Rhône engine. Delivered in January 1918, it was one of 100 built by The British Caudron Co. Ltd of Cricklewood Broadway, London, constructed in Alloa, Scotland. With this machine he consistently flew for the rest of the war and performed his best work in the Allied cause.

Mick Davis, in his contribution on Camel markings in *The Camel File*, cautiously stated 'It has been reported that the legendary D.V. Armstrong had his 78 Squadron Camel, C6713, painted overall red at one stage,' and this is certainly true.[1] The photograph below, taken very early in 1918, shows DVA seated in C6713 – 'don't miss the smile!' says the caption – almost certainly the earliest photo of this aircraft. The dark colour cannot be confidently ascertained

View of DVA's A Flight of Sopwith Camels at Sutton's Farm, 1918.

as red, but contemporary sources confirmed that it was painted all-red (apart from the burnished aluminium cowling) as early as January 1918. One feature is clearly absent in this picture: the white painted name 'Doris' which soon arrived on the fuselage below the cockpit. Doris Evison was the girl he had met during his HD duties in England and planned to marry. Those who knew her said she loved to dance – 'a beautiful person and beautiful to look at'.

Many lucky onlookers were treated to some unforgettable exhibitions at Sutton's Farm that year. A remarkable first-hand account was penned by a Mr T. Clarke, who described himself as 'very keen on stunt flying' – and at this time during the war, with several aerodromes being within reach, he had a good chance of seeing some of the best.[2]

On one visit to Sutton's Farm in January 1918 Clarke was lucky enough to catch a mock battle between DVA in his red-painted Camel and a Sopwith

Another early view of C6713, again before the addition of the name 'Doris': note the particular style of lettering chosen for the fin serial number, which is echoed in the specially crafted identification plate shown in Plate 15.

Triplane flown by an RNAS officer. From DVA's album we can see this very Triplane serial N5351 (opposite) which was flown over to Sutton's Farm from Fairlop by Captain H.S. (Hubert) Broad, on Monday 14 January, and after the joust was put through its paces by Armstrong himself. Broad was on instructional and test-flying duties at the time while recovering from injury. 'Scrap with Armstrong in Camel' is noted in his log-book. Later he would become a test pilot and celebrated aviation sportsman. The qualities of the delightful Sopwith Tripe have been described in Chapter 4.

Shortly after the mock dogfight, Mr Clarke recounted how the entire personnel were then treated to a solo show by Armstrong in his Camel. 'He took off with a loop off the ground, and after doing every stunt possible and impossible, proceeded to chase everyone off the tarmac.' Seeing Clarke and his friend Parks still standing their ground, he then rushed towards them across the aerodrome and flicked over in a roll so low that his wing nearly touched the ground. Clarke described the onrush of air as so great it threw the pair of them right back against the boundary fence. DVA then rocketed upwards, performed a handful more stunts, and departed.

Hubert Broad must have taken advantage of a rare lull in the January weather, for no sooner had the snow thawed than the wintry spell culminated in a heavy downpour of rain, snow and sleet. This was caused by 'a small but intense cyclonic disturbance of considerable intensity' which made its

way across from south-west England to concentrate in the Kent area on the 16th, causing westerly gales in the Straits of Dover. This weather prolonged the inactivity of the German bombers, and hence the HD squadrons, throughout January.

In tracking the interesting progress of D'Urban Armstrong's wartime wardrobe, we can see from the photograph on page 142 that he was well prepared for foul weather, having armed himself with a coat of the specially patented, tightly woven wind- and water-proof cotton being produced for this purpose. This was much favoured by aviators in preference to the mackintosh variety of trench coat that we know today, whose rubberised lining made it quite stiff to wear. DVA's choice can actually be identified as the very field coat – single-breasted and belted – advertised for sale by Aquascutum as 'Waterproof yet Self-Ventilating' ('thousands of satisfied wearers') available at their Regent Street establishment where a large stock of military waterproofs was 'kept ready for immediate wear'. More pliable and comfortable than the trench coat, though unsuitable for flying, it could be supplied with a detachable warm woollen lining. The Camel in the photo is less easy to identify, and may have been a random aircraft he was requested to stand next to.

At No. 6 in DVA's flight was Lieutenant W.F. (Frank) Kendall, already an experienced Camel pilot, and another member who became an equally good friend was Lieutenant Idris 'Jimmy' Meredith Davies. They are seen together in the photograph on page 143, with DVA now sporting yet another model of flying jacket, double-breasted this time with shoulder and cuff straps. It

This photograph may have been taken by a member of the public after witnessing one of DVA's memorable performances at Sutton's Farm. [courtesy of National Museum of the Royal Navy]

would have been brown leather lined with wool, which was much lighter in weight than the shearling-lined leather jacket from the previous year, and evidently another new addition to the Armstrong wardrobe. The muffler will be noticed as a regular accessory, perhaps knitted by Doris.

No. 78 Squadron's full complement of flight commanders and their dates of command have not been conclusively identified, but those at the outset would have been drawn from among men like Captain A.E. 'Steve' Godfrey (later Air Vice Marshal), Captain Stanley Cockerell and Captain N.E. (Noel) Chandler.

Cockerell, initially DVA's deputy flight commander, and Chandler, a New Zealander, had previously flown with No. 112 Squadron from which a few other pilots had transferred to No. 78, including Jimmy Meredith Davies. They appear in a group photograph in DVA's album (see page 144) showing eighteen of No. 78 Squadron's personnel with his red Camel 'Doris' in the background. The squadron's complement was continually fluctuating, for obvious reasons, and it seems there were major changes in March when this photograph was probably taken. The identity of only one man – not wearing pilot's wings – is unknown. DVA is standing fourth from the left, evidently enjoying an exchange of pleasantries with someone in the front row.

So far as can be ascertained, the following additional members of No. 78 Squadron appear in records or have been traced to the squadron during DVA's official dates of posting: Captain F.L. (Francis) Luxmoore; Lieutenants D.J. 'Dinger' Bell whom we shall meet on page 153, L.L. (Laurence) Carter and H.R. (?Henry) Clarke; Second Lieutenants V.C. (Victor) Chapman, C.G. (Cyril) Joyce (died

Jimmy Meredith Davies (L) with DVA (R).

in flying accident May 1918), C.W. (Charles) Middleton, R.A.J. (Roland) Sadler (died September 1918), and C.G. (Cyril) Salmond.

A development not to be overlooked is that on 1 April 1918 a new service, the Royal Air Force, was formed by the amalgamation of the Royal Flying Corps (the Army's air corps) with the Royal Naval Air Service (the naval air arm), whereupon the RFC ceased to exist independently. D'Urban Armstrong's rank became 'Lieutenant, Aeroplane and Seaplane Officer, RAF, and Temporary Captain'. The new force was the brainchild of Lieutenant General Jan Christian Smuts, the eminent South African whose vision for the future of aviation had engendered the SAAC in his home country in 1913. Appointed to the Imperial War Cabinet in 1917, he had been given the lead in addressing the defence of London against the Gotha raids. From this vantage point he could see the parlous situation of inter-service bickering, duplication and rivalry for resources between the RFC and RNAS which was undermining the war effort. Recognizing the huge potential efficiencies of amalgamation under a single command, he managed to achieve the establishment of the Royal Air Force in the teeth of entrenched opposition, a feat in which Winston Churchill (Minister of Munitions) declared that never in all the vicissitudes of his career had the General stood more in need of tact and adroitness. Despite its obvious necessity it was not widely welcomed, and the new uniform remained a thorny problem until its essentials were resolved in 1919.[3]

No. 78 Squadron RFC, L–R [Back row]: G.N. (Giles) Blennerhassett, Stanley Cockerell, C.G. 'Billy' Williams, D.V. Armstrong, M.H.G. (Matthew) Liddell (died April 1918), Noel Chandler, G.M. (Geoffrey) Boumphrey, Jimmy Meredith Davies, [unidentified], T.L. (Thomas) Tibbetts, R.F.W. (Ralph) Moore, G. 'Sherry' Clapham; [Front] William Algie, D.G. 'Baby' Lewis, S.P. (Sidney) Gamon (died March 1918), Will Hubbard, W.J.G. Barnes, F.D. (Frederick) Hudson (died April 1918)

The portrait photograph of Armstrong in the colour section (Plate 13), which was taken upon his transfer to the RAF with the rank of captain, shows his brand new uniform. It was still khaki at this stage, since it was argued that most of the air effort was over land; but the new design entailed the RFC wholly abandoning its uniquely-styled plastron jacket, which as a result gained lasting iconic status as synonymous with those early young men of the pioneering Corps. Over the ensuing year the uniform for the new service went through a succession of changes, as Arthur Gould Lee reflected with some heat:[4]

> When these innovations came we did not welcome them, for they had been thought up by a Committee strongly biased

towards naval practice, with the result that a service which had been predominantly military was given a distinctly nautical image.

Those of us with the Army background particularly resented losing ranks such as captain, major and colonel in exchange for flight lieutenant, squadron leader, wing commander and group captain, all distinctly salty, and we also much disliked giving up our rank stars and crowns for sleeve stripes and vertical gilt bars on either side of the cap badge – these last evoking such ridicule that they were soon abandoned.

The first RAF uniform was in khaki in RNAS style, but this became a light blue (chosen according to rumour by a popular actress) with gold stripes; but again ridicule, aided by the oil and dirt in aeroplanes, forced the adoption of a more practical darker blue with black braid rank stripes. We had to carry not swagger canes but yellowish walking sticks with curved handles, which collectively made an absurd sight on parade. Years later these were abandoned too.

Fortunately, while the war lasted no pressure was exerted to compel the adoption of these new-fangled notions, and most of us clung to our sentimentally precious regimental tunics and RFC maternity jackets, which we patched with leather until they were worn to tatters. Even when we were eventually forced to adopt the new blue, we still for some years wore breeches and puttees, while officers of squadron leader rank and above sported black field boots.

It was in 1918, when Armstrong was recognized not only as the RFC's celebrated stunt artist but also a practitioner of night combat tactics, that Harold Balfour remembered meeting up with him again 'when I landed a Bristol Monoplane at 78 Squadron Home Defence airfield in Essex. By that time he had pioneered night flying with a Camel and greatly distinguished himself as introducing this to the Royal Flying Corps. He then had his all-red Camel and, in fact, escorted me in my Bristol Monoplane over to Hounslow.'[5]

Though the lasting fame of Captain Armstrong to this day has rested on his extraordinary gifts as an aerobatic virtuoso, this leading role in the specialist field of night combat has not been widely appreciated. The following extract from an address by General Jan Smuts refers to how

Bristol Monoplane at Sutton's Farm.

he recognized DVA's qualities and exploited his ability not only to develop this new capability but to train others:[6]

> Shortly after my arrival in London I was asked to be responsible for the Air Defences of London. The great air raids had just started and it was a difficult problem to deal with. I undertook the task of arranging the air defences of London. In the course of this work I wanted a man, a fine man who was efficient to take charge of the night fighting and the night flying, which as you know is quite the most serious and dangerous of air work. I made enquiries and I found that the best man in the British Air Force was young Armstrong. Well, I selected him and put him in charge of this night flying and night fighting. He undertook the job of training squadrons, and he did this work in a most efficient way, and he became an outstanding example of what could be done in this line and achieved very much more than had been thought possible in this direction.

DVA would pursue these instructional activities at home in England and subsequently with French and American units in France, gaining considerable fame in the process. It would not be an overstatement to say that by training and fostering night-flying skills, as well as by bringing on pilots able to wring the utmost out of the Sopwith Camel, Armstrong contributed in no small way to the Allied effort in the aerial war.

As the requirements of that war continued placing high demands on men and machines, improvements for night combat were constantly sought. The Sopwith Camel in its various configurations has been acclaimed as the most important British fighter of the Great War. It is credited with nearly 1,300 known victories from its introduction in June 1917 until the Armistice of November 1918, more than any other individual fighter in any air force of the war.

Many were now being converted to Comics, the twin Vickers being replaced by two Lewis guns mounted above the upper wing section, as the muzzle flash of the Vickers guns by night could blind a pilot's aim. They could now fire directly forward or upward at an angle of 45 degrees, and it was easier to manipulate the Lewis-gun mountings with the cockpit repositioned farther aft. Even those unmodified now favoured larger centre-section cut-outs for better upward view along with additional equipment for night visibility and, importantly, to aid signalling and landing after dark. By the end of the war some Camels were even fitted with wireless.

DVA opted for the enlarged centre-section cut-out, but his Camel 'Doris' (C6713) otherwise remained of the standard variety as seen in the close-up of her nose on page 159. This configuration clearly offered the best aerobatic capabilities, an activity he continued to find irresistible and which was encouraged by the authorities who valued his morale-raising and confidence-boosting demonstrations.

An often overlooked advance in pilot safety had been made earlier in 1917 with the advent of the four-piece Sutton harness invented by Captain Oliver Sutton, which had come into its own with the mercurial Sopwith Camel in which pilots routinely found themselves in all conceivable flight attitudes. The Sutton fighting harness had secure shoulder straps as well as lap straps, all fitting into a simple but cleverly designed quick-release cone-and-pin fastening that could be undone even when the pilot was upside down. It was not yet installed as standard, and Sutton received no official recognition for his invention, but it was gratefully welcomed by pilots who were well aware of accidents, sometimes fatal, resulting from insecure lap straps. Anyone regularly exhibiting low, slow and smooth aerobatics like Armstrong, and especially with his mind attuned to ultimate performance, would have been eager to adopt the modification. 'The combination of the Camel and the Sutton harness,' Oliver Stewart commented, 'gave those aerobatically inclined their greatest opportunity.'

Grenville Manton, who was a lieutenant in the RFC and later enjoyed a long career in the motor and aviation world, found Armstrong's aerobatic displays so memorable that he later described them in detail in enthusiasts'

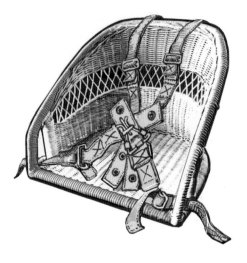

Sutton harness with quick-release fastening.

magazines. He even painted an illustration of how he remembered one of those sensational flick rolls performed low enough to disturb the grass. A conflation of Grenville Manton's recollections runs as follows:[7]

> I first witnessed his extraordinary ability to exploit the astonishing manoeuvrability of the Camel in unusual circumstances. I was coming in to land at Waddon (Croydon) in an Avro 504 one evening in 1918. The sun was setting and it seemed I had the clear blue sky to myself. Then, immediately below me, I spotted a Camel scudding across the aerodrome at zero feet chased by its own long shadow. It headed straight for the boundary hedge and reared up in a tremendous vertical climb immediately in my line of flight, drawing level with me and then inverted right over my head. It then disappeared behind my tail to complete the lowest, neatest and tightest loop I had ever seen. 'I must keep my eye on this gentleman,' I thought as I prepared to slip off the last 200 feet. And then he did it again and yet a third time as I taxied in. 'Who's that?' I asked the flight-sergeant, pointing to the departing Camel. He didn't know. It seemed that this visitor had just come from nowhere, thrown five consecutive loops starting at an altitude of one foot and made his exit without so much as a hand wave.
>
> A week later he came a second time and it was then that I saw aerobatics such as I had never seen previously and, I am certain, shall never see again. Imagine the scene. A hot

summer morning on a wartime aerodrome. Avros, Pups and Camels are lined up outside the Bessonneau hangars. A fitful breeze flicks the windsock against its pole. The air is laden with a reek of dope and castor oil. There is a lull in the general hubbub that hangs around the place, and into that brief stillness there comes the growing roar of a Le Rhône. Casual eyes turn in the direction of the sound. It is a Camel coming fast and low towards the hangars. The machine approaches the tarmac, flying parallel with the hangars, and suddenly with a rapidity that makes one blink it flicks over in a roll.

Now, this is no 'old pilot's tale'; that evolution was done at no more than fifteen feet from the ground. We caught a glimpse of the greasy belly of the Camel's fuselage, saw the wing tips miss the ground by a matter of twelve inches, gaped as the little kite swung round the right way up again, and, as one man, we let out a blasphemous ejaculation as we watched it sweep up and away in a terrific climbing turn.

The hum of the engine ebbed and flowed as the pilot ground-strafed the fields around the aerodrome. And then he came by again. The sun glinted on the spinning disc of the propeller as

Grenville Manton's painting which appeared in Motor Sport with the caption 'A Flick Roll Ten Feet Up!'[8]

he roared towards us; we could hear the wail of Rafwires as the Camel gathered speed. A rabbit ran in terror as the low-flying plane whipped the grass into fluttering agitation. And then again – that flick roll.

So for a quarter of an hour that Camel held our attention. Three times the pilot pulled a loop so low that, as he swept inverted above our heads, we could see for a few fleeting moments intimate details within the cockpit: the instruments glinting in the sun, the green canvas belt, the wings on the fellow's tunic, black, sleek hair and a hand gripping the stick. Meanwhile the Le Rhône was running at full bore, its note falling and rising, falling and rising as the machine climbed and dived three times. ... And then he slipped away, leaving a faint smoke trail while we stood and watched, shook our heads and laughed.

Piece by piece in the years that have passed since Armstrong's flying gained for him a peculiar reputation, I have gathered tales about him. All around the 18th Wing his staggering flick rolls and his amazing loops became the talk of the tarmac and the Mess. ... From time to time I have met people (including an ex-pilot of the US Army Air Corps) who have enquired as to whether I had ever seen 'a fellow named Armstrong' fly a Camel. I remember, too, Sir Christopher Quintin Brand saying to me that Armstrong was, in his opinion, the finest and most accomplished Camel pilot he had ever met. Major Oliver Stewart, who knows all there was to know about a Camel – for he did all the special tests on it at Martlesham when it was a suspect, dreaded and loathed by many – agrees that no other pilot could fly the little beast with such superb judgement and accuracy as Armstrong did. As Stewart says, the fellow had the hands of a surgeon.

Stewart was often rated together with Armstrong as the two most brilliant Camel pilots of the war, and in 1928 Oliver Stewart went on to publish one of the earliest books describing how to fly aerobatics.[9] In its pages he commented that 'the slow roll was not then known', which confirms he was unaware of DVA's mastery of it. Stewart recalled those earlier times when 500 feet was considered a dangerously low altitude for rolling:

This belief was prevalent when, at a home defence aerodrome near London, I first saw Captain Armstrong giving his Camel an airing, and so I received a shock such as no exhibition of aerobatics has ever given me before or since. For I believe I am right in saying that Armstrong was the first man to introduce really low aerobatics. He flew across the aerodrome, the wheels of his machine skimming the grass. Suddenly, yet without any jerk, the machine reared up, turned completely upside down without raising itself above the level of the shed roofs, and flattened out with the wheels again skimming the grass. Had there been the slightest error of judgement the machine would have struck the ground.

I do not wish to suggest that this kind of extremely low stunting is a good thing. But when the pilot appears who has studied aerobatics carefully and scientifically, and who rolls low because he believes that for him such a manoeuvre is safe, then it is impossible not to admire the perfection of his flying technique.

Amusingly, despite this cautionary note, Stewart's little handbook is decorated with a series of diagrams in which every manoeuvre terminates ten feet or less above the roof of a hangar.

Another depiction of one of Armstrong's grass-cutting flick rolls, by artist Laurie Bagley, appeared on the cover of AeroModeller *magazine in 1958*

CAMEL PILOT SUPREME CAPTAIN D.V. ARMSTRONG DFC

In his tribute quoted above, the comment 'without any jerk' goes to the heart of what is innately recognizable as proficiency in aerobatics: it is precisely this smooth and cohesive performance that distinguishes to this day the great exponents of the art. Armstrong's exceptional skill was such that, despite wrestling with the Camel's fierce gyroscopic forces, his display flying was utterly seamless. Many gifted wartime pilots perfected their own special stunts, being so familiar with aerodrome structures that they could perform tricks like rolling their wheels on hangar roofs, but when DVA gave a performance it was a coherent sequence designed to present a series of ever-growing effects, one after another, often playful, always masterly. This, of course, was the product of long and continuous usage until he grew to be at one with the aircraft. Frank Kendall, his comrade in A Flight, 78 Squadron, said that DVA could fly a perfect loop in the Camel without ever straining a wire 'because he became a part of the machine'.

Another account was penned by John Underwood in his 1972 publication *Aerobats in the Sky*. He cited remarks by Wing Commander Norman Macmillan, the First World War flight commander, flying instructor, subsequent test pilot and prolific aviation author, saying: 'Macmillan rated Captain D.V. Armstrong the greatest aerobatic pilot of his day, bar

A Flight of No. 78 Squadron still finding time for high jinks. L: Moore and DVA; R: DVA (centre) carrying an assortment of bodies.

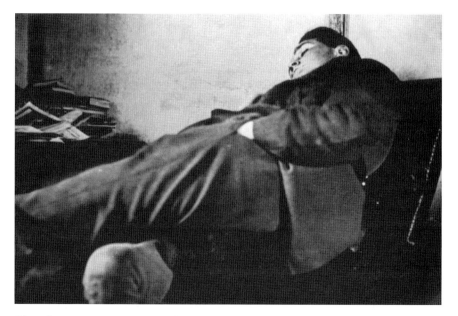

The above snap is captioned 'DVA asleep on Algie [William Algie DSO] in Ante-room'.

none.' Often, he wrote, when taking his Camel aloft Armstrong would come streaking across the field, thump the wheels on the turf and flick roll. 'Witnesses swore time and again that his wing tips swept the grass. His loops were nearly as dramatic, beginning and ending virtually on the deck. Never had such flying been seen before and few have matched it since.'

Like all the Home Defence squadrons whose task was to protect London from aerial attack, No. 78 Squadron was located close enough to town for the pilots to make occasional visits to theatres and night-clubs. They got to know a lot of the girls from various London shows and invited them over to lunch at times. On one such occasion after DVA had given his usual display, 'Dinger' Bell, who'd had far too much to drink, boasted he could do those famous rolls low down just as well. Everyone tried to stop him by rendering his own machine unserviceable, secretly undoing an ignition wire. Furious at being unable to start, he got into another Camel, took off and crashed. To the surprise of all, he only broke his legs (see DVA's photo of the crashed machine overleaf).

Relating to the serious business of operational flights with 78 Squadron, regrettably we have few accounts for the early months of 1918: of DVA's actions we can trace around four records of night-fighter interception patrols between January and May.

Intriguingly, on 7 March, DVA was recorded on a sortie flying Camel serial number D6401. Perhaps this was because C6713 was out of service: he had reported 'engine u/s' and 'guns u/s' on 17 February.

On his last recorded sortie with 78 Squadron, the night of 19/20 May, the raiders consisted of over forty bombers headed for London, and Armstrong in Camel C6713 finally found a target at 23.55: a Gotha flying at 12,000 feet near Orsett.[10] It was to be the last raid on London by the Germans in the First World War, the biggest they had ever mounted, and the most disastrous for them. A force of forty-three German bombers, three of them Giants and the rest Gothas and smaller machines, took off from the Ghent area at five-minute intervals from 22.42 until 01.30. Over southern England for the best part of the night there was a continual flow of hostile aircraft, many of them being pursued by fighters.[11]

A total of eighty-four night-fighters were engaged from the HD aerodromes that night, of which ten Camels took off from Sutton's Farm, one of them flown by Armstrong. On patrol between Tilbury and South Weald he sighted a Gotha G.IV (of *Bosta 18/Bogohl 3*) below him when he was north-west of Orsett. He attacked it repeatedly from above and below until his ammunition was exhausted. The Gotha lost height, and the return fire from both front and rear positions became erratic. After attacking continuously for twenty minutes he broke off between Hainault and Sutton's Farm.

At this moment Second Lieutenant A.J. (Anthony) Arkell and his gunner/observer AM1 A.T.C. (Albert) Stagg in a Bristol F.2b Fighter of No. 39 Squadron attacked the Gotha from underneath at very close quarters, and at 1,500 feet the bomber burst into flames and crashed at Roman Road, East Ham. For this remarkable achievement Arkell was awarded the MC

The 19-year-old Anthony Arkell and gunner/ observer Albert Stagg with Gotha wreckage.

and Stagg the MM.[12] In the account by Squadron Leader H.T. Sutton, DVA is credited as 'took part in destruction of Gotha'.[13]

In describing the same engagement, Frank Cheesman comments that the official history does not seem to tally exactly with the pilots' reports. At 23.55, while north-west of Orsett at 12,000 feet Armstrong sighted the Gotha below, which proved to be carrying a very alert gunner. As he positioned his Camel carefully behind and beneath, he came under immediate fire down the bomber's fuselage tunnel, then, as he zoomed up over its tail, the gunner smartly switched to the upper position. Armstrong made a complete right-hand circle, the Gotha remaining clearly visible in the moonlight, then closed to fifty yards and fired several bursts until his gun jammed. Clearing the stoppage he fired the rest of his ammunition at point-blank range with no result, except that the return fire became rather wild. Having fought the Gotha down to 9,000 feet he left it between Hainault and Sutton's Farm at 00:15. By that time the very experienced Arkell reported already having chased his opponent for ten minutes (since 00:05), and the discrepancy lay in whether two fighters – one with a second pair of eyes in the rear cockpit – could have attacked the same bomber at the same time without noticing one another.

This is not, however, impossible, as comparisons with other incidents reveal. No chicanery is suggested, merely a mis-match of reporting. Squadron Leader Sutton's account was later confirmed by another pilot who remembered that the engagement took place on Whit Sunday, 19 May. He reported that DVA closed with a Gotha and expended all his ammunition in repeated attacks without visible result (by which he probably meant visible damage), and that his target was later shot down over East Ham, which accords with both reports. So the victory was ultimately Arkell's.

As previously commented, it is too much to expect 100 per cent accuracy from mission reports in the context of frenzied wartime night-fighting, and it was not uncommon for victories to be shared for this reason. Cheesman remarked that Armstrong's gunnery suffered from his machine's buffeting by the Gotha's slipstream and at one point he momentarily lost control. Plus, of course, he had to fly the single-seater himself whilst firing, break off to clear his own jam, and then resume his attack. The whole episode makes more sense if DVA's length of engagement is simply adjusted to nearer ten minutes than twenty, whereupon, having run out of ammunition and no longer spitting bullets, his small departing Camel was scarcely noticeable in the clouds upon Arkell and Stagg's arrival: their concentration would have centred on the huge twin-engined German bomber with its two gunners who were both still busily firing as opportunity offered. It took Stagg 350 rounds until a final burst set its starboard engine on fire and it spun into the ground.

An animated group of 78 Squadron pilots at Sutton's Farm: centre group L-R Algie, Clapham (facing camera) and Armstrong (wearing helmet). [Alex Revell]

In the citation for Armstrong's later DFC award his commanding officer, Lieutenant Colonel B.C.D. Small, stated that he had taken part in the defence of London against *all but three raids* by enemy aircraft between September 1917 and June 1918.

Armstrong's demonstration/instruction activities were interspersed with his 78 Squadron duties, and by mid-May he had spent nearly twelve months on Home Defence during which he had been occupied by night flying since September. Apparently the authorities now decided to relieve the pressure by detaching him for a specified period. At any rate, on 19 May 1918 Tryggve Gran received a posting to No. 78 Squadron to replace Armstrong as second in command to Major Allen, taking over as flight commander of A Flight – this to be effective from 20 May, the date of DVA's last combat sortie over English soil. In his reminiscences, Gran noted that Clapham and Carter were with him in A Flight, and Captains Clarke and Boumphrey commanded B and C Flights.

Gran also reported that as the summer of 1918 progressed there was something of a lull for the pilots on HD duties. This would have contributed to freeing DVA from any imminent need to return, and would have left

A noticeably careworn group of pilots from 78 Squadron indicates the toll taken by months of night-flying duties: L-R Frederick Hudson, D'Urban Armstrong, Jimmy Meredith Davies.

157

Tryggve Gran [John Barfoot]

him at liberty to tour a variety of units in his all-red Camel giving demonstrations of advanced flying as well as introducing pilots of all levels of experience to night combat techniques. It was, by the way, quite normal by then for pilots to paint their machines in bright colours and adorn them with artwork: in comparison, DVA's plain red was positively restrained. Gran reported that the machines in his A Flight of 78 Squadron were all green with red noses, while B Flight was dark and C Flight was blue. 'My own bus was scarlet with a silver nose, a more elaborate animal I have never seen.'

In connection with DVA's exhibition flying we know he had 'Doris' fitted with a second Rotherham air pressure pump on her undercarriage, which is seen to advantage in the photograph below. Evidently he was experimenting with improvements or adjuncts to her fuel supply system. Without a schematic of the pipework it is not apparent how the second pump contributed, but at first glance it would likely be for redundancy in case the usual pump failed – which dire event required the pilot to change hands on the stick and work hard hand-pumping for the rest of the flight. More intriguingly, it is not impossible that he and his fitter had piped it in such a way that the fuel tank would feed during periods of inverted flying, of which the Camel was capable of a little over thirty seconds unaided. Oliver Stewart had been interested in such a possibility during his experiments at Orfordness: 'At first I had no inverted fuel system and no one at that time seemed to have any useful ideas on how one could be devised, though ideas flowed soon afterwards when "cigarette tin" inverted systems allowing several minutes of inverted flight with full power were introduced.'[14] This presumably refers to the installation of a small auxiliary tank; certainly rudimentary inverted fuel systems were being developed at this time, and in 1919-22 an RAE test team at Farnborough carried out lengthy investigations into inverted flight under Roderic Hill.

In an extract from *War Birds: Diary of an Unknown Aviator* (mentioned earlier, Chapter 6) we have already met John Grider at the School of Aerial Fighting and Gunnery in Ayr, Scotland, where he described a terrible series of pilot training deaths on Camels in mid-March. Being precisely the type of unit where Armstrong's handling skills would have been invaluable, it is possible that he was sent there in haste to join the team of instructors (in his ferry-pilot days he was already accustomed to flying between England, Scotland and France). So it is interesting that Grider's diary mentions an 'Armstrong'

Nose end view of Camel C6713, showing non-standard twin wind-driven air pressure pumps, one on the front port undercarriage strut as well as the other on the more normal front starboard centre-section strut.

on a number of occasions, sometimes describing him as Australian. Even today it is quite common to find confusion among Americans between the South African, British and Australian accents, so this in itself does not rule out the possibility that he is referring to DVA.[15]

We first meet Grider's 'wild Australian' in late January 1918 on a night out in London when the revellers are listed as 'Capt. Pentland, the wild Australian, Fry, Cal, Springs and myself'. But this particular outing is dominated by the foolery of Captain Jerry Pentland, who actually *is* an Australian (but pretends to be Russian), and historians have usually taken Grider's descriptor on this occasion to relate to him.

Nevertheless it is worth looking at further references, and there is one passage in which we find 'Armstrong, the wild Australian' at Ayr. It is dated 22 March, but the dates in this part of *War Birds* are not necessarily exact because it is not so much a diary as a catalogue of harum-scarum adventures of young American volunteers on the loose during their training (later compiled into a book by one of their number, Elliott White Springs).

On this occasion, 'Armstrong came back tight and got into the WAACs residence by mistake'; so this particular Armstrong could very well be our man, in residence at the School as an instructor/demonstrator but unfamiliar (or claiming to be unfamiliar!) with the exact lie of the land. His old companion from 60 Squadron, Duncan Bell-Irving, was also known to the American lads. He had become an instructor after injuries prevented his return to combat, and is mentioned in one of the *War Birds* escapades as instructing at Thetford in January 1918. He would later become chief flying instructor at Gosport. It is entirely possible that between these postings he, too, was sent to instruct for a while at Ayr, where the training casualties were becoming so lamentable, and if so it might have been through Bell-Irving that his friend Armstrong's presence was procured.

By the end of that month the American flyers had completed their courses and moved to Hounslow; and this is where one of Grider's references to 'the Australian' is certainly identifiable as D'Urban Armstrong, demonstrating not only the merits of the Camel but also the techniques of night combat. In the diary entry of 10 May, Grider gives a typically laconic description of his sensational flying:[16]

> Armstrong, the Australian stunt pilot, was over at Hounslow the other day in his specially rigged Camel and gave an exhibition for us. He's certainly a wonderful pilot. He runs his wheels on the ground and then pulls up in a loop and if he sees he hasn't got room enough, he just half-rolls at the top. I saw him land from a full roll, and he glides and does S turns upside down. I don't think he has long to live, tho, just the same. He says night flying is not so difficult after you get used to it. And he says it's just as easy to fire at night as in daytime. I don't see how he figures that tho.

As well as noting the easy familiarity of tone, it is remarkable that Grider, on seeing him fly at Hounslow, should describe DVA as Australian *if they were not already known to each other*. Although Armstrong's nationality sometimes crops up in historical material, it is hard to find it mentioned at all in accounts of his flying by contemporary spectators, or even in reminiscences by fellow pilots who knew him personally (there is no such mention in *Sagittarius Rising*). Had Grider made enquiries about DVA upon first encountering him at Hounslow, he would not have heard this mistake made about a famed pilot. And he would scarcely have detected any accent

L-R: John McGavock Grider,
Elliott White Springs,
Lawrence K. Callahan, 1918.

in quasi-formal interactions with a stranger. This is because in DVA's home circles in the Natal Colony there was minimal influx of Afrikaans-speakers with their recognizably accented English: his entire public-school education had taken place at an English-influenced colonial boarding establishment. Thus he would have sounded very much like members of other white communities in colonies such as Rhodesia and Kenya, and even more like his fellow officers in the RFC, among whom he had been living for well over two years.

However, Grider could easily have been repeating his assumption that Armstrong was Australian if they had already known each other informally at Ayr, and if one or more of those previous 'wild Australian' anecdotes really did refer to DVA. When sharing horse-play or a night out with Grider's group, some of Armstrong's Natalian slang – or even Zulu expressions – might have been flung into the mix, baffling the American ear. With our present state of knowledge it cannot be ruled out.

It was probably this very demonstration given by DVA at Hounslow that was remembered by Billy Bishop, recently promoted to major and about to take No. 85 Squadron (the 'Flying Foxes') to the Western Front:[17]

> He came over to my squadron at Hounslow a few days before I took it to France in May 1918 to give an exhibition of flying, and it was beautiful. The pilots of the night flight, of which he had charge, were all trained by him, and the whole lot of them could fly extraordinarily well, but of course not up to his standard. I doubt if any person will ever equal him as a stunt pilot.
>
> Some time in May '18 he led his flight down the Thames River from Hornchurch [Sutton's Farm] to the Sopwith Plant at Brooklyn [Brooklands], and they flew under all the bridges en route. This was a most marvellous performance and showed wonderful judgement, as the bridges are very, very narrow and it is practically impossible to get through. ... He was possibly the most wonderful pilot in the world. We all looked on him as such, and although I have seen all of our best pilots fly, and the best of the French and Italian, I have never seen anything to equal the exhibitions of flying he used to give.

Billy Bishop pictured in August 1917; by May 1918 he was Major W.A. Bishop VC DSO* MC and Commanding Officer of No. 85 Squadron

CHAPTER 8

151 SQUADRON & 3RD AIC: MASTER OF NIGHT FLYING

Since September 1917 the Germans had become formidably aggressive in night-bombing. But the success of England's Home Defence squadrons had defeated their hopes of terrorizing her civilian population, and incursions over south-east England became sporadic and weather-dependent. In the night raid of 19/20 May 1918 they lost seven aircraft: it was their largest and their last. Forced to re-think their strategy, they withdrew the Gothas to operate on the Western Front, where their night-time raids not only hit bases like aerodromes, ordnance depots and ammunition dumps, but also targeted railways and even Allied hospitals.

In response to this grim development No. 151 Night Fighter Squadron was formed on 12 June 1918 at Hainault Farm, equipped with Sopwith Camels.[1] They were placed under the command of Captain Gilbert Murlis Green DSO MC, who will be remembered as having dared to lead Camels of No. 44 Squadron into the night sky in their first (unauthorized) attempt to counter German night-time incursions. Since then, the minimal instruments and almost non-existent illumination available for night flying had been replaced by increasingly sophisticated equipment and navigation aids including radiumized instruments, navigation lights and Holt flares for landing.

This new 151 Squadron, to be based with the British Armies in France, was the first unit charged with a specifically offensive night-fighter role on the Western Front, escorting night sorties by Allied bombers, intercepting German night bombers behind Allied lines, and attacking occupied airfields on the German side. Thus No. 151 is remembered for pioneering a technique later to become common in the Second World War, flying intruder missions over enemy airfields, attacking the sites and the bombers themselves as they returned from raids.

There were three flights of Camels, one each from 44, 78 and 112 Squadrons, and they included many of the finest pilots from the three parent units. Armstrong joined on 15 June as their most senior flight commander, and brought with him 'Doris', C6713, now darkened with camouflage for night flying: an example of this severe overpainting can be seen on the Comic illustrated on page 105. He had by now earned his spurs not only as the RFC's foremost Camel exponent, but also as a seasoned tactician able to embrace and develop the scope of night-fighting techniques.

	A Flight	B Flight	C Flight
Flt Commanders	Capt. D.V. Armstrong	Lt S. Cockerell	Capt. W.H. Haynes
	Lt C.R.W. Knight	Capt. A.B. Yuille	Lt J.H. Summers
	Lt R.M. Darney	Lt E.P. Mackay	Lt A.A. Mitchell
	Lt L.S. Cook	Lt A.V. Blenkiron	Lt W.G.D.H. Nicol
	Lt W.F.H. Harris	Lt W. Aitken	Lt L.C. Sheffield
	Lt A.C.Macvie	Lt F.C.Broome	Lt H.S. Bannister

By June the German bombers had moved to concentrate on the bombing of Allied airfields in France. On two nights in July alone, they made sixty-three attacks involving the dropping of 170 tons of bombs. With anti-aircraft fire making little impact, France sorely needed some form of night defence.

On 23 June No. 151 Squadron flew from Marquise in France to its base at Fontaine-sur-Maye aerodrome north-east of Abbeville in Picardie. Almost immediately, from 25 June to 1 July, DVA's A Flight was temporarily attached to No. 101 night-bomber squadron of 5 Brigade at Flixecourt which lay a few miles farther south and closer to Amiens (see map on p. 168). No. 101 had been the second RFC specialist night-bomber unit, under the overall command of Brigadier General Lionel Charlton, later Air Commodore (pictured opposite), and they had been operating in France since September 1917; in fact they had mounted some of the first offensive aerial operations against German supply lines and communications centres.

While the other flights of 151 Squadron were responsible for defending Abbeville, A Flight under the command of Armstrong was tasked with special offensive duties at Famechon, south of Amiens, in support of 101 Squadron's FE.2b night bombers: to patrol enemy areas at night-time and when their searchlights were exposed, to attack them with 20lb bombs and machine-gun fire. On the lighter side, during this secondment

DVA's duties extended to giving the brigadier general lessons in flying the Camel he had acquired for his own use. Charlton recalled how DVA also visited some of the airfields nearby, 'and it was no uncommon sight to see all the pilots of a squadron attracted from their quarters and diversions to see his arrival and departure always accompanied as it was by a little display of trick flying, which showed his wonderful command of his machine to the amazement even of the oldest hands. On one occasion he visited a neighbouring French aerodrome and being asked to "stunt" proceeded to the performance of

Brig Gen L.E.O. Charlton DSO.

such amazing evolutions as startled the French pilots completely from their self-possession and caused them to look away fearing he had lost control of his machine.'

Lionel Charlton had conducted Armstrong's interview when he first joined the RFC on 26 December 1915, and remembered him when subsequent reports of his skill in flying the Camel started reaching him in France. Now, whilst on attachment to No. 101, DVA achieved the first recorded victory for No. 151 Squadron, bringing down an LVG bomber as described more fully below; it would herald the start of his most significant contribution to the aerial war. Charlton later attested 'with what conspicuous success his efforts were attended and how his name became a watchword on the ground and in the air to the French and British armies'.

He also emphasized the great boost given by such aerial success to men on the ground: 'He must have indirectly received the blessing of many hundreds of thousands of men unknown to him ... to whom the spectacle of a German multi-engined night bomber crashing from out of the sky in flames meant a surcease from the endless nerve-rack of being bombed at night.' Importantly, this also helped to weaken the enemy's morale, 'and in this respect ... was the means of saving hundreds of men from death and wounds'.[2]

The Allied front line advance August-September 1918.

At this point it would perhaps be helpful to clarify that the Allied front line, running roughly from the river Somme to the northern coast of France, had come under severe pressure from the German Spring Offensive of 1918 but had been able to repel the attack aided by the arrival of much-needed fresh troops from the USA. As the summer progressed the Allies

Amiens Cathedral during bombardment.

pushed their front line farther east (towards Belgium) while their concern inland, where DVA was based, concentrated on the ancient city of Amiens with its vital rail junction which was under persistent bombing. On 8 August the strategically decisive battle of Amiens marshalled multi-national forces, mainly from Britain, the Commonwealth and USA, in a surprise offensive supported by nearly 2,000 aircraft including 600 RAF fighters attacking enemy positions. This became the German Army's 'Black Day' during which six of their divisions collapsed and entire units surrendered, allowing valuable territory east of Amiens to be re-taken.

Thus it will be seen why 151 Squadron was repeatedly tasked with targeting important enemy-occupied airfields in these areas, countering the attacks by German night-bombers. Within four weeks the Allies had achieved command of those targets most often indicated in 151 Squadron's offensive operations, such as Moislains, Estrées-en-Chaussée, Guizancourt, etc., and the German forces were in retreat. Soon they were forced back to the Hindenburg Line, the position from which they had begun their costly Spring Offensive. Their defeats and losses on the Western Front were aggravated by mutinies, while in Germany itself civilians were starving to death and revolution was in the air; they would sue for peace in November.

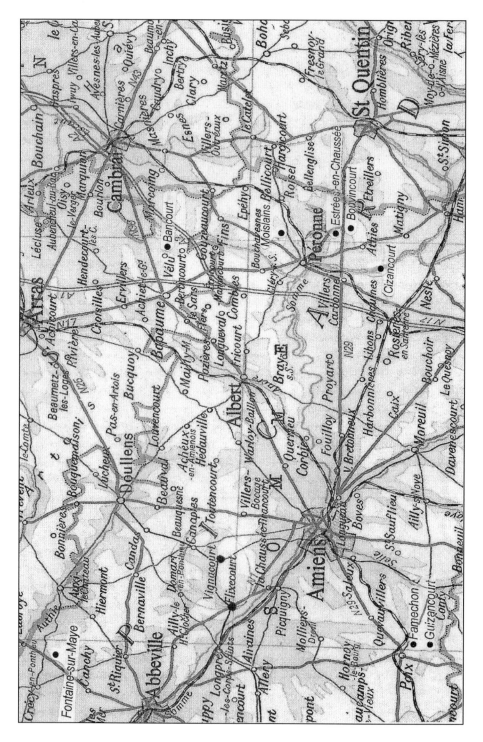

151 SQUADRON & 3RD AIC: MASTER OF NIGHT FLYING

Offensive activities of the sort carried out by 151 Squadron were very different from DVA's previous night flying, when his squadrons were primarily engaged in intercepting the enemy's bombing attacks, a much more random affair of reacting to alerts and attempting to sight and repel incoming threats. Such defensive sorties against German fighters as well as bombers continued unabated on the Western Front, but 151's pilots were now taking the attack to the enemy in new ways, carrying out offensive night patrols themselves, flying at low level after dark to attack and bomb targets in enemy territory.

The events of this momentous summer had only just begun when, on 1 July, Squadron Commander Murlis Green was recalled to England to resume Home Defence duties. Command of No. 151 Squadron passed to Major Quintin ('Flossie') Brand DSO MC, who had been promoted as OC No. 112 Squadron in February, and whose illustrious career continued with distinction on the Western Front.

It was on the previous night, 29/30 June 1918, that DVA had made contact with German bombers to achieve the squadron's first victory, attacking and bringing down a solitary LVG two-seater caught by Allied searchlights as it returned to base from a bombing raid. This was in the vicinity of the German-occupied airfield at Estrées-en-Chaussée near St Quentin (location marked in black on the opposite map). Armstrong opened fire and the German aircraft put its nose down, then after several hundred more machine-gun rounds it went down vertically and was recorded as 'Driven Down Out of Control' on the enemy side of the lines. Timed at 23.25, this victory occurred just six days after their arrival in France. The squadron's tribute on the website *From Camel to Hawk* commends Armstrong's 'courage, skill and fine judgment in all his flying, these qualities being used to good effect in air-to-air combat'.[3]

Although these accounts of 151 Squadron generally concentrate on combat reports, it is also the case that nightly patrols by the squadron (weather permitting) continued on a regular basis even if no enemy aircraft were sighted. As an example, DVA performed eight such patrols during early July, sometimes twice a day.

His next reported damage to the enemy came a week after his 21st birthday, on the night of 31 July/1 August 1918, in a night intruder attack by Armstrong on the Estrées-en-Chaussée aerodrome itself, which housed the bombers of *Bogohl 7*. He went in low at 500 feet to drop all four bombs and achieved the satisfaction of putting the landing lights out of use for returning German bombers.[4]

Soon afterwards, during further operations behind enemy lines, the aerodromes at Estrées-en-Chaussée and Guizancourt were targeted for low altitude night-flying attacks on 6/7 August 1918 by bombing with 20lb bombs and strafing with machine guns. DVA had dropped three of these Cooper bombs on and near the hangars at Estrées-en-Chaussée when in the early hours (01.20) he observed a German two-seater aircraft above him coming in to land. He followed it round the circuit and positioned himself to open fire under its tail when it was down to about 700 feet. The enemy observer answered fire erratically, then ceased. Its nose was well down by now, and Armstrong continued firing until the aircraft 'appeared to do a bad nose-down turn'. Almost immediately it crashed on to the aerodrome, bursting into flames as it struck the ground. DVA aimed his fourth bomb at the wreck to put it permanently out of commission, returning to his aerodrome with all ammunition spent.[5]

Effective attacks on pinpoint targets like this demanded a technique that had to be learnt by painstaking practice. Ground strafing itself was hated by many pilots as you were an easy target for ground defences. Similarly, bombing at night in such conditions gave you scant chance of doing calm and careful aiming. You had to dive at the target and release the bomb at exactly the right moment: too low and you could be hit by fragments from the explosion yourself; too high – as was the temptation when under fire – and you'd miss, which was a waste of the entire effort. Plus the extra bomb-load rendered your aircraft unfit for optimal air-to-air combat, particularly when out of balance after releasing three 20lb bombs with the fourth still suspended in the rack.

Many other engagements were of course initiated by the brave and skilled pilots of 151 Squadron which cannot be afforded a place in this biography: they can be found in official reports and in shared sources such as the renowned journal for First World War aero enthusiasts *Cross & Cockade International* and its American cousin *Over the Front*, as well as in online resources of which the Great War Forum is a leading example. Equally important is the fact that a victory (i.e. an enemy aircraft 'Destroyed/Driven Down/Out of Control') was never the sole criterion of success: machines put out of action or driven away from their targets served a vital purpose as far as the beleaguered Allied forces on the ground were concerned, who would otherwise have suffered heavier losses.

An action on the night of 7/8 August involved Brand and Armstrong, when both flew to Estrées-en-Chaussée and bombed hangars. Brand then spotted a bomber coming in to land and followed the large two-seater for

DVA's Camel C6713 snapped at Bertangles aerodrome, France, visiting No. 24 Squadron which was based there between 14 August and 8 September 1918. 'Doris' carries a bomb-rack and is now repainted for night-fighter duties, with darkened inner white rings of cockades on undersurfaces of the dark-painted lower wings, which have flares mounted below them. [Mike O'Connor]

some time, and in an account of 151 Squadron in *Cross & Cockade* he is said to have been able to get in a good burst of fire, whereupon 'the bomber immediately fell away in flames'.[6] However, Brand's combat report says he followed the German to another aerodrome but had to turn away to avoid the very active gunnery there, contenting himself with firing 100 rounds 'in the vicinity where EA was last seen'.[7] This is just one among many illustrations showing how records and memories can diverge. But such small discrepancies take nothing away from the nightly feats of navigation, airmanship and indomitable courage displayed as a matter of routine by Allied pilots in the quest to counter the onslaughts of German bombers and their deadly payloads.

On the following night, 8/9 August 1918 (the night of the Amiens offensive), Armstrong was officially commended for his determination in the face of horrendous flying conditions. Despite a very low ceiling with cloud cover down to about 500 feet 'he flew to the same hostile aerodrome [Estrées-en-Chaussée], but finding no activity there and seeing no lights whatever, he flew on to Cizancourt Bridge dropping his four bombs upon it from 500 feet. On this night he was unable at any period to fly at over 800 feet owing to low driving clouds and very strong wind.'[8]

Cizancourt was a key bridge on the Somme which can be seen on page 168. That it was singled out in his DFC citation indicates the 'exceptional skill', as the commendation says, this night's work displayed. To fly for any reasonable distance after dark at 500 feet, i.e. at half today's conventional circuit height, would be a nerve-racking prospect in a modern light aircraft with the comfort of a canopy. To do so in high winds and low clouds in an open-cockpit Camel, spattered with oil and wrestling with a folded map (see below), all the while presenting an easily-spotted gunnery target from the ground, required nerves of steel. And all this in pitch-black conditions with no visible horizon or moon or ground lights to navigate by, nor even a reliable compass – and then to turn from your plotted course and find your way to an unplanned alternative objective – by today's standards would be little short of astounding.

Yet such was the job in hand, and theirs the mission to accomplish it. With no let-up in the pressure, a large number of machines were airborne on the night of 10/11 August when shortly before midnight a multi-engined German bomber was seen illuminated by spotlights north of Amiens. The various combat reports show that several pilots had to manoeuvre to avoid others closing in to attack, and after bursts were fired by Knight, Summers and Aitken it was Yuille who delivered the *coup de grâce* firing from underneath at almost point-blank range. His victory was confirmed

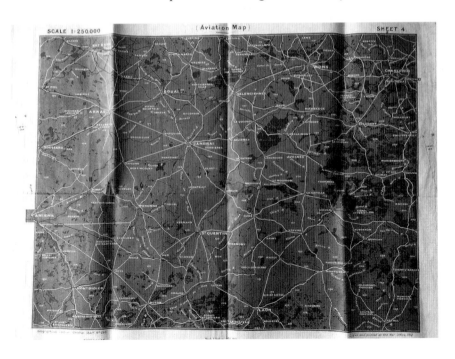

by Armstrong as senior flight commander who observed the engagement from 1,000 feet below and reported that Yuille was 'exceedingly close when firing'. Only after it crashed in flames behind Allied lines was the machine identified as one of the rare 5-engined German 'Giant' bombers, the Zeppelin-Staaken R.XIV, which became a subject of immense interest.

Another account by 151 Squadron pilots describes an attack on Moislains aerodrome at about this time; the date is not identified, but the references to bright moonlight place it around the full moon of 20 August. Armstrong, Brand, Haynes and Cockerell took part in a concentrated bombing operation in which at first they met little ground opposition, but by the time Brand attacked again, fully illuminated in the light of the moon, 'they opened up against him with just about every gun on the establishment. Miraculously he was unhurt, and on his return to base it was seen in the bright moonlight that his machine had been riddled by bullets, including several through the windscreen and cockpit.'[9]

Armstrong was next reported as attacking Moislains again on the night of 21/22 August 1918 at 03.15 to 03.30, dropping two incendiary and two Cooper bombs from 400 feet on hutments and tents, 'although subjected to the most accurate and fierce machine-gun fire from the ground, and his machine being brightly illuminated in the glare of the Incendiary bombs'.[10]

A couple of nights later, on 24/25 August 1918 at 22.20, DVA shared a victory with Lieutenant F.C. 'Tommy' Broome of B Flight, who would go on to achieve two more victories the following month and earn the DFC and AFC. They were on patrol when Broome saw a Gotha G-type of *Bosta 15/Bogohl 3* in searchlights west of Arras at about 7,000 feet and attacked from the rear, firing a burst of twenty rounds. He remained on its tail firing another twenty rounds while the Gotha took evasive action, whereupon he 'got in its backwash' (slipstream) and fell into a spin.

Meanwhile Armstrong had also seen the machine and closed to within twenty yards of it, but had to turn sharply away when Broome opened fire from directly behind him. Observing his comrade's aircraft shot by return of fire, DVA closed again and poured 240 rounds into his target, coming so near that he had to turn aside to avoid a collision. Broome then fired another sixty rounds and reported seeing the tracer going through the fuselage of the Gotha which spun down to about 3,000 feet.

This is a fine example of the nature and accuracy of their combined attack in which, without prior preparation, they managed to complement each other's manoeuvring while keeping up a continuous assault. Clearly at one point neither pilot noticed the other, Broome firing despite Armstrong's

A Gotha G.V of the type probably targeted by Broome and Armstrong.

having approached the Gotha so closely that he had to dodge his friend's line of fire. The latter was aiming at a greater distance and in very much shorter bursts, while Armstrong's tactic was to close to minimal range and blaze away. It was unlikely, however, that DVA's 240 rounds were discharged in one long burst, which would risk overheating. The rate of fire of the Vickers was 600 rounds per minute (or 1,200 from the Camel's twin installation), so Broome's initial two bursts of twenty rounds took exactly one second each. Armstrong probably also fired in bursts as he closed almost to collision point, possibly four successive bursts of three seconds each, with the Gotha pinned in his sights. Then he again broke away as Broome fired his longer closing burst of sixty rounds, taking about three seconds, and finally, with his machine and engine badly hit, Broome then had to return to base.

DVA watched the enemy aircraft fall into a left-hand spin and followed it down. 'I imagine I saw a fire start,' he recorded, but it failed to develop, and he last saw the Gotha still spinning at 2,000 feet. Reported 'Shot Down', the machine crashed on the Allied side of the lines near Arras where its crew were taken prisoner.[11]

Armstrong also acquired a Parabellum machine gun as a souvenir from the Gotha, an unusual opportunity since the favourable tailwind usually gave German aircraft every likelihood of getting back to Hunland even when damage resulted in a crash-landing.

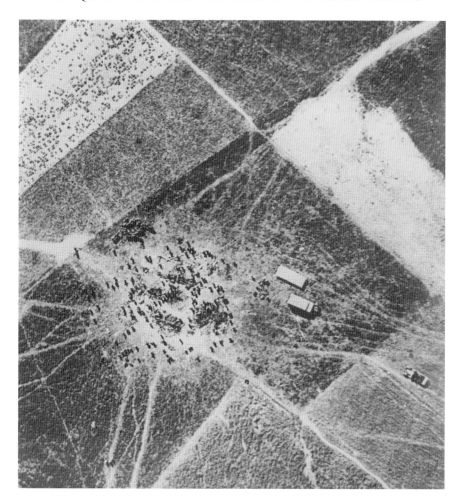

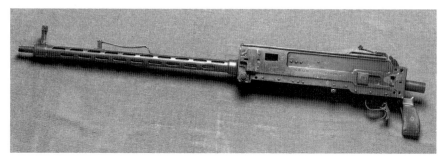

Within a fortnight the Allied push had succeeded in establishing its new forward position as shown on the operational map above (p.166), and had liberated the formerly occupied areas including airfields.

Wreckage of the Gotha being surveyed by some very relieved and gratified ground forces.

Concurrently with this there was a lull in aerial activity for over two weeks due to bad weather, followed by a strategic emphasis on defence against bombing and other incursions by the Germans after dark.

On the night of 10/11 September 1918, learning that an enemy aeroplane was threatening the Allied Front in his squadron's operational area, Captain Armstrong volunteered to go up. The weather conditions he encountered were atrocious, with rainstorms and winds of 50mph, yet he climbed into the darkness and remained on patrol for over an hour. Such determination did not go unnoticed, with his DFC commendation singling out his 'remarkable skill and resolution in night operations'.[12]

Combating adverse weather seems to have been an Armstrong speciality: in fact Wing Commander M.G. Christie recalled, when DVA was A Flight Commander with 78 Squadron earlier that year, his exceptional mastery of his machine 'in almost any weather any night. He was one of my best leaders when it was a question of giving practice to the searchlights on cloudy unfavourable nights.' On one occasion Christie had hastened to telephone 78 Squadron 'to forbid any of our Camel pilots going up' as he considered the weather 'far too rough for single-seater scouts to ascend'.[13]

Another shot of C6713 at Bertangles showing that all markings have been severely painted over for night operations. As in the previous snap, she has the centre-section cut-out extended to 3 ribs, non-standard twin fuel pumps, and wheel covers removed. A bomb carrier for four 20lb Coopers is fitted under the fuselage. [Mike O'Connor]

The reply came that I was too late: Armstrong had gone up and one or two of his braves with him. They all landed safely and after that I felt no compunction about Armstrong's patrol pushing off under almost any conditions. Thus he assisted very materially in developing the art of night flying which culminated in his being selected as senior Flight Commander in the First Night Flying Squadron that went overseas in summer 1918 [No. 151 Squadron] and which became famous. ... His prowess as a pilot was supreme; his sense of measure, rhythm and timing was superb, and for sheer flying ability I consider he had no equal in the world. On the ground he knew his job and could inspire his officers with just that élan which conquers every obstacle.

From mid-month onwards 151 Squadron enjoyed a most successful September, racking up a dozen or so victories. One week after DVA's lone patrol in the teeth of gale force winds came an extraordinary occurrence on the night of 17/18 September 1918. The official records show victories for Armstrong and Brand before midnight, with DVA having encountered

177

and shot down a Friedrichshafen G.III night bomber of *Bosta 8/Bogohl 6* south of Arras. He observed the G.III at 22.40 caught in a concentration of searchlights with a Camel behind it which apparently was not engaging from a close enough range, so Armstrong dived down, coming in on the enemy's starboard side. He closed right in and fired 100 rounds into the bomber which immediately burst into flames and crashed a few miles east of Bapaume, which was now Allied territory, of course.

In recollections from fellow pilots the encounter was remembered as much more bizarre than this bland report. Flying at 8,500 feet on a cloudy and overcast night, DVA had engaged the bomber and set it on fire, but after taking evasive action he temporarily lost his sighting. He then observed what he thought was his target falling in flames, terminating in an enormous explosion when it was down to about 6,000 feet. He duly returned to base and made his report. Quintin Brand then landed soon afterwards and claimed the same machine, at which there ensued a heated debate. Eventually the explanation became clear 'when eye-witnesses, who had been aloft at the same time, reported exactly what had happened. ... There had been TWO enemy aircraft flying side by side, and these had been shot down simultaneously by Major Brand and Captain Armstrong'. DVA, un-sighted due to his evasive manoeuvring, had re-sighted on Brand's target as he watched it fall. Both had been so occupied with their tasks that they had been oblivious of each other's actions. Each was therefore able to claim one Gotha 'Destroyed', with DVA's at 22.40 and Quintin Brand's at 22.41.[14]

DVA's combat report on file at the National Archives can be seen to contain an extra sentence, evidently to clear up the confusion, which has been added in fresh typing to the original and all carbon copies including this one: 'I could not pinpoint the spot [of impact] owing to the large explosion and fire on the machine which Major Brand brought down at this moment.' The timing of the event on DVA's report has also been altered by a couple of minutes in fresh typing, while Brand's remains unchanged.[15]

The photograph (opposite) of Armstrong's shot-down G.III appears in his album and has been identified by Frank Cheesman with the comment 'there appear to be only two members of the RAF visible in the photograph, and these were probably stationed there to guard the wreckage or were members of the salvage/investigating team'.[16]

At this point in September the squadron moved its base forward to Vignacourt, north of Amiens, to support a stealthy relocation of Allied searchlight defences made under cover of the adverse weather that was keeping German aircraft grounded. The result of this tactic was highly

Friedrichshafen G.III brought down by DVA east of Bapaume; two RAF personnel at centre wearing field caps.

satisfactory, taking the enemy completely by surprise when they resumed nocturnal operations.

Armstrong's final combat report details an action on 23/24 September 1918 at 23.50 when he engaged with a two-seater enemy aircraft at 10,500 feet. Diving on it he fired 150 rounds whereupon it immediately went into a vertical dive, as a result of which 'what appeared to be the observer shot out over the top plane'. He continued following the aircraft down to 8,000 feet but lost it while it was still hurtling in its descent, so was unable to define any other result from the encounter, which was marked 'Details insufficient to form an accurate opinion'.[17]

By the end of the war, No. 151 Squadron had claimed sixteen enemy aircraft destroyed at night on the Allies' side of the lines, five destroyed on the enemy side and confirmed, and another five probables, making a total of twenty-six successful engagements without loss. During the five months in which the squadron had taken part in hostilities overseas the total number of hours flown by night was 1,443 hours 26 minutes, without the loss of a single machine or personnel casualty to enemy action.

Men (and puppy) of C Flight, No. 151 Squadron, France, 1918 [Trevor Henshaw].

Throughout all these encounters the squadron's pilots could not have remained combat ready without total confidence in the skill and professionalism of the men who maintained their weapons, nursed their mercilessly thrashed engines, and kept their aeroplanes airworthy. In the photograph in plate 11 it is plain to see the easy familiarity of DVA with Evans, his fitter and Fowle, his rigger, born of shared adversity and mutual respect.

Another photograph (above) shows the ground crew of C Flight, 151 Squadron, all essential members of the often overlooked teams on the ground that worked constantly to keep the machines and men in the air. Bill Taylor, whom we met earlier flying Pups in 1917, wrote of his gratitude to his own crew when the time came for him to be posted home:[18]

> I knew how McFall and the others had repeatedly worked all night to get new engines in for me as the Le Rhônes chewed themselves to pieces under the stresses of the unmerciful treatment we had to give them. I remembered how the armourers had checked every round before loading the clips for the Vickers to give me the best chance of firing with a minimum of stoppages. I saw these patient, skilful, decent men: friends whose unsung work had kept me in the air and had had a big part in bringing me back from more than a

hundred patrols and escorts and private wars – and I knew
that anything I could say would be inadequate.

D'Urban Armstrong was cited three times in official RAF communiqués
for his work in 151 Squadron,[19] and by the time he had served with them
for three months he was granted a period of leave. It was recorded as
27 September-11 October 1918, but the events described below indicate that
the leave actually lasted only one week, ending on 4 October. This would
explain why DVA's service record has him attached to the French Aviation
Corps from 5 to 10 October. His duties there were to assist the French with
defence, including protection of hospitals which were still being bombed by
the Germans. At the end of the war General Jan Smuts recollected the key
importance of this attachment:

> When the air raids started in Paris they wanted us to send a
> man to take charge of their night work also. I sent Captain
> Armstrong where he trained the French airmen as he had
> trained our airmen to a proper standard until the Germans no
> longer ventured to attack Paris either by day or by night.

Lieutenant General Jan
Christian Smuts pictured
in 1918.

CAMEL PILOT SUPREME CAPTAIN D.V. ARMSTRONG DFC

During his attachment the news arrived that he had been awarded, on 6 October, the Distinguished Flying Cross for consistently outstanding work over the past year. The citation in the *London Gazette* of 3 December 1918 reads partly as follows (the full account may be seen in Appendix II):

> A brilliant pilot of exceptional skill. His success in night operations has been phenomenal; and the service he renders in the training of other pilots is of the greatest value, personally supervising their flying and demonstrating the only successful method of attack by night. On the night of 10-11th of September, learning that an enemy aeroplane was over our front, he volunteered to go up. The weather conditions were such as to render flying almost impossible, the wind blowing about fifty miles an hour, accompanied by driving rainstorms; despite this, Captain Armstrong remained on patrol for over an hour, his machine at times being practically out of control. The foregoing is only one of many instances of this Officer's remarkable skill and resolution in night operations. ...
>
> [The citation concluded] This Officer has been the right hand of his Squadron Commander since the formation of his Squadron, and has by his wonderful flying, taught the pilots of No. 151 Squadron more than any other Instructor could possibly have done. He has demonstrated to all pilots daily the only successful method of attack at night against E.A., by personal supervision of their flying. As a Flight Commander I cannot speak too highly of him and his wonderful spirit at all times. His bravery as a Pilot at all times and in all weather conditions cannot be surpassed, and I am unable to recommend him too strongly for this decoration.

The British national newspaper *The Daily Mirror* carried a news article on 4 December 1918 recording DVA's award. Although the main headline was devoted to him, the article also brought to notice the deeds of several other equally brave officers, including Captains McClaughry and Brand, as well as two exceptionally valiant chaplains, the Reverends Lusk and Tron, awarded Bars to their MCs for attending and evacuating wounded soldiers on the battlefield under heavy fire.

CHASED HUN AIRMAN IN ROARING GALE

British Captain's Dashing Feat in Driving Rain.

A brilliant pilot of exceptional skill has won fresh lustre for the 'cavalry of the air'. This gallant officer is Lieutenant (A/Captain) D.V. Armstrong, who has just been awarded the Distinguished Flying Cross.

On the night of September 10, learning that an enemy aeroplane was over our front, he volunteered to go up.

The weather conditions were such as to render flying almost impossible, the wind blowing about fifty miles an hour, accompanied by driving rainstorms. Despite this, Captain Armstrong remained on patrol over an hour, his machine at times being practically out of control.

'His success in these adventures has been phenomenal,' records the London Gazette, *'and the services he renders in training other pilots is of the greatest value, personally supervising their flying and demonstrating the only successful method of attack by night.'*

It was not only the pilots of British and French forces who had cause to be grateful to D.V. Armstrong for morale-boosting pilot training and support in night combat. A mere twenty-four hours after ceasing his duties with the French Aviation Corps he received a posting on 11 October to proceed to Issoudun for attachment with the 3rd Air Instructional Center, American Expeditionary Force (AEF), where he remained from 13 October until the end of the month.

Meanwhile, during those two weeks of DVA's leave and French attachment, the Allies' last great push – the Grand Offensive – had been launched to devastating effect, with the participation of 1.2 million men of the AEF employed for the most part in the Meuse-Argonne offensive of 26 September. By 5 October the defences of the Hindenburg Line had been broken along its entire length, and the Germans were completely overwhelmed in the brief battle of Cambrai from 8 to 10 October. Despite the enormous numbers of casualties taken by the AEF, it would have been known at Issoudun that their countrymen had made a decisive contribution to forcing the realization on the German high command that their dreams of victory were over.

We are now nearing the date of Armistice Day, 11 November, and from the preserved tail-fin of DVA's Camel C6713 (see Plate 15), which is coloured bright red with serial number outlined conspicuously, it is clear that by then 'Doris' had shed her drab overpainting and emerged in full colour again. There is considerable evidence of painting and repainting of First World War aircraft at unit level, which seems to have been readily performed for any number of purposes – whether purely cosmetic, or for the more serious necessity of changing or disguising squadron/flight markings, etc. Aeroplanes and their insignia were routinely darkened for night flying, for which the squadrons had temporary paint available. Records show that C6713 went in for maintenance at the end of September, during DVA's time on leave and in Paris, and this appears to have been precisely the right moment for her reversion to red livery in anticipation of that three-week instructional attachment with the American forces. It is also quite possible that the fully-darkened camouflage was already being discontinued by night-flying units at this time, since it was found to present a starkly silhouetted target – especially at low level – against a background of clouds, or when illuminated by the moon or caught in searchlights. Thomas Martyn's memoir of his time with No. 102 Night Bomber Squadron in France tells of how his informal tests suggested a much lighter colour was preferable. On presenting his findings to his CO, Harold Wyllie, a painter himself and son of a famous Royal Academician, Martyn recorded that the authorities accepted his subsequent recommendations with little procrastination. 'Thereafter, all night-flying planes were painted an apple-green, a much more effective camouflage in the light phases of the moon and against probing searchlight beams in the dark.'[20]

The 3rd Air Instructional Center (AIC) at Issoudun lay south-west of Bourges in the Indre department of central France (circled on map below). It had been formed to transition US pilots to wartime flying from their basic training received at home, where they lacked appropriate aircraft and instructors with combat experience. The training methods developed by Armstrong and other seconded instructors produced a complete course in advanced flying and aerial tactics for the war in Europe, in which American pilots eventually were to receive about sixty hours of training including night-flying, night attack and night landing. In the final stages of the war, by the time these recruits had also completed the on-site aerial gunnery school they averaged over 100 hours of training, nearly triple the number of hours with which pilots of the RFC had

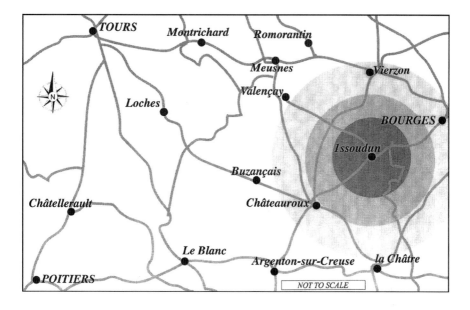

been reporting to their combat units two years earlier. And Issoudun had become the largest air base in the world.

We have some surviving reminiscences from American pilots who knew DVA as an instructor there, organizing some of the earliest courses of training with the American Expeditionary Force. Among them was Lieutenant T.N. (Temple) Joyce who wrote an article declaring that Armstrong should be credited as the originator of the classic 'Roll-off-the-Top' (that manoeuvre still too often known nowadays as the 'Immelmann Turn').

There are many types of ascending turn essential to every fighter pilot's repertoire; they consist of a turning climb or half-loop, combining height gain with change of direction (a key principle being not to find yourself upside down at the mercy of your opponent). Max Immelmann's ascending turn in the early years of the Great War was advanced for its day and named after him in admiration, but it was never his intention to execute a pleasing aerobatic figure as Joyce saw demonstrated by D'Urban Armstrong at Issoudun, i.e. pulling a graceful half-loop until inverted at the top, then returning upright by performing a half slow roll (aileron roll) – see illustration (b) overleaf.

Immelmann, having only the Eindecker controlled by wing-warping, could never have delayed banking his wings until the top of his climb, nor was his height gain sustained; he would have needed an immediate dive to make good his escape. His climbing turn, as described by his brother and others who saw it, resembled the wing-over as depicted in (a) below, which he entered from a dive to climb, fire under his opponent's tail, then dive away with a banked turn in a different direction.[21]

In subsequent years, with pilots able to exploit ever more advanced machines, techniques were developed culminating in aerobatics as skill, as art, as display and as sport. At Issoudun Temple Joyce was the regular exhibition pilot, keen to develop his art just like Armstrong and Stewart before him, and always looking to learn new manoeuvres – such as the flat spin which he mentioned having learnt from one of the French instructors. As well as to entertain, the aim of the exhibition pilot was to please the eye with geometrically symmetrical lines and angles, a concept that underlies the criteria for judging competition aerobatics today.

In *Cross & Cockade* Temple Joyce gave a taped interview describing how DVA earned a unique reputation among trainee US pilots when he was assigned to Issoudun as instructor at the 3rd AIC's newly opened night pursuit school.[22] Armstrong was well known as a 'hot' pilot and would give spectacular displays of aerobatic flying in his red Camel which sported the name of his fiancée, Doris, painted on the front. 'He would come diving down at the field, level off about two feet from the ground, pull up into a

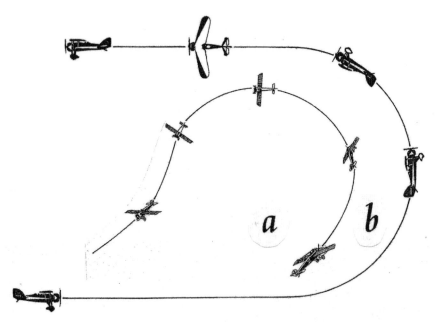

(a) The Immelmann Turn (a wing-over), the most the German's Fokker E.III could have managed; (b) Armstrong Roll-off-the-Top which the E.III could never have performed.

loop, and when he reached the top, he would roll out and go on his merry way.' This was the first time Joyce had seen a half aileron roll out of the top of a loop, so when DVA landed he asked, 'Armstrong, how do you do that? Do you kick the rudder or what?' 'You fly it through, Joyce. It's a good trick – go up and try it,' was the answer. No matter how many times Temp would ask, all Armstrong would say was 'You fly it through'.

Temp fell into ten or so outside spins before he realized that you did exactly what Armstrong had advised: you were in normal aerodynamic flight even though inverted, so you just aileroned, added top rudder to keep the nose up, and 'flew it through'. To Joyce it had appeared to be a half-flick because of the Camel's high rate of roll ('it had the highest rolling moment from aileron control of any plane in existence'), and flicks were by now second-nature in the latest powerful machines. Joyce claimed to be the first American to replicate Armstrong's manoeuvre, and even after the war was still being asked how to execute it. When congratulated on his prowess he always said how he had learnt it from Captain Armstrong.

'In memory of the finest acrobatic pilot I have ever seen,' he wrote in 1962, 'I recommend that the manoeuvre be henceforth called the Armstrong rather than the Immelmann.' Sadly, even in Britain and his native South Africa, the Roll-off-the-Top is not remembered as Armstrong's invention.

In an earlier chapter we observed that in all the months and years he spent practising aerobatic skills, Oliver Stewart failed to slow roll his Camel. 'Here is a curious historical fact,' he wrote in 1967;[23] 'at the time I was concentrating upon aerobatics ... the slow roll had not been developed. ... Flick rolls were common, but the slow roll, in which the aircraft is flown all

Issoudun Aerodrome Field 3, 1918.

the way round, was still unknown. ... I did not do a slow roll until shortly before I wrote my book on aerobatics. ... I had only discovered it a short time before my book appeared in 1928.'

This is probably because Stewart was acting in isolation at Orfordness. It so happens that from 1918 at the Royal Aircraft Establishment, Farnborough, a team assembled by Roderic Hill was investigating inverted flight, initially looking at inverted spins, but also casting the net wider to encompass the aerodynamics of flying inverted.[24] Various methods were recorded in the process of deliberately turning upside down, all involving half-rolls, and at the outset their inverted spin trials were overwhelmingly entered from a half flick roll with gyroscopic forces already in play. However, like Armstrong before them, Hill's team soon appreciated that a 'flown' half-roll could be achieved with careful co-ordination of aileron and rudder, and by the time they issued their final report *The Manoeuvres of Inverted Flight* (1922) they had thoroughly examined the aileron roll and devoted a complete section to it. 'The slow half roll,' says the report, 'seems most adapted to the flying qualities of the Camel.'

> Attaining the inverted position by means of a half [slow] roll is a quieter manoeuvre. It is possible to roll over upside down, fly inverted for some time and roll out on to an even keel in normal flight ... the pilot need never lose sight of the horizon, thus retaining a more continuous sense of where he is.

In joining the two separate half-rolls into a full 360-degree roll, the report adds, the aim should be to achieve 'an even rate of roll from start to finish. ... The two halves of the manoeuvre should blend perfectly into a continuous whole.' Yet even after years of investigation, the Farnborough test pilots considered that 'the pilot must find by experiment' the correct synchronization of controls for the slow roll in his particular aeroplane, each man having employed a different combination that suited himself.

This method of joining two half-rolls, discovered in the early 1920s, exactly mirrors the way in which a pilot like Captain Armstrong would have gradually developed the slow roll technique which he had perfected at least two years earlier, relying on innate sensitivity and 'feel' for the performance of his machine. Once having mastered his half slow roll from the top of a loop, he must inevitably have continued his experiments by piecing it together with the other half to achieve that blend 'into a continuous whole' which constitutes the classic slow roll. Given the Camel's lightning-quick

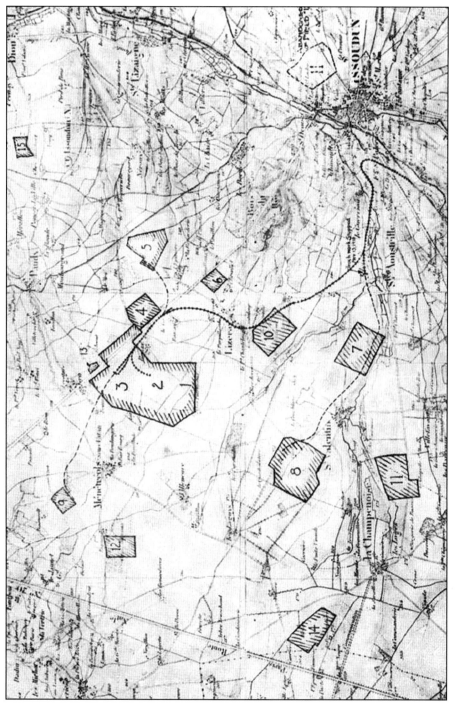

Layout plan of the 15 fields at Issoudun.

rate of rotation, onlookers would scarcely have taken note that DVA had made this breakthrough, and would merely have assumed it was a remarkably smooth and in-line version of the flick roll they were accustomed to seeing. Any notes that Armstrong may have made have unfortunately disappeared, and there remain only piecemeal accounts of the manoeuvres he developed.

An example of one such account is the following narrative by Colonel Hiram Bingham (above), CO of the 3rd AIC from August to December 1918, who also wrote of DVA giving instruction in night flying at Issoudun.[25] 'Hunting the Hun in the dark was a favourite sport of Captain Armstrong, Commanding Officer [actually senior flight commander] of the first British Night Pursuit Squadron at the Front. He himself had a record of having brought down more than fifty Hun machines [*sic*!], including the gigantic five-engine Gotha.' (N.B. DVA did not claim involvement in this engagement by 151 Squadron, but observed and reported it.)[26] Here is how Bingham related seeing D'Urban Armstrong arrive at Issoudun:

> One day I was crossing the street from my quarters to my office, when the unaccustomed sound produced by a plane looping near the ground called my attention to the extraordinary antics of a Sopwith Camel. It made loop after loop over Headquarters,

missing the roofs of the buildings by only a few feet, finally coming so close to the ground as to cause us all to hold our breath as the marvellously skilful pilot pulled his ship out of a loop within a few inches of the ground, fairly touching the long grass. Then the machine was pulled straight up into a 'zoom' of unparalleled magnitude. It stalled, fell like a leaf, fluttering from side to side, recovered, made a tight spiral incredibly near the ground, lit as gracefully as a butterfly, and hardly rolled more than a few inches. Then a small dog bounded out of the cockpit from the pilot's lap to the ground, while the pilot himself with a novel under his arm and a smile on his face walked nonchalantly across the aerodrome. Thus did Captain Armstrong announce his arrival. ... [He] was the most graceful and skilful flyer that I have ever seen.

One of the greatest differences between the Royal Air Force and our own was that they believed in encouraging morale and stimulating their pilots to recklessness by such exhibitions as these, even though the most skilful pilots occasionally met their death in this fashion. ... There is no question but that there was a far higher morale among the pilots in the British squadrons than in our own.

By now – indeed since 1917 – instruction in pilot training in England had been completely overhauled by the Smith Barry Gosport System which promoted flair and assurance in absolute mastery of one's mount. The school's Mobile Flights, staffed by excellent instructors, flew their good-tempered Avro trainers to the limit with utter confidence, and the small Gosport 'pep circus' was dedicated to looking for new stunts and giving spirited demonstrations of old ones ... although high spirits occasionally got the better of

Robert Smith Barry.

Issoudun Aerodrome, Field 7.

common sense: 'An order was issued,' wrote Harold Balfour, 'to the effect that flying through the moat of the Fort [Rowner] must cease as it broke the telephone wires "which showed bad judgment".'[27]

The Americans had wholly embraced these methods and recognized their value: 'Instructors should be encouraged to give exhibition stunting,' wrote Major R.H. Fleet of the US Army. 'Thus may students learn that flying near the ground is safe, and thus may their ardour, enthusiasm and desire to learn be kept at the top-most notch. Too many rules of the air, too many prohibitions against reckless flying ... are against the very purpose of flying training, namely to make courageous flyers and aerial fighters.'[28]

During his three weeks at Issoudun DVA made an indelible impression. He was hosted by Captain Richard S. Davis (later Major R.S. Davis, Croix de Guerre avec Palme), officer in charge of Field 7 on the HQ staff under Colonel Bingham. Field 7 was near St Valentin, a few miles from the main fields at Issoudun, and was used for formation and night-flying work.

Richard Davis could never forget the day Armstrong arrived in his Sopwith Camel and gave his trademark little display: 'What a sensation he caused. Never had we seen such flying, and we were supposed to be experts! And then his dog hopped out – a little white Scottish terrier – and then after three brief weeks he was gone. But in that time, during which he organized a course of night pursuit flying, the first with the American Air Force, he endeared himself to every one of my men and officers. The entire camp was just raised – as if by a divine spirit – a few steps higher in morale and cheerfulness and the *will to do*. He was by far the most wonderful pilot I have ever seen, and I have trained and seen many hundreds.' Davis held on to mementos of Armstrong's stay including his thank-you note, received after DVA had returned to 151 Squadron, in which he said that his three weeks at Issoudun were 'by far the finest and happiest he ever spent in France'.[29]

It seems that Armstrong found his ultimate role at Issoudun, instilling confidence and prowess in his US trainees. His main duty was to devise a course of initiation into the occult arts of night flying – something which had never before been taught systematically. The following is Bingham's brief summary of how his night training proceeded:

> We were most fortunate in being able to secure [Armstrong's] services in starting our instruction in night pursuit. Half a dozen of the most skilful pilots began practising landings at night in an Avro with Captain Armstrong in the instructor's seat. ... After the student had shown the necessary proficiency on the Avro, he was sent up in the Sopwith Camel, the machine preferred by Captain Armstrong as being most effective for night pursuit.
>
> After the technique of night flying in small pursuit planes was mastered, the most interesting part of the work began, namely, practice in attacking night bombers. The night bomber is picked up by listening devices, his position is given to the searchlight operators, and the pursuit pilot is sent up to his known elevation and into his approximate location. He gives the signal and immediately the searchlights are turned on the bomber, who is then held in the powerful rays. The pursuit plane comes up in the blackness behind and shoots from a distance of about 20 yards and at an angle of about 10° below. He has plenty of time to fire deliberately and with care. Captain Armstrong used to say the results were so satisfactory as to be 'hardly sportsmanlike'!

N.B. Clayton Knight, whose reminiscences have already been quoted above, appears to have mis-identified the dog in question. Knight had rejoined DVA at the formation of 151 Squadron to fly as his No. 2 once more in A Flight (other old friends who joined the squadron included Laurence Carter and Frank Kendall from No. 78). Knight brought down a Gotha and a Friedrichshafen in August, then joined 206 Squadron but was shot down in October 1918 and taken prisoner. Fortunately he emerged to become a well-known aviation artist and illustrator, his artwork appearing in *The New Yorker* as well as a large number

of books including the original edition of *War Birds: Diary of an Unknown Aviator*.

In Knight's recollections from his days with No. 44 Squadron he wrote: 'Our hero Captain Armstrong always flew with a little mongrel dog named "Dickebusch", a souvenir of his earlier days in France.' It had become quite common, as Billy Bishop confirms in his book *Winged Warfare*, for RFC airmen to care for stray or injured dogs picked up near their base. However, records show that this particular little mongrel dog was actually associated with Lieutenant W.A. (Walbanke) Pritt of 44 Squadron, pictured here, whose Camel B3859 sported an amusing cartoon of a running dog with its leash towing the cockade on its fuselage. First adopted while he was with 66 Squadron in France, and subsequently smuggled home, Dickebusch was named by Pritt after the lake which formed an important landmark for flyers on this part of the Front. He made it his mascot by marking red, white and blue roundels on each of the dog's sides.

In 1918 Armstrong had been one of the officers under the command of Colonel John Salmond, GOC, RAF France, and Salmond was responsible for selecting him for instructional duty at Issoudun:[30]

> I had seen him flying before at home, and I was impressed then and later with his exceptional skill. I recollect considering him the best pilot of his time, and when asked by the American Aviation to send a picked officer down to instruct in night flying, and in the work that our night-flying squadrons were doing, I chose him as the best possible officer for the job.
>
> I received from the American Aviation a glowing account of his work, his personality and his wonderful piloting, and they were frankly amazed at the wonderful skill that he showed. He was one of the best and bravest pilots in the Royal Air Force, and his great spirit was always tempered by self-control.

On 1 November 1918, as the war moved to an end, DVA returned to No. 151 Squadron which in the interim had moved to Bancourt aerodrome,

Issoudun Aerodrome, main area.

east of Bapaume, in the wake of the retreating German Army. And again the evidence of C6713's tail fin is a reminder that her colour was not required to be changed, even though his duties included flying patrols at Le Quesnoy-en-Santerre on the evenings of 9 and 10 November. No enemy aircraft were making any appearances at this time, and 151 Squadron's final air victory had been achieved by Major Brand ten days previously on 29 October. With the enemy retreating east it is likely that German night bombing in their area had virtually ceased by the end of the month. Cecil Lewis reported that on arrival in France with the newly formed 152 Squadron around 23 October he did no fighting whatsoever.

The signs of Germany's defeat were already clear by the end of October, when Turkey collapsed, having been fatally undermined by the Armistice of Salonika signed by its ally Bulgaria. The German Army's high command had been urging an armistice since September, and Austria-Hungary was next to surrender on 3 November. By this time German unrest at home had led to an uprising in Berlin which put an end to the Kaiser's vacillation and on 9 November Kaiser Wilhelm's abdication was proclaimed. The Armistice of 11 November ceasing all hostilities at 11.00 a.m. was signed on a cold, drizzly morning in a railway carriage in the Compiègne Forest.

At the end its tour, 151 Squadron returned home to great acclaim for its success in operations and especially in pioneering night intruder tactics. It was stationed briefly at Gullane, Scotland, before eventually being

disbanded in September 1919. But D.V. Armstrong was not destined for the tranquil moorings of civilian life.

Over the years many different and often exotic stories have been told of how Captain Armstrong died accidentally in C6713 two days after the Armistice. The most credible version is that recounted by members of No. 151, who report that he crashed whilst giving an exhibition of aerobatics on a visit to a neighbouring squadron.

Their son's death was conveyed to his devastated parents, George and Ethyl, who had recently retired to their new home in Durban. A mere twelve days later their elder son, Athol, would die and be buried in a country churchyard in England. D'Urban was laid to rest at Tincourt Cemetery, a little east of Péronne. His burial service was conducted by the Reverend C.M. Schooling, the chaplain attached to 58 Casualty Clearing Station. His grave (number VI, D.9) can be found at Tincourt among the countless other graves of lost young men of 1914-1920. At his death he was aged 21 years and less than 4 months.

The tributes to D.V. Armstrong were many, and several are reproduced in Appendix III. The words of those who flew with him are perhaps most meaningful. 'The loss of such a magnificent pilot to the RAF was very sad,' says the 151 Squadron tribute. 'He was well known in the Corps and his cheerful disposition and courage made him respected by all who knew him.' All such accolades and recollections agreed universally on similar qualities in the man, which may be summed up as a magnificent pilot, a courageous fighter, and a cheerful and unassuming comrade in arms. In a cable of condolence to his parents, General Smuts wrote: 'Your fine boy will be remembered for his skill and modesty.'

CHAPTER 9

IN RETROSPECT

It was on 13 November 1918, two days after the Armistice was signed, that D'Urban Armstrong took up Camel C6713 for a cross-country flight, leaving Bancourt at 14.20. High pressure had followed the cold, wet start to the month, and with the arrival of the sun he felt in celebratory mood as he headed for Bouvincourt aerodrome,[1] south-east of Péronne (home to No. 1 and No. 43 Squadrons), some sixteen miles from Bancourt by air. A fine day accompanied by a mood of relaxation, perhaps tinged with incredulity that the war was over at last; so a pleasant little excursion – less than ten minutes at a cruising speed of about 120mph – maybe to visit friends at Bouvincourt for the afternoon.

Captain Armstrong was known to announce his arrival by performing a few eye-catching aerobatics overhead his destination. 'He commenced to stunt over that airfield as only he could', according to one source. Little enough to go on, but if there is one thing a seasoned aerobatic pilot never does, it is try out new manoeuvres near ground level over unfamiliar territory. So we may be confident in the knowledge that he would be performing tried and tested figures.

Whilst on the subject, it may also be assumed that he had his own equivalent of today's pre-aerobatics HASELL safety checks (Height, Airframe, Security, Engine, Location, Lookout); he would not have been selected to carry out extensive supervision and instruction had he not been conscientious in how he approached matters of safety. Schooled in 60 Squadron under the rigorous influence of the great Smith Barry, he impressed Colonel John Salmond with his 'great spirit always tempered by self-control'. This was not an irresponsible lad showing off.

Nevertheless, after a three-year career with never a single mistake, accident or other airmanship blot on his record, on this one occasion his Camel mysteriously failed to recover from a spin. 'Error in judgement,' says the Casualty Report. 'Machine spun to earth.'[2] We will return to review this conclusion later.

D'Urban died instantly, and was received at No. 58 Casualty Clearing Station 'dead on arrival'. Aside from multi-injuries, the casualty card contains no further detail. Nor has it been possible to establish whether an inquest took place – these were normal in Britain, but apparently not in war-ravaged France. Consequently we are left wondering what caused that terrible accident.

An irrecoverable spin is a recurring theme in many accounts, but not universally so. One much-quoted comment from an unnamed American source, which appears *inter alia* in the book *Sopwith Camel: King of Combat*, asserts that 'the Camel never recovered from a near-vertical spin and dove straight into the earth at full power.'[3] This is impossible: it is completely ruled out by the unmistakably flattened appearance of the photographed wreckage.

Many and varied alternative ideas have been put forward. A clutch of hypotheses favour a misjudged rolling manoeuvre, e.g. Harold Balfour's assertion that 'his wing-tip touched in the middle of his roll';[4] or he snagged a wire attached to a hangar, or hit the hangar itself, e.g. Hiram Bingham's 'stunting too close to a hangar'.[5] However, it is fruitless to conjecture with these theories since we have no direct eyewitness report. The official version 'spun to earth' is likely to be the truth, but the mere occurrence of a spin provides no answers; least of all because straightforward spinning presented no challenge for the combat pilot and/or aerobatic specialist. Recovery would have been second nature to Armstrong in a machine whose habits he knew intimately. A spin was equally the most likely outcome if an unstable aircraft like the Camel suffered a failure, whether involving engine, airframe, controls, or any combination of the three.

As to spin recovery, it is true the Camel gained a reputation from the start for its tendency to spin if mishandled, but once combat pilots knew how to control and recover from these tendencies the jinx was lifted and they prized it as the most successful fighter of the war. Wing Commander Norman Macmillan, who was very alive to the need to treat the Camel with respect, gave the following example of how a trainee pilot tamed his Camel simply because he was sufficiently well trained in how to handle a rotary in a spin. The pupil was practising at 1,000 feet on a blustery day when on entry to a dive his Camel went right over on its back, stalled, and spun inverted. The pilot knew the necessary recovery actions but, being unused to the Camel, he over-corrected and his mount immediately switched from an inverted left-hand spin to an upright right-hand spin. Again the pupil corrected but, seeing the ground so much closer now, tried to pull out too quickly, stalled again, and promptly spun to the left. This time he made the correct recovery inputs and waited. Despite being so close to the ground he held the dive until his Camel had gained enough speed to be restored to level flight without another stall, its wheels brushing the ground as it did so. 'What aeroplane but the Camel,' Macmillan asked, 'could spin three times in three different ways between 1,000 feet and the ground and emerge undamaged, especially in the hands of a pupil?'[6]

By the same token, how likely is it that Armstrong, the most proficient Camel pilot of his day, knowing to the last millisecond how to handle any spin in any attitude, would suddenly on this occasion misjudge his recovery? Was it really pilot error, as stated in the Casualty Report? Perhaps it is time to interrogate this verdict and maybe even acquit an acclaimed pilot of a slur on his flying reputation.

The report itself was issued six days later and signed by the CO of 151 Squadron, Major Brand, but he had not seen the incident; he would merely have recorded whatever information was received from a senior officer at Bouvincourt. It is not known whether that officer in turn had personally seen the event or merely derived his information from a witness who happened to be out on the aerodrome. Further, the expertise of that witness, and whether he had flying experience, or was aware of the exceptional flying record of the visiting pilot, is also unknown. Was it a rush to judgement? In a full air accident inquiry it is very difficult indeed to establish that an error has been made by a pilot – certainly not without a thorough investigation to rule out failures in the machine itself. There is no record of any such investigation taking place. So it is not surprising that nagging doubts remain.

Before impugning Armstrong's capabilities we must take account of his well attested proficiency flying Moranes and Camels in combat over a span of three years, both widely categorized as death-traps, and his most recent year or more on night operations which included providing instruction in night-fighting. 'By personal supervision', to quote his commanding officer, 'he taught the pilots of No. 151 Squadron more than any other Instructor could possibly have done.' The assessment penned by 151 Squadron on the website *From Camel to Hawk* is worth quoting in full: 'Captain Armstrong was well known throughout the RAF for his skills in aerobatics, particularly flick rolls and loops at low level. He showed courage, skill and fine judgement in all his flying, these qualities being used to good effect in air to air combat.' This was a pilot of enormous experience and acute judgement, for whom aerobatics had become a routine activity. And indeed he claimed, as did Oliver Stewart, that he could safely perform them at low level because he had worked out how to recover from any likely predicament. Stewart himself, who knew all there was to know about aerobatting the Sopwith Camel, wisely never ventured an opinion about DVA's accident.

That Armstrong was a superb pilot is a theme that runs consistently through his career – some observers went so far as to call him the best.

Before handing over Camel B3826, he noted that he had done 123 hours flying on her without straining a wire. *Without straining a wire* on a stick-and-rag biplane throughout six solid months of war work interspersed with aerobatic demonstrations. This very remark shows he was acutely aware how critical it was to ensure he was in complete control throughout every manoeuvre, and how closely he kept a check on his machine's condition.

If these reflections seem to garland him with praise, they do so only because at his sudden death in a foreign land there lacked voices at hand to speak out for him, voices whose care should have been to reject hasty conclusions. Even after the passage of a century, his reputation calls for serious probing of the assumption of pilot error, at least in theory, against the likelihood of undetected failures in engine or airframe.

Was there an engine problem? Certainly this was the view of Wing Commander W.M. (Willie) Fry MC (although Fry thought he was rolling rather than spinning when he met his end): 'He was killed doing a roll in a Sopwith Camel near the ground, a stunt he had performed many times before. On that last occasion the engine failed.'[7] Fry was merely recounting an explanation he had heard. But Cecil Lewis had heard a different one, and given the popularity of his First World War memoir the view he expounded has been widely believed, especially thanks to its invented circumstantial detail. Lewis thought he left it too late to recover from a spin, and went into detailed speculation as to the mistakes he supposed Armstrong made.[8] Yet neither Fry nor Lewis was there to see it happen, and Lewis even assigned the wrong date to the accident. Once again we must beware of relying on third-party accounts. Interestingly, however, Lewis was as concerned as Fry about the danger of engine failure when stunting near ground level.

How recently had C6713's engine been overhauled? So far as we know, the time between overhauls (TBO) prescribed for the 130hp Clerget and the 80hp/110hp Le Rhône was the same: twenty hours. For the record, the TBO is the manufacturer's specified number of running hours before the engine requires to be completely disassembled, its components inspected and problems rectified. As the overhaul point approaches, even without the failure of any one component the engine may show loss of power output, probably arising from poor compression in the engine cylinders or poor spark-plug condition indicating excessive oil fouling or excessive mixture richness. Realistically, an engine used and misused in aerial combat for much of its life ought never to exceed the manufacturer's advisory TBO, and probably they never did: it is thought they would usually need stripping before twenty hours anyway, due to power loss from carbon build-up, etc.

Experts on these rotary engines say they were by no means 'fit and forget' – they were subject to continual supervision and tuning. The pilots themselves were well aware of deterioration through loss of revs, and some whose skills were up to the task were known to strip their own engines regularly, if only to decarbonize the cylinder-heads and valves.

C6713 was withdrawn for maintenance around 30 September when its engine was overhauled and probably replaced.[9] Apart from this its overhaul records are unknown. But the US fitters at Issoudun were as constantly employed keeping aero engines in top condition as in any front-line squadron, and were well served by an efficient supply system. So there seems little reason for anxiety about the condition of the engine.

The position is different when it comes to the machine's airframe. Armstrong cited 123 hours on B3826, but compare this with C6713 for which his Casualty Report gives a total flying time of 256 hours 30 minutes, more than twice that total, and a very great deal indeed for a Camel. Issoudun had a number of Camels on strength and presumably the riggers were up to speed on them, but would they have been familiar with the crucial necessity of checking bracing wires at all times and keeping them fully taut? Moreover DVA had been training tyro pilots, and if any of them flew C6713, might there have been heavy landings they failed to report?

Observations about landings and bracing wires may seem a little arcane, but if we bring in Norman Macmillan's expert opinion again, he considered they were relevant to the Sopwith Camel's unpredictability. Writing in 1960, he commented that despite the skill of its greatest exponents, though most of the time it would perform manoeuvres identically, yet once in ten, twenty or perhaps fifty times it would unaccountably behave differently.[10] This was a characteristic that Macmillan found disturbing, and in 1969 he published another book in which he explored this question further, and even suggested a possible reason:[11]

> Sir Sydney Camm, the famous designer of Hawker fighters ... told me he believed many Camel crashes were due to the [cabane] struts between the fuselage and the upper centre-section not having been pinned but merely fitted into sockets, *which meant they were held in position only by the bracing wires.* If these wires were slack, he said, the centre-section struts could move, and end-loads applied to the upper wing spars in flying manoeuvres could cause the spars to curve between the interplane struts and the centre-section struts, *perhaps even to a degree which might lift the upper socket off*

the centre-section [cabane] strut. This was enough to explain the then inexplicable fatal accidents not only to pupils but to the most skilful pilots. [Emphasis added]

Bad landings, Macmillan said, could be particularly responsible for this dangerous loss of tension for the following reason: the cabane struts sloped upwards from the upper ends of the same fuselage vertical struts whose lower ends accepted the undercarriage loads. Thus a bad landing often slackened the centre-section bracing wires, which must be tautened or trouble would follow.

Dodge Bailey, chief pilot of the Shuttleworth Collection, who is one of the few living exponents of the rotary-engined Camel, confirms that he is familiar with Camm's views as recounted by Macmillan, i.e. that insufficient tension in the cabane bracing wires could cause the Camel's cabane struts to become unseated from the centre-section sockets under positive *g*, resulting in the centre-section parting company from the struts. Knowing of C6713's 256 hours, he feels it is conceivable that pulling *g* in his manoeuvres at Bouvincourt could have precipitated a cabane strut of Armstrong's well-used Camel becoming unseated, allowing the top wing to dislodge.[12] As Camm observed, under positive *g* the upper wing spar could curve, and indeed it could be seen visibly to bow out of shape. No more than an inch – probably less – of the upper end of the cabane strut actually lodged inside the socket, and it would take very little slackening of the bracing wires for

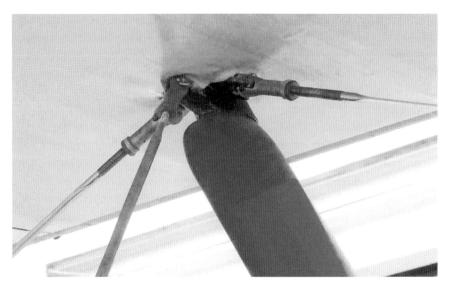

Less than 1 inch at the top of the Camel's cabane struts rested in these sockets.

the seating to become loosened. Perhaps as little as three-quarters to one inch maximum was all the main wing-spar needed to curve at the centre-section for the socket to be lifted right off the strut.

Anecdotal evidence suggests that some Camel pilots encountered this and recognized what had to be done. The US pilot Elliott White Springs wrote numerous books and articles drawing on his experiences with the RFC and RAF and, in one of his novels, *Above the Bright Blue Sky*, the main character is concerned at the abject performance of a comrade's Camel in an engagement with Fokker D.VIIs. Upon testing it himself 'the wings flopped like an ornithopter,' he says. 'I thought I was going to lose the centre section in that last spin. It's rigged all wrong. Get the crew to work on it right away.' If Armstrong had encountered, earlier in his career, those effects of poorly rigged bracing on his Camel, it would have been a salutary lesson learnt to his advantage. But if he had not – and bearing in mind he prided himself on never straining a wire – he would be unaware of what might happen in the circumstances outlined by Sydney Camm.

Without going into further detail it is readily apparent that for aerobatics this area of the Camel's rigging was critical. Any maintenance or engine overhaul process could afford an opportunity for incorrect tensioning and trueing-up. At war's end it is not impossible that C6713's usual rigger(s) had been given leave or redeployed, and with the cessation of aerial combat maybe their replacements never gave thought to aerobatic *g*-forces and the need for assiduously maintaining the tension of bracing wires. If so, one of Armstrong's quite routine pull-ups might have found the cabane struts insufficiently braced and unable to remain snugly in their sockets, allowing the top wing to move, which then prevented the normal recovery procedures from a spin he had safely performed innumerable times.

And not only are we concerned with bracing wires: in an aeroplane of the design standards of 1918 being constantly subjected to stress and torsion, a key factor is the *accumulated stress* on all components over time; metal fatigue in particular reduces component life exponentially. In a machine worked constantly for over 250 flying hours, the accumulated effect – invisible to the naked eye – could substantially weaken much of the structural integrity.

These examples suggest just a few of the problems that might beset a well-worn aircraft during aerobatics. That he personally misjudged his spin recovery should be the last assumption applied to D.V. Armstrong rather than the first, especially bearing in mind that spinning down to the ground was for him a favourite method of descent.

As a final comment on the Casualty Report's conclusion 'Error in judgement', compare the full investigation that took place into the accident that killed Lieutenant George Craig in England on 19 August 1917. Lieutenant Craig was one of Armstrong's comrades in No. 44 Squadron on Home Defence duties, and his accident was the subject of a coroner's inquest. He was killed while engaging in flying practice with a fellow pilot, in the course of which he had spun the machine down twice and brought it out of the spin each time. 'But immediately after the last occasion the machine spun in the opposite direction ... and crashed to the ground.' Despite the incident occurring at 'a great height', he was completely unable to recover – plenty of altitude in hand was no help at all in his predicament. The jury decided that death was due to misadventure. 'Error' was not mentioned.[13]

A note on spinning the Sopwith Camel

Spins and spinning occur many times in this book. Most pilots today will have learnt about spins as part of their instruction, and a luckier few will have been taught aerobatics, precision spinning, and recovery from unintentional spins. It is safe to say that almost without exception they will have been taught to initiate and recover from spins by the use of elevator and rudder only. Both power application and aileron usage are forbidden until after recovery (unless flat spins are part of the curriculum).

In contrast, the method of spinning a Camel in the First World War differed radically from modern techniques, as did methods of recovering. It is consequently very difficult to determine precisely what recovery actions were considered judicious or injudicious: opinions probably varied with individuals and circumstances. The following is a description of Camel spinning written by Major W.G. Moore in *Early Bird*, published in 1963, relating to his time in command at Turnhouse in mid-1918.[14]

> To put a machine into a spinning nose-dive you throttled down your engine, keeping in level flight until she stalled and tried to fall out of the sky nose down. You would then pull back the elevator control into your stomach. If you wanted to spin fast you would put on full aileron and rudder the way she wanted to spin. Nearly all machines spun more naturally one way, but you could force some of them to spin the opposite way by using opposite aileron and rudder control but you spun more slowly. It was quite an effective spinning nose-dive if you could spin a number of turns right-handed and then a number left handed. ...

The only way to get out of a spinning nose-dive was to make the machine move faster – much faster – through the air so that your controls took effect. It was certainly a hard choice which took some nerve near the ground. First you pushed your joy-stick hard forward, then opposite aileron and rudder and full engine; as soon as controls got a grip on the air from your increased speed you centred everything in a powered dive and hoped you had not left it too late to pull out before you hit the ground.

A possible explanation of Captain Armstrong's accident

Throughout the years during which this account of Captain Armstrong was being assembled, a valuable contributor of information has been Rob Fletcher in South Africa, whose credentials include not only being an aerobatic pilot but also a qualified accident investigator. Until recently it was felt that the cause of Armstrong's accident must remain a mystery, but this changed when the above photograph came to light. It has been vouched for as authentic, and as having been taken after his crash on Bouvincourt aerodrome. The following conclusions are therefore proposed; they are based on detailed analysis by Rob Fletcher of what can be ascertained and conjectured from this photograph, taking into account all known data about the aeroplane and its pilot. The intention here is to offer a brief summary of what it seems can be learnt, while his full analysis and conclusions are presented in Appendix I.

Visually, the most striking thing he notes about this photograph is the very flat and compact wreck. This is unusual in an aircraft accident, where normally fragments litter the line of the flight path. There was some forward velocity, but apparently not a great deal. Even if some scattered items may have been retrieved and placed alongside, yet it gives no impression that the area was strewn with wreckage: most of the aeroplane seems to have landed and remained in one spot, and not been flung far and wide as would happen if the machine had, for example, cartwheeled as the result of coming to grief during a rolling manoeuvre.

As summed up in his memorable description, looking casually at the photograph gives an impression as if a giant hand had pushed down against a Camel that was standing on the ground, exerting vertical pressure to flatten it whilst twisting rapidly to the left, leaving the aircraft crushed on its belly with flattened wings. Almost the only component that we can measure with confidence from the photograph is the cross-section of the fuselage behind the cockpit, and this would probably reach only to waist height – say a little over three feet. The Camel is an aeroplane that stands 9 feet 6 inches at rest on the ground. Which suggests that the vertical forces compressed the machine to about one-third of its normal height.

This aspect of the image outweighs all else when seeking the cause of the crash. There is only one manoeuvre that will result in the configuration of the composite wreckage in the photograph, and that is a well-developed spin; but more than that, it has to be a well-developed *flat spin to the left*. Which no aerobatic pilot will deliberately programme into a low-level aerobatic routine. This flat spin, with a very high rate of rotation, constitutes the giant hand pressing the Camel flat with the linear energy given over to the rotational energy.

In examining the Casualty Report we may also note the recommendation to salvage the aircraft's engine for repair and re-use: it has been observed by an expert on the Sopwith Camel that the fact of its being considered repairable further suggests a flat spin.

A previous incident can be found on page 133 where Tryggve Gran describes his own Camel accident – a classic entry into a flat spin which he has failed to recognize. It will be remembered that Gran was saved by some advice Armstrong had given him: 'As a last way out of it I bust the motor,' i.e. giving a very short burst of power to throw more air at the rudder, thereby rapidly increasing its effectiveness in killing the rate of yaw. In his case the advice evidently worked. However, if the power were to be left on a little too long in an established spin (rotating at, say, two seconds per turn) it could raise the nose, flatten out, and double the rate of rotation until the view outside the cockpit is just a blur. The rate of descent may be somewhat less than a conventional spin, but the flat spin is never planned as a low-level manoeuvre because even for the expert the recovery process takes several turns longer; and if the flat spin is inadvertent, reactions may also be impaired by disorientation.

We may imagine, therefore, that Armstrong planned to end his routine at Bouvincourt with a left-hand spinning descent, but for some reason the usual inputs to counteract the spin at his desired point failed to work. Realizing he was losing height fast, he followed his own advice and gave a burst of power, but found instead that the spin went flat leaving him out of altitude and out of recovery options. His machine impacted while rotating rapidly to the left, partially nose-down but in an attitude much flatter than a normal spin, almost parallel to the ground, resulting in the wreckage as seen in the photograph.

And here we encounter the key question: *why was this highly proficient pilot unable to recover using customary inputs in a conventional left-hand spin?*

There could have been several factors that resulted in something amiss with C6713 in Armstrong's last flight, but since Sir Sydney Camm believed the dislodgement of the centre-section was to blame for many unexplained Camel accidents, and directly linked it to the after-effects of stress from g-loads, the application of Ockham's Razor suggests this as an obvious contender. It cannot be claimed evidence actually exists that a cabane strut became unseated from its centre-section socket, for it would have taken a forensic investigation – of which there was none – to discover whether this happened. What is far more likely is that the report from Bouvincourt was based on a witness's description of the incident rather than a careful examination of the wreckage. Sir Sydney's insights as to the insufficiencies of the strut/socket system would be unlikely to occur to a casual observer unfamiliar with the loads placed on the Camel by accumulated stresses. Moreover, if the centre-section had become dislodged from the cabane struts it would be scarcely discernible when viewed from below, as the Camel's top wing became visibly distorted anyway with the application of g-forces.

Probably all the witness would have registered was the sudden burst of power and the transition from a normal spin to a very fast flat spin descending dangerously close to the ground, which might very well convey the impression that the pilot had simply misjudged his recovery point and left it too late, i.e. an error in judgement.

Yet we have every reason to believe Sir Sydney Camm, designer of the Hawker Fury, Hurricane, Typhoon and Tempest, and to deduce from his analysis that even after eighteen months of constant familiarity on the type by its most acclaimed and skilled exponent, it was probably the Sopwith Camel itself that claimed the life of Captain D.V. Armstrong.

LAST FLIGHT

So there it is – airfield's in sight, nicely on track and hardly any wind, sun a little high to the SW, not in my eyes but bouncing off the cowling and prop disc. Soon it'll hide behind the wing. Look around the cockpit – height about 1,000 feet but I'm going down to ground level anyway, harness tight, goggles tight and clean ... change hands, pump air pressure, right on 2psi ... airframe feels good, nothing unusual through the stick, not too much forward pressure, normal vibrations. Airstream battering me through the guns and around the windscreen trying get under my goggles and helmet. Damn but it's cold in November, soon this winter flying will be over and we can spend time in the Mess round the fire ...

Bouvincourt boundary coming up just under the nose and left wing. Look high, nobody else aloft. Rock wings and skid slightly left and right. Look below the nose as we yaw, all clear, nobody below — ah, they've got the message, people over there watching near the hangers and ... down we go ... this should wake them up. Field's tilting up, accelerating, accelerating, getting closer, closer and closer, about centre field now, just above the grass, 150 on the clock, ready for the pull-up. Ease back on the stick, some left rudder, more left rudder, and now zoom straight up. Keep it straight, look left, check left wing 90 degrees to the horizon, no yaw ... Wait nicely, wait nicely, she's almost stopped ... NOW! Hard left rudder and she pivots beautifully to the left, nose aiming straight at the grass. Catch it with right rudder and she sails straight down. Not at all bad, let the dance begin.

Straight down, make it a long line ... wait, wait ... speed building, hand on throttle, mixture richer, ever so ever so slightly ... now gently back, back on the stick as she curves to level out, grass below coming fast ... Grass, grass, keep the stick pressure, watch the nose coming up to the horizon, shadows flickering below just in front of the right wing, speed back on 150 and again gently back, back with the stick and curve the loop up, left rudder coming on, keep it straight, check the left horizon, more left rudder, judge the curve ... smoothly on to our back, look forward, pin the cowling just on the horizon and yes, exactly now, roll left ...   ...

... Catch it with stick and rudder and keep the nose pinned right there as the throttle comes back, now balance it, balance on the pin-head and feed in that full right rudder and aileron with the stick coming right back ... Altimeter lagging but we're looking good at about 800 feet ... There, she breaks, right wing rotates and nose goes down into the spin, steeply, steeply and the rotation starts, fast, fast, faster, faster. It's nice, a good one, fine and normal, about two secs per turn and going down about the usual rate ... I reckon four or five turns, these two to the right, then two to the left and out we come, that'll be my exit point, maybe 150 / 200 feet to correct ... then we'll fly her down to the grass, throttle off, back on the stick for a three-pointer, a surprise flick roll and land.

Look down at the grass, look straight over the engine and guns, count, count. Two turns to the right coming up now, anticipate, wait for it, now go left, rudder and aileron, power off, third turn, fourth, getting ready to recover, getting ready, nearly there ... Bloody Hell, what's that, the centre-section moved, I saw the bloody centre-section lift and move! ... The right wing's flexing, get out of this, NOW! ... Stick hard forward, hard right aileron and full power quick, bust the motor ... Come on, come ON ... nose is nearly up on the horizon, still rising but she won't stop going left, she's accelerating faster and faster, that bloody wing is twisting ... everything just a blur ... stop, stop, STOP, power OFF ...   ...

From across the aerodrome men come running, running, running towards the descending, roaring, rotating noise, shards of sunlight flashing now and then as it spins, spins, spins, down, down, down ...

Then the awful **THUD**, loud as a cannon ... and the awful, awful **SILENCE**. And the flat red wreck, half the height of a man, lying on the grass with the sun glinting here and there on its crushed, polished metal ...

And frightened by the running feet, a small bird flies away, into the sunlight ... unknowing that an exceptional man with dazzling abilities has died, a once-famous name that will leave only faint and fading footprints on the years of past and future history.

APPENDIX I

CRASH ANALYSIS

Preamble. The only visual evidence of Captain D.V. Armstrong's fatal crash is a single photograph, taken at the crash site on Bouvincourt aerodrome on, perhaps, 13/14 November 1918. The basis of the proposed conclusion is therefore what can be both ascertained and conjectured from this photograph, subsequently reinforced or modified by material derived from the Bibliography and Expert's Opinions.

Photographic Analysis
1. Wings
    1.1. Left Wing Top Plane Upper Surface
        1.1.1. A reasonable portion of this surface is visible and appears more intact than the remainder of the airframe. The LH upper wing has separated from the centre-section at the left-hand keel plate, and the LH leading edge of the upper

wing has broken inwards/rearwards at about the 4th rib outboard of the keel plate attachment. This approximates to the fitting where the LH leading cabane strut is attached to the upper LH wing panel front spar. The remainder of the visible upper wing panel is in reasonable condition with the upper fabric torn away at about the 10th rib station outboard of the LH keel plate. This approximates to the attached position of the leading LH wing interplane strut.

1.1.2. What is taken to be the remains of the centre-section lies immediately to the rear of the two Vickers machine guns. The visible portion is likely to be the leading edge of the centre-section and its appearance suggests that the cut-out was the wider 3-rib option. The section has come away from its mating keel plate at each wing and has been forced rearwards and down to the RH, ending very close to further wreckage on the ground. There are crush marks at the assumed leading edge and heavy creasing in the upper fabric which is taken to have occurred when the twin Vickers machine guns were forced upwards and rearwards into the centre-section.

1.1.3. Nothing is visible of the LH lower wing, but the appearance and visible structure of the LH upper wing suggest that the lower wing was probably lying flat on the ground with broken interplane struts and some degree of integrity. This is, of course, speculation.

1.2 Right Wings

1.2.1 There is virtually nothing identifiable from any portion of the RH wings except what might be that part of the upper RH wing trailing edge supporting the centre-section cut-out. Nothing is visible from the RH lower wing.

2. Fuselage

2.1. The cowling/engine/propeller/spinner combination is seen indistinctly to the lower right of the RH machine gun with sundry bracing wires to the rear of this gun. What can be seen of the cowling/engine combination appears to be virtually horizontal and lying flat on the ground, but this is speculative. If correct, the engine may still be attached to the aluminium firewall/engine back-plate, suggesting both a heavy rotational force to the LH and an upward force applied to both the engine and the engine bay back-plate/firewall at time of impact. These in combination would force the two Vickers machine guns upwards, rearwards and to the RH, into the leading edge of the centre-section as a result.

2.2. The initial strike described above would have included the undercarriage, the remains of which are not visible. The undercarriage wheels and V-struts with spreader bar probably vanished rearwards and/or sideways almost coincident with or just prior to the engine strike; in the process their removal probably destroyed the lower longeron and the cockpit flooring and vertical spacers on both sides of the fuselage.

2.3. The cockpit area and its surrounding panels appear to be destroyed and the entire section may be lying in the foreground, fragmented. This again implies that the entire undercarriage was removed early in the impact, and at that moment the upper and lower longerons may have been destroyed together with the seat bearers and fuel tank bearers, the cockpit floor, and the vertical spacers; so that the pilot's seat and the main fuel tank were ejected through the RH side of the now broken-sided fuselage together with the strut supporting the hand-operated fuel pressure pump. This strut is seen in the photograph to the RH of the pilot's seat, lying on the ground or on wreckage.

2.4. There is no evidence that the gravity fuel tank was ejected with the main tank and it probably remained in the fuselage.

2.5. The main fuel tank has been badly dented on its front face and the LH end of the tank has burst open with the tank ending up standing on its RH end. The burst suggests that the tank was only partly full at the time of impact.

2.6. The fuselage has broken comparatively cleanly at the station behind the fuel tank bay and the fuselage starboard side fabric has been torn away, probably from around the RH side of the engine cowling backwards to the station behind the fuel tank bay, in what seems to be more or less one long strip. Broken RH side longerons/ spacers can be seen both above and almost touching the fuel tank which appears to be still attached to its floor/pilot's seat bearers.

2.7. The pilot, despite being initially restrained by his seat belt/ harness, would, coincident with the impact, have jack-knifed violently forward into the rear butts of the guns and his legs, with muscles probably severely contracted, would have come out of the rudder-bar straps and been thrown upwards against the carburettor air intake system and whatever other cockpit furniture was adjacent.

2.8. Very shortly afterwards, the pilot's seat plus the pilot and his belts were probably propelled violently backwards and to the right, to impact against the main fuel tank which had probably broken free from its mountings and was moving forward, thus causing the dent in the tank.

2.9. The forwards and LH sideways impact of the a/c would then have propelled the pilot and his seat backwards and sideways to the RH from the disintegrated cockpit through the upper right longeron, also broken, taking the hand-operated fuel pump and its mounting spacer with them. See the position of this fuel pump and its spacer in the crash photograph.

2.10. This further suggests that the a/c was rotating positively to its LH side at a velocity sufficient to generate forces large enough to break the relatively robust mounting frame and floor-plate, which would allow the combined masses of pilot, fuel tank and machine guns to depart through the RH side of the cockpit and to the RH of the a/c on impact.

2.11. The Sutton 4-point harness had been in use since 1917 and a pilot regularly performing aerobatics would almost certainly have adopted it; however the photograph shows no evidence of any harness or lap strap, which one would expect to have been cut away to extract the pilot from the seat.

2.12. The rear of the fuselage appears to have broken away more or less cleanly from the remainder of the badly crushed and collapsed front section.

2.13. There are 2 hinged panels that appear prominently in the upper decking which may be access panels.

2.14. It is estimated that the height of the upper decking is no more than 3 feet above the ground, giving an indication of the degree of crush sustained by the a/c in the accident.

3. Comment

3.1. The foregoing description implies that the a/c was in either a flat or a somewhat nose-down rotation to its left at impact.

3.2. The following photograph of an undamaged Camel attempts to show the above-mentioned major forces as black arrows and the damaged, departed major portions of the airframe as faded-out sections.

4. Summary

4.1. This analysis, if not contradicted by further photographic evidence, is suggesting that the final attitude of C6713 just before contact with the ground was *rotational to the left* with *right wing low* and *nose-down but not excessively so* (i.e. closer to the horizontal than the vertical).

4.2. In this position, the lower RH wing would probably have made the initial ground strike at high rotational velocity, the impact probably removing it, the undercarriage and the upper RH wing in short order whilst, almost simultaneously, the nose of the a/c struck the ground, applying the forces described that collapsed the upper LH wing on to the lower LH wing and broke open the cockpit and fuselage longerons.

4.3. The destruction of the a/c as described suggests high energy forces in directions not parallel with the principal axes of the a/c and suggests reduced forward linear velocity by comparison with a high rotational velocity to the left.

4.4. In more colourful terms, looking casually at the photograph suggests a very flat wreck, as if a giant hand had pushed down hard against a Camel standing on the ground and flattened it in a vertical direction whilst twisting rapidly to the left, leaving the a/c crushed on its belly without undercarriage or RH wings and with flattened LH wings.

5. Conclusion

The above analysis suggests a fully developed flat spin to the left, of at least one if not two turns, right wing low with the nose nearing the horizon, as C6713's final manoeuvre.

R.N. Fletcher BSc (Mech. Eng.) MBL DMS
January 2018

APPENDIX II

DFC CITATION

London Gazette 3 December 1918
Awarded the Distinguished Flying Cross

ACCOUNT OF DEED

A brilliant pilot of exceptional skill. His success in night operations has been phenomenal; and the service he renders in the training of other pilots is of the greatest value, personally supervising their flying and demonstrating the only successful method of attack by night. On the night of 10-11th of September, learning that an enemy aeroplane was over our front, he volunteered to go up. The weather conditions were such as to render flying almost impossible, the wind blowing about fifty miles an hour, accompanied by driving rainstorms; despite this, Captain Armstrong remained on patrol for over an hour, his machine at times being practically out of control. The foregoing is only one of many instances of this Officer's remarkable skill and resolution in night operations.

At 10.40 p.m., on the night of 17-18th September 1918, whilst on patrol East of Bapaume, Captain Armstrong observed a Gotha Biplane caught in a concentration of searchlights at 8,500 feet, with a Camel machine behind it. Seeing that the Camel was not engaging the EA [enemy aeroplane] from a sufficiently close range, this Officer dived down, coming in on EA's right. He closed right up under its tail and fired 100 rounds into it. The EA then burst into flames and dived to the ground, where it burst into pieces just East of Bapaume.

On the night of 10-11th September 1918 on receipt of a report that an EA was over the Fourth Army Front, Captain Armstrong volunteered to go up, although the weather was practically impossible for flying, the wind blowing at about 50 miles an hour, accompanied by driving rain storms. In spite of this Captain Armstrong remained on his patrol for 1 hour 5 minutes, although his machine was practically out of control on several occasions. On landing his machine had to be held down to prevent it being blown over.

DFC CITATION

On the night of 6-7th August 1918 Captain Armstrong attacked Estrées-en-Chaussée Aerodrome. After dropping 3 Cooper bombs on the hangars from 600 feet he observed an EA coming in to land. Captain Armstrong then closed under the EA's tail and opened fire from 15 yards range, when at 700 feet. The EA's Observer answered the fire, and then suddenly ceased altogether. Captain Armstrong continued firing until the EA suddenly turned to the right with nose down, and crashed on its aerodrome, bursting into flames as it struck the ground. This Officer then dropped his 4th bomb on the wreck and fired a further burst into it, returning to his aerodrome with all ammunition expended.

On the night of 8-9th August 1918, although the clouds were at about 500 feet this Officer flew to the same hostile aerodrome, but finding no activity there and seeing no lights whatever, he flew to Cizancourt Bridge dropping his 4 bombs upon it from 500 feet. On this night he was unable at any period to fly at over 800 feet owing to low driving clouds and very strong wind.

Captain Armstrong attacked Aerodromes as follows on dates shewn:-

Moislains: 3.15 a.m. to 3.30 a.m. on 21-22nd August 1918, dropping 2 Incendiary and 2 Cooper bombs from 400 feet on hutments and tents although subjected to the most accurate and fierce machine-gun fire from the ground, and his machine being brightly illuminated in the glare of the Incendiary bombs.

Estrées-en-Chaussée: on the night of 31 July 1918-1 August 1918, dropping all 4 bombs on landing lights from 500 feet.

Captain Armstrong took part in the defence of London against all but 3 raids by EA between September 1917 and June 1918.

This Officer has been the right hand of his Squadron Commander since the formation of his Squadron, and has by his wonderful flying, taught the pilots of No. 151 Squadron more than any other Instructor could possibly have done. He has demonstrated to all pilots daily the only successful method of attack at night against EA, by personal supervision of their flying. As a Flight Commander I cannot speak too highly of him and his wonderful spirit at all times. His bravery as a Pilot at all times and in all weather conditions cannot be surpassed, and I am unable to recommend him too strongly for this decoration.

Lieutenant Colonel B.C.D. Small, Commanding 54th Wing, 9th Brigade
151 Squadron, 54th Wing, Royal Air Force
Date of Recommendation 19 September 1918
Awarded 6 October 1918

APPENDIX III

POSTHUMOUS TRIBUTES

Captain D.V. Armstrong's medals have been donated to his school, Hilton College in KwaZulu Natal, where they are displayed on public view together with a bronze by the noted First World War sculptor John Tweed. Other memorabilia of his war service include the tail fin of his Camel, C6713, and the Parabellum machine gun from a German Gotha bomber he shot down. In addition, many written tributes have been preserved from those who knew him and counted it a privilege to have done so. Several are transcribed below. Those whose lives were touched by him seem never to have forgotten his great heart, his tireless fighting spirit, and his wondrous and seemingly effortless mastery of the air.

Extract from address by General Jan Smuts, 26 August 1919, at the luncheon given in his honour by the Durban Council Chamber

Some of the most brilliant airmen that we have had in the whole of the Air Force came from Natal, and I remember today especially one young man named Armstrong, who must be enrolled amongst the greatest heroes of Natal. ...

Shortly after my arrival in London I was asked to be responsible for the Air Defences of London. The great air raids had just started and it was a difficult problem to deal with. I undertook the task of arranging the air defences of London. In the course of this work I wanted a man, a fine man who was efficient to take charge of the night fighting and the night flying, which as you know is quite the most serious and dangerous of air work. I made enquiries and I found that the best man in the British Air Force was young Armstrong. Well, I selected him and put him in charge of this night flying and night fighting. He undertook the job of training squadrons, and he did this work in a most efficient way, and he became an outstanding example of what could be done in this line and achieved very much more than had been thought possible in this direction. When the air raids started in Paris they wanted us to send a man to take charge of their night work also, and I sent Captain Armstrong where he trained the French airmen as he had trained our airmen to a proper standard until the Germans no longer ventured to attack Paris either by day or by night.

Then you know what happened. Just when the war had ended Armstrong met his death in an accident while flying, and by the death of this young hero the Empire lost one of its most brilliant airmen, one of the most brilliant men the Empire has produced in the War. I mention Armstrong's name just to illustrate the value and quality of the Natal men in the War. You can produce quality and great leadership which was exactly what was wanted in this great effort. Let us always remember what these heroes, some of them no longer amongst us, contributed towards the victory which we now enjoy.

Air Marshal William A. (Billy) Bishop, in letter dated 25 June 1920

I knew your son very well, but although we were at various times engaged in the same work it was never at the same time; as when I was on the defence of London he was in 60 Squadron in France, and then when I went to 60 Squadron he had returned to England and, I believe, was employed in ferrying, so that I cannot tell you very much about his work.

As doubtless you have been told on many occasions, he was possibly the most wonderful pilot in the world. We all looked on him as such, and although I have seen all of our best pilots fly and the best of the French and Italian, I have never seen anything to equal the exhibitions of flying which he used to give. He came over to my Squadron at Hounslow a few days before I took it to France in May 1918, to give an exhibition of flying, and it was beautiful. The pilots of the night flight, of which he had charge, were all trained by him and the whole lot of them could fly extraordinarily well, but of course not up to your son's standard. I doubt if any person will ever equal him as a stunt pilot.

Some time in May 1918 he led his flight down the Thames River from Hornchurch to the Sopwith Plant at Brooklyn [Brooklands], and they flew under all the bridges *en route*. This, as you know, was a most marvellous performance and showed wonderful judgement, as the bridges are very, very narrow and it is practically impossible to get through.

It was with the greatest regret that I read about his death after the Armistice was signed, and I know there are no words of mine which can express my deep sympathy for Mrs Armstrong and yourself, both in the loss of the lad I knew, and his brother. The War has indeed hit you hard, but one can only say that they died doing their duty, which is the greatest thing a man can do, and their names will never be forgotten. I am sure that when the next generation is born there will be many tales told to youngsters on their fathers' knees of the exhibition flying and marvellous work at the Front which your son did in the Royal Air Force, and the tales will be told scores of years from now by thousands who did not know his name of that glorious night in 1918 when he shot down the first five-engined Hun machines flying over our lands on a bombing expedition. It occurred at the time when the Huns were bombing our hospitals and the feeling was very bitter on our side, so that the wonderful sight of seeing this giant machine go down in flames that particular night did a tremendous lot not only to encourage the thousands and tens of thousands of soldiers who actually saw the blazing mass fall, but it cheered up our people all over the Empire.

My very best regards to Mrs Armstrong and you, and I hope you will allow me to say that you both have every reason to be the proudest people on earth.

Air Commodore Lionel Charlton, Air Attaché, British Embassy, Washington DC, in letters dated 22 May 1920 and 30 March 1921

I think no one of my young friends in the Royal Air Force is deeper in my memory than your son. I was his Commanding Officer when he first joined up, and at the end of the War found myself again his Commanding Officer in the famous 151 Squadron of which he was the leading light.

You need have no fear lest his memory should fade in the annals of the Royal Air Force, not only on account of his magnificent pilotship, his extraordinary fearlessness and his successful combat career, but also because his nature was one to win friends universally, being in fact, to my mind, the beau-ideal of what a British boy should be. Personally, apart from my admiration of his *professional* qualities, I had a deep friendship for his *personal* ones, and congratulate you, his parents, on having given his services to the Empire in its need.

POSTHUMOUS TRIBUTES

It gives me great pleasure at last to write to you on the subject of your gallant son and to embody in this letter a few personal recollections, an appreciation, and a record of his movements and appointments ...

I was in command at South Farnborough, the Headquarters of the Royal Flying Corps, when he joined on the 26 December 1915, and well recollect the excellent impression he made on me in his introductory interview, and I marked him then as likely, in my opinion, to fulfil as he did the highest expectation.

After a short period as pilot attached to the Aircraft Section at Farnborough, and a few weeks with No. 22 and 45 Squadron for the purpose of completing his training, he was drafted to France to join No 60 Squadron on 25 May 1916. Waldron, Somers [*sic*] and Smith-Barry had undergone a very severe handling in the hands of the enemy without loss of morale and nothing was so conducive to a continuance of this satisfactory condition than the advent of young Armstrong who proved himself, from the outset, keen and fearless and efficient.

When No. 60 Squadron was withdrawn from the line for rest and replacement of machines, your son was posted to Paris and the Machine Gun School on the French coast for temporary duty and finally was posted to the Home Establishment on 20 December 1916, until 15 June 1918.

During this interval he was successively a Ferry Pilot, engaged in flying machines to France for reinforcement purposes, and a member of the 39th, 44th and 78th Home Defence Squadrons, and on 1 March 1918, promoted to the Command of Flight with Captain's rank.

I remember rumours of his marvellous skill in flying the Camel reaching us in France. Although this duty was most honourable and demanded a high measure of skill and courage in night flying, his chance really came when he was posted to No. 151 Squadron on night-flying Camel scouts and attached, under my command, to No. 101 night-flying squadron of the 5th Brigade, then quartered between Amiens and Abbeville, a position to which it had been forced to retire by the success of the German advance in March 1918.

You know with what conspicuous success his efforts were attended and how his name became a watchword on the ground and in the air to the French and British armies. He must have indirectly received the blessing of many hundreds of thousands of men – unknown to him, but not he to them – to whom the spectacle of a German multi-engined night bomber crashing from out of the sky in flames meant a surcease from the endless nerve-rack of being bombed at night. Moreover, he helped chiefly to weaken the enemy

221

morale in this respect and therefore indubitably was the means of saving hundreds of men from death and wounds.

Nothing finer was ever done in the air than the intrepid efforts of this young man to cope, and successfully cope, with this scourge by night. During this period it will amuse you to know that he became my instructor for a short period. No. 151 Squadron was stationed very near my headquarters at Flixecourt and I had recently acquired a Camel which I didn't know well enough to fly. Young Armstrong used then to come and give me tuition and afterwards, more often than not, came back with me to headquarters for tea or for dinner according to weather or circumstances.

During the daytime he would visit other squadrons by air and it was no uncommon sight to see all the pilots of a squadron attracted from their quarters and diversions to see his arrival and departure always accompanied as it was by a little display of trick flying which showed his wonderful command of his machine to the amazement even of the oldest hands. On one occasion he visited a neighbouring French aerodrome and being asked to 'stunt' proceeded to the performance of such amazing evolutions as startled the French pilots completely from their self-possession and caused them to look away fearing he had lost control of his machine.

On the 13 November 1918 he was received at No. 58 Casualty Clearing Station, 'accidentally killed', and a brilliant career full of future promise was closed. His death caused a universal sense of loss among all who had known him, however slightly, for in addition to his bravery and skill his charm of manner, courtesy of address and general manliness had endeared him to everyone in his surroundings.

With me it was, alas, too common an occurrence to lament the death of young men trained to fly under my command who had become personal friends, but in no instance did I regret more deeply such a case than that of your boy. The event is too long ago now for me to offer you my condolences, and I will instead offer you congratulations on having been the parent of so noble a son.

Wing Commander M.G. Christie, in letter dated 25 June 1921

I first remember him as a pilot in 60 Squadron where at the time (1916) I was spending a week as a new Squadron Commander to learn tactics. He was promising well in those days and had gained a good reputation for exceptional flying ability. I lost sight of him till I came to the 49th Wing at Upminster in spring 1918 and found him a Flight Commander in one of my night-flying anti-Gotha squadrons round the western environs of London – No. 78 – at Sutton's Farm Aerodrome. He was then reaching the zenith of his flying skill, and much is due indeed to him that the London Aerial Defences proved so successful to us and so costly to the enemy, that after the last disastrous attempt to raid London in May 1918 the Gothas never revisited this country.

Your son delighted in 'taking the air' in almost any weather any night: he was one of my best leaders when it was a question of giving practice to the searchlights on cloudy unfavourable nights. I remember indeed one dark windy occasion when an enemy machine was reported 'on the way'. I went to phone 78 Squadron to forbid any of our Camel pilots going up as I felt sure that the German machine reported was a myth and that the weather was far too rough for single-seater scouts to ascend. The reply came that I was too late: Armstrong had gone up and one or two of his braves after him. They all landed safely and after that I felt no compunction about Armstrong's patrol pushing off under almost any conditions. Thus he assisted very materially in developing the art of night-fighting which culminated in his being selected as Senior Flight Commander in the First Night Fighting Squadron that went overseas in summer 1918, and which became famous as you will know.

Your son's prowess as a pilot was supreme; his sense of measure, rhythm and timing was superb, and for sheer flying ability I consider he had no equal in the world. On the ground, he knew his job and could inspire his officers with just that 'élan' which conquers every obstacle. In his early death aviation lost one of its greatest artists, and the RAF was poorer of a fine and devoted personality.

Air Marshal John M. Salmond (later Marshal of the Royal Air Force Sir John Salmond), in letter dated 22 March 1924

Your son was working in my Command during the time I was GOC, RAF France at the end of 1917-1918. I had seen him flying before at home, and I was impressed then and later with his exceptional skill.

I recollect considering him the best pilot of his time, and when asked by the American Aviation to send a picked officer down to instruct in night flying and in the work that our night-flying squadrons were doing, I chose him as the best possible officer for the job.

CAMEL PILOT SUPREME CAPTAIN D.V. ARMSTRONG DFC

I received from the American Aviation a glowing account of his work, his personality, and his wonderful piloting, and they were frankly amazed at the wonderful skill that he showed. He was one of the best and bravest pilots in the Royal Air Force, and his great spirit was always tempered by self-control.

Report of Air Vice Marshal Sir Leslie Brown

For nine years Urban Armstrong lived the life of a Hilton boy amongst us, and no name is written so widely across the records of our school as is his. Whether we look to the class lists, or to the records of House and School in the various activities of Public School life he is always a central figure, taking a leading part among his fellows in every stage of his school career. Bright and happy by nature, he was very popular amongst his companions, while his unfailing courtesy and manliness won for him the friendship and affection of his elders. Few boys have left Hilton with a brighter promise of a great career, and the brief years that have since elapsed have splendidly fulfilled that promise. 'Your fine boy will be remembered for his skill and modesty' are the words of General Smuts in a cable of condolence to his parents, and no nobler epitaph could be penned.

The youngest son of Mr and Mrs G.S. Armstrong, of Empangeni, D'Urban Victor Armstrong entered Hilton at the age of 8 years in 1905. He early showed promise, both in the class room and on the playing field. In December 1910 he came second in the Scholarship Examination and was made an honorary scholar of the school. In 1911 he had reached the 2nd XI, and was made a School prefect at the unusually early age of 14 years. From then onwards until he left in 1914 he took an increasingly prominent part in the life of the school, and in his last year he was Head of Pearce's, a sergeant in the Cadet Corps, Captain of the XI, and vice-Captain of the XV. He matriculated in the 2nd class in December 1914.

Upon leaving school he volunteered for active service in German South West, but was rejected owing to a football knee. He then passed all the tests for Motor Transport Service but was again rejected as being under age. Not to be daunted, he then succeeded in joining the Royal Air Force, and sailed for England in 1915. In May 1916 he was selected for service in the 60 Squadron of Fighting Scouts. This squadron lost heavily at the Somme, and Armstrong was the only member of his flight left and one of the sole remaining five of the squadron. He was credited with the destruction of

6 machines and one balloon during these operations. After being employed for some time testing new machines and flying them across to France – on which duty he crossed the Channel 88 times – he was promoted Flight Commander in 1917 and selected for Home Defence over London in the night flying squadrons, and was instrumental in bringing down three Gothas near London.

Capt Armstrong at the time of his death was on active service as a Flight Commander in France, and had earned the reputation of being one of the most daring and skilful airmen in the Empire. He was awarded the Distinguished Flying Cross shortly before his death.

NATAL ROLL OF HONOUR, 1918

Captain D.V. Armstrong DFC, Royal Air Force

The astounding news of the accidental death of Captain D.V. Armstrong ('Urban'), youngest son of George S. and Mrs Armstrong, Empangeni, Zululand, will be received by his many friends with the most profound regret, happening as it did on the 13 November, two days after the signing of the Armistice with Germany.

At the age of 8 years he went to Hilton College where he passed his 'Matric.' and won a Scholarship. Shortly afterwards the War broke out and although 17½ years of age he felt the call to 'do his bit', volunteering for service in German South West, but was rejected on account of a slight weakness of one knee received while playing football, of which sport – and cricket – he was very fond. He afterwards passed all tests for Motor Transport Service but was again rejected, being under age.

Nothing daunted, he proceeded to Cape Town where he succeeded in joining the Royal Air Force, sailing for England with his widowed sister, Mrs Royds, about three years ago. He made his first flight in December 1915 and three months afterwards was instructing others. In his fourth month he was flying machines across to France. In May 1916 he was selected to join the noted 60 Squadron of Fighting Scouts for active service in France, landing there on 26 May and fighting until the battle of the Somme, in December 1916. This squadron lost heavily at the Somme. He was the only member of his flight left and one of the sole remaining five of the squadron. In the course of these operations he brought down six machines and one balloon. In recognition of their services the French Government wished to decorate the squadron and lots were drawn by the five survivors as to who should possess the award. The member who gained it has already received the Military Cross. With the remaining four he was sent back to England and was there employed testing new machines, flying them across to France and leaving them there for service. On this duty he crossed the Channel 88 times, flying some of the machines from Glasgow to the Channel ports and then over to France.

He was promoted to Captain, or Flight Commander, in 1917 and was selected with others for Home Defence over London in the Night Flying Squadrons in Sopwith Camel aeroplanes, and with three other officers brought down three Gothas near London. After this the hospitals in France were being bombed by the Germans and he was included as a member of a Special Night Flying Squadron set for the defence of these hospitals. This squadron did excellent repressive work, accounting for a large number of enemy bombing machines from 20 June to 22 September 1918 and is officially credited with over a quarter of those brought down.

He was awarded the Distinguished Flying Cross only a few weeks back.

Although flying for three years, often in most trying weather, he enjoyed good health and was always in the best of spirits. He was of a bright and cheerful disposition, beloved by all who knew him – old friends as well as new – keen at his profession and of him a famous General has said 'He will be long remembered for his skill and modesty'.

RAF MUSEUM, LONDON

Half a century later it came to the notice of J.M. Bruce, Keeper of Aircraft and Aviation Records for the Royal Air Force Museum, that Hilton College had custody of Captain Armstrong's memorabilia including the tail fin of C6713, his medals, and the captured Gotha Parabellum machine gun. On 6 November 1973 he wrote to the then Headmaster, R.G. Slater in the following terms, asking if the College would consider allowing them to be exhibited at the RAF Museum:

> To anyone who knows anything at all about military aviation of the First World War, the name of Captain Armstrong is synonymous with the most extraordinary and outstanding aerobatic flying ever done anywhere in the world during that strenuous period of conflict. As you doubtless know, his favourite aircraft was the Sopwith Camel, and the accounts

of his flying left by those who were fortunate enough to witness it indicate that he was a pastmaster in the handling of that remarkably temperamental aircraft, notably at very low altitudes. He was also a night fighter pilot of considerable distinction at a time when even night flying was regarded as more than unusually difficult. ...

This Museum, which was opened only in November of last year by Her Majesty the Queen ... is the only British national museum devoted to the study and recording of aviation history in all its aspects.

In this context, these relics of Captain Armstrong would fill a unique and fascinating place. My purpose in writing to you, therefore, is to enquire whether we might, at some time of your choosing, be allowed to add these remarkable relics of an outstanding pilot to the collections of this Museum. As our aircraft display happily includes a complete and almost perfect specimen of the Sopwith Camel, it would be wonderful if we could display here relics connected with the Camel's greatest exponent. ... If they were displayed here in this Museum they would be seen and appreciated by an enormous and interested public who would have the name of D'Urban Victor Armstrong brought before them in the most vivid manner possible.

It appears the Headmaster passed on this request to Urban W.M. Campbell, a nephew of Captain Armstrong, the essence of whose reply was as follows:

Thank you for your letter about the request by the RAF Museum ... I agree that they would probably be better in a museum, but I am sure that my late grandfather would have preferred that they remain in South Africa. I can recall well the conversation in our home ... that General Smuts had requested that the relics be handed over to the nation for safe-keeping, but my father jumped in and asked that Hilton be given first option. As you know, Hilton 'won'. During the course of the conversation grandfather had mentioned that the War Museum, I think at Kensington, London also wanted them, but he expressed the wish that they remain in South Africa. However, may I suggest that in view of the above they be offered to the South African War Museum and should they turn the offer down, then send them over to London.

Whatever course of action followed this exchange is not known, but the items have remained ever since at Hilton College.

* * *

WAR MEMORIALS

The names of Captain D.V. Armstrong and his brother Lieutenant A.L. Armstrong appear on the Zululand War Memorial at Eshowe, along with many others, 'In Proud and Grateful Memory of men of Zululand who fell in the Great War'.

In the smaller township of Empangeni a different memorial to the fallen was conceived, urged by the district surgeon, Dr Moberly: a much-needed hospital would be built. Hitherto his only place of healing was a shack in his own back yard. Among the donors were the Armstrong family's Zululand Sugar Milling Co (£259) and Sir James Liege Hulett & Sons (£100). The family also endowed the Armstrong Ward and donated a plaque on which were inscribed the names of the men who died. The plaque is missing, but no doubt those names commemorated their two lost sons. The first patients were admitted in 1920 and 1921.

ACKNOWLEDGEMENTS

This biography began to take shape in the 1980s during research for my publication *Flight Fantastic: The Illustrated History of Aerobatics* in which Captain Armstrong earned a place of honour. His nephew, Nat Royds, was particularly proud of his uncle's achievements and encouraged my aim to produce a full biography, to the extent of readily permitting me to illustrate it with Armstrong's wartime photograph album, for which he gave me a complete set of photographic copies.

Meticulously captioned, the album is annotated with brief comments that vividly recall the experiences of that young man, newly introduced to a world of flight, of warfare, of aircraft technology and weaponry, of comrades and laughter and sudden death. His references to himself are few, and the progress of his career is only sketchily outlined. His log-books do not appear to have survived, and sadly it seems that since the death of Nat Royds the family have not preserved his original album.

The details of his service (aside from cursory official records) have been pieced together from personal and historical records of the war and from the writings of those who served with Armstrong or witnessed his wonderful flying. To these I am therefore deeply indebted, as well as to the many aero enthusiasts and historians who have been without exception eager to help ensure that Captain Armstrong's life and career were properly appreciated.

Before proceeding to thank them by name, I must first acknowledge one person without whose support this biography would have languished as it was left, unfinished and without a publisher, thirty years ago. Rob Fletcher, fellow admirer of D.V. Armstrong, is an *alumnus* not only of Hilton College but also of Pearce, Armstrong's old House, and he introduced me to the many items of memorabilia donated to the school by Armstrong's family. A pilot since the age of 13, Rob participated in Competition Aerobatics for many years (Pitts S2A, Zlin 50, Sukhoi 26 and Yak 52), in which he represented South Africa in 1995. In addition to his insights as a pilot – uniquely evident in Armstrong's imagined 'Last Flight' – his expertise also lies in mechanical engineering and an apprenticeship in airframe servicing. In quasi-retirement he is now heavily involved in accident investigations (mainly vehicles, rolling stock and the like) for which his qualifications include a Diploma in Forensic Investigation and Criminal Law from the University of KwaZulu-Natal. In the past seven years he has satisfactorily completed over 130 investigations, most of which went to court for judgement.

His wish to commemorate Captain Armstrong's centenary in November 2018 enticed me away from the fifteenth century, and his assistance in carrying out research in South Africa has been invaluable, not to mention his technical advice when it comes to the Sopwith F.1 Camel.

The following list of names must be headed by Mick Davis of *Cross & Cockade International*, who greatly assisted with the identification of photographs, read drafts of the text, and gave unstinting advice when asked, particularly in relation to the Sopwith F.1 Camel. *CCI* is dedicated to using its expertise and resources to spread knowledge about the aero history of the First World War and generously permitted use of several images in this book, for which Colin Huston's help was greatly appreciated. I am also grateful to John Barfoot for very kind assistance during my research in the 1980s, at which time the late Frank Cheesman and Chaz Bowyer also contributed their incomparable knowledge of First World War aviation.

Trevor Henshaw gave generously of his time, encouragement and support, and he and Colin Huston did wonderful work improving old photographs. Dodge Bailey uncomplainingly shared his abundant knowledge of flying the Shuttleworth Collection Camel. Special thanks go to experts Norman Franks, Andrew Nahum, Piet Nutt and Alex Revell for patience and forbearance in the face of all my calls for assistance.

The following alphabetical list is small enough recognition for the valued help of every individual named, each of whom contributed something to make this tribute possible: Jill Bush, Andrew Ross Dinnes, Tim Lambon, Stuart Leslie, Michael O'Neal (American Aviators of WWI), Alex Rice, Andrew Traist and Brian Weaver. Technical help was gratefully received from Dr Catherine Ross of the Met Office National Meteorological Archive, and from Geoff Butler and Alan Brown of Farnborough Air Sciences Trust and Museum.

In South Africa, thanks go to Russel Addison and Barry Lane who are historians dedicated to preserving records of the early sugar industry, and Dewald Nel also gave assistance. Of DVA's family Gale Hancock, Colin

ACKNOWLEDGEMENTS

Armstrong and Faith Armstrong were especially helpful in constructing the family tree and attempting to engage the interest of other family members, although sadly with little success. Appreciation goes to Hilton College, and to Bev Davidge, Curator of Hilton College Museum; to Ann Crowder of Durban High School, Nigel Lewis-Walker, Captain, Natal Mounted Rifles, Mariette Botha of Deon Boshoff Attorneys, and Emily-Anne Krige, Senior Archivist, Campbell Collections, University of KwaZulu-Natal.

Membership of the excellent Great War Forum was invaluable in these researches, and many co-members put themselves out to assist. For detailed comments on uniforms and other clothing I am indebted to the incomparable knowledge of 'Frogsmile'. Space allows me to mention only a handful of other members' names which include: 'Grid', Mike Meech, 'Nieuport11' (Andrew Pentland), 'Interested' (Phil), 'PRC', and 'Topgun1918'.

For Mousehold Heath's military history I thank Anj Beckham (Norfolk Historic Environment Service, Norfolk County Council), Paul Holmes, Huby Fairhead and Les Whitehouse (all experts on the history of Boulton Paul), Norfolk Record Office, Norwich Heart (The Military in Norwich), The Royal Norfolk Regimental Museum.

In the course of thirty years spent piecing together a century of history it is inevitable that some material (anecdotes, images, etc.) have passed through many hands to reach my own; where the originators and/or copyright holders are known they have been acknowledged, and where possible made aware of the usage made of such material in this work. Several friends agreed to read and critique my drafts, and to them I give special thanks; should any omissions or errors remain, I take full responsibility and offer my apologies.

IMAGE ACKNOWLEDGEMENTS

A special thank-you to artist/illustrator Lynn Williams, who has put many generous hours into illustrating this book and its cover. He shares my admiration for Captain Armstrong and brings a pilot's understanding to his artwork. Lynn is a particular enthusiast of aerobatic biplanes and designer of same, his 'Flitzer' being built from plans and flown worldwide in various configurations. He has also found time to write the first in a projected series of aviation-based adventure novels spanning time and space, taking in real and imagined conflicts including the Great War.

CAMEL PILOT SUPREME CAPTAIN D.V. ARMSTRONG DFC

Gratitude goes to the publishers of Haynes Manuals, *AeroModeller* and *Motor Sport*, and to the following list of individuals who either supplied or attempted to supply images, which involved putting themselves out to help make this the best possible memorial to Captain Armstrong:

Russel Addison, Michael Badrocke, Dodge Bailey, Chaz Boyer, Frank Cheesman, John Childs, Mathew and Peter Craig, Gordon Cruikshank, Andrew Ross Dinnes, Jonathan Falconer, Rob Fletcher, Norman Franks, Alan Harman, Trevor Henshaw, Philip Jarrett, Peter Kilduff, Polly O'Connor, Michael O'Neal, Alex Revell, and Alex Rice.

BIBLIOGRAPHY

Bailey, Roger (Dodge), 'IKANOPIT', *Propswing,* 2017

Balfour, Harold, *An Airman Marches: Early Flying Adventures, 1914–1923* (Greenhill Books, London, 1985)

Baring, Maurice, *Flying Corps Headquarters 1914-1918* (Buchan & Enright, London, 1985)

Barker, Ralph, *The Royal Flying Corps in World War I* (Robinson, London, 2002)

Bingham, Hiram, *An Explorer in the Air Service* (Yale University Press, Yale, 1920)

Bishop, W.A., *The Courage of the Early Morning* (McClelland & Stewart, Toronto, 1965)

Bowyer, Chaz, *The Age of the Biplane* (Hamlyn, London, 1981)

— *Sopwith Camel: King of Combat* (Glasney Press, Falmouth, 1978)

Bradley, John, *The History and Development of Aircraft Instruments 1909 to 1919 and the Scientists involved* (PhD thesis via FAST)

Bridgman, Leonard & Stewart, Oliver, *The Clouds Remember* (Arms & Armour Press, London, 1972)

Bruce, J.M., MA, *The Aeroplanes of the Royal Flying Corps (Military Wing)* (Putnam, London, 1982)

—— 'Sopwith Camel' Pt 1, *Flight*, 22 April 1955

Carson, Annette, *Flight Fantastic: The Illustrated History of Aerobatics* (Foulis/Haynes, Sparkford, 1986)

Carson, Annette and Müller, Eric, *Flight Unlimited 95* (Carson, Morningside, 1995)

Cole, C. and Cheesman, E.F., *The Air Defence of Britain 1914-1918* (Bodley Head, London, 1984)

Davis, Mick, 'Night Flying Camels & Comic Conversions', *Cross & Cockade International*, 48/3, Autumn 2017

Fry, Wg Cdr W.M., MC, *Air of Battle* (William Kimber, London, 1974)

Franks, Norman, *Fallen Eagles* (Pen & Sword Aviation, Barnsley, 2017)

Goetzsche, Eric, *The Official Natal Mounted Rifles History* (Interprint, Durban, 1971)

Grinnell-Milne, Duncan, *Wind in the Wires* (Jarrolds, London, 1971)

Hamilton-Paterson, James, *Marked for Death* (Head of Zeus, London, 2015)

Hawker, Muriel, *H.G. Hawker: Airman* (Hutchinson, London, 1922)

Henshaw, Trevor, *The Sky Their Battlefield* (Grub Street, London, 1995)

Hill, Sqdn Ldr Roderic, MC, AFC, *The Manoeuvres of Inverted Flight*, R&M No 836 (Royal Aircraft Establishment Experimental Flying Dept., 1922) (Also R&M No 617 (1919), KR 1493 (1920), KR 1581 (1920))

Immelmann, Franz, *Immelmann: The Eagle of Lille* (Greenhill Books, London, 1984)

Jarrett, Philip, *Pioneer Aircraft: Early Aviation Before 1914* (Putnam, London, 2002)

King, H.F., 'Fighting Breed', *Flight*, 30 November 1951

Lee, Arthur Gould, *No Parachute* (Grub Street, London, 2018)

—— *Open Cockpit* (Grub Street, London, 2018)

Lewis, Cecil, *Sagittarius Rising* (Peter Davies, London, 1942)

Macmillan, Wg Cdr N. OBE MC AFC DL, *Great Airmen* (G. Bell & Sons, London, 1955)

—— *Great Aircraft* (G. Bell & Sons, London, 1960)

—— *Into the Blue* (Jarrolds, London, 1969)

Martyn, T.J.C., *Aviation Adventures: The True Story of the World War 1 Royal Flying Corps Pilot Who Founded Newsweek* (Purple Plum Press [digital], 2015)

Miller, H.C., *Early Birds* (Angus & Robertson, London, 1968)

Moore, Major W.G., OBE, DSC, *Early Bird* (Putnam, London, 1963)

Nahum, Andrew, *The Rotary Aero Engine* (Science Museum, London, 1987)

O'Connor, Mike, *Airfields & Airmen: Cambrai* (Leo Cooper/Pen & Sword, Barnsley, 2003)

Revell, Alex, *Baptism of Fire, The Royal Flying Corps at War: The First Year in France 1914-1915* (Wickford Books www.wickfordbooks.co.uk, 2018)

—— *No. 60 Squadron RFC/RAF* (Osprey, Oxford, 2011)

Scott, A.J.L. and Warne, D.W., *Sixty Squadron RAF 1916-1919* (Greenhill Books, London, 1990)

Shores, C., Franks, N. and Guest, R., *Above the Trenches* (Grub Street, London, 1990)

Smuts, J.C., *Jan Christian Smuts* (Cassell, London, 1952)

Springs, E.W., *Above the Bright Blue Sky* (John Hamilton, London, 1935)

BIBLIOGRAPHY

Springs, E.W. and Fulford, H., intr. Hillier, M., *War Birds, The Diary of a Great War Pilot* (Frontline Books, Barnsley, 2016)

Stewart, Oliver, MC, AFC, *Aerobatics* (Pitman, London, 1928)

—— *Words and Music for a Mechanical Man* (Faber & Faber, London, 1967)

Sturtivant, Ray and Page, Gordon, *The Camel File* (Air-Britain, Kent, 1993)

Sutton, Sqdn Ldr H.T., *Raiders Approach* (Gale & Polden, Aldershot, 1956)

Taylor, Sir Gordon, GC, MC, *Sopwith Scout 7309* (Cassell, London, 1968)

Tredrey, F.D., *Pioneer Pilot: The Great Smith Barry Who Taught the World How to Fly* (Peter Davies, London, 1976)

Underwood, John, *Aerobats in the Sky* (Heritage Press, Glendale, California, 1972)

Vaughan, D.K., ed., *Letters from a War Bird: The WWI Correspondence of Elliott White Springs* (University of South Carolina Press, Columbia, 2012)

White, C.M., *The Gotha Summer* (Robert Hale, London, 1986)

Williams, Neil, *Aerobatics* (Airlife, Shrewsbury, 1975)

War Birds: Diary of an Unknown Aviator (Anonymous, John Hamilton, London, 1927) [For authorship see D.K. Vaughan *Letters* above]

Yeates, V.M., *Winged Victory* (Sphere, London, 1969)

Journals:

Aero Modeller
Cross & Cockade GB
Cross & Cockade USA
Cross & Cockade International
Flight
Motor Sport
Over the Front
Popular Flying

Websites:

www.151squadron.org.uk, *From Camel to Hawk: A Diary History of 151 Squadron,* in honour of G.D. Kelsey, DFC

www.prcraig.com, in honour of Lt George Robert Craig, MC

www.theaerodrome.com, The Aerodrome Forum

www.airhistory.org.uk/rfc, Air History: The Royal Flying Corps

www.britishbadgeforum.com, The British & Commonwealth Military Badge Forum

https://www.greatwarforum.org, The Great War Forum

NOTES

Chapter 1

1. With acknowledgements to www.huletts.co.za/ops/south_africa/mills/felixton. asp; Barry Lane; and UVS historian Russel Addison.
2. AVM Leslie Brown, RNAS.

Chapter 2

1. The term Reserve Aeroplane Squadron was altered in January 1916 to Reserve Squadron (RS).
2. Wing Commander William M. Fry MC, *Air of Battle.*
3. Fry, *Air of Battle.*
4. Personal communication, 8 May 1985.
5. Our Dumb Friends League, now The Blue Cross, was founded in 1897 to care for working horses on the streets of London, and in 1912 extended its care to animals at war.
6. Eric Goetzsche, *The Official Natal Mounted Rifles History.* Appreciation for technical advice to Tim Lambon, former Rhodesian mounted officer.
7. 'The Essential Characteristics of Successful and Unsuccessful Aviators, with Special Reference to Temperament', penned by a doctor – Captain T.S. Rippon (RAMC) – and Lieutenant E.G. Manuel (RAF), *The Lancet*, 28 September 1918.
8. 3 October 1918, pp. 1117–18.
9. A further disappointing result was that despite the written testimony of two eyewitnesses to Hawker's spin tests (Hiram Bingham and Horrie Miller), his achievements were dismissed in the 1960s when the magazine *Aeronautics* sought to identify the first airman to perform deliberate spins and recover from them. Their chosen candidate was Sir Geoffrey de Havilland, although corroboration for this claim remains absent. Harry Hawker, of Hawker Aircraft fame, was largely responsible for ensuring the responsiveness and manoeuvrability of the Sopwith machines and in 1919 was the first civilian to be awarded the AFC for his magnificent war work. See Carson, *Flight Fantastic: The Illustrated History of Aerobatics*, pp. 62-4.

NOTES

10. Despite universal use of the hyphenated form Smith-Barry, it is clear from the opening page of Tredrey's biography that his family, descended on his father's side from the 4th Earl of Barrymore, used the form Smith Barry. It is possible that RRSB bowed to the inevitable and adopted a hyphen himself: only the sight of his signature will determine whether this is so.
11. J.M. Bruce, *The Aeroplanes of the Royal Flying Corps (Military Wing)*. Appreciation to Alex Revell and Trevor Henshaw who took on the research into these two fascinating Moranes.
12. Harold Balfour, *An Airman Marches*. B.C. Hucks and Gustav Hamel were celebrated pioneers of early flight in England; Claude Grahame-White was an even more famous pioneer and builder of aircraft, who had started his flying school at Hendon in 1911. He invested in aviation as a business, and urged the importance of aeroplanes in the forthcoming war.
13. With thanks to Philip Jarrett for this information from *Pioneer Aircraft: Early Aviation Before 1914* and for kindly providing the photograph.
14. Baring, *Flying Corps Headquarters 1914–18*.

Chapter 3

1. Every attempt has been made to indicate each individual's rank at the time he is discussed.
2. A.J.L. Scott and D.W. Warne, *Sixty Squadron RAF 1916–1919*.
3. Baring, *Flying Corps Headquarters 1914–1918*. The figure known today as a barrel roll came into popular use only in the 1930s, by which time the French had developed new terms to distinguish between the various *tonneaux* in the aerobatic repertoire: e.g. *tonneau déclenché* for flick roll, *tonneau lent* for slow roll, *tonneau barriqué* for barrel roll.
4. Gosport closed down with the Armistice but the Gosport System was adopted at the post-war Central Flying School in the 1920s and became the worldwide gold standard of flying instruction. In his speech at a reunion dinner in 1938, reported in the *Aeroplane*, Marshal of the Royal Air Force Viscount Trenchard described Smith Barry as 'the man who taught the air forces of the world how to fly'.
5. Lee, *Open Cockpit*.
6. Scott and Warne, *Sixty Squadron*.
7. Balfour, *An Airman Marches*.
8. *Cross & Cockade International*, Vol. 45 No. 2.
9. Alex Revell, *No. 60 Squadron RFC/RAF*.
10. Lewis, *Sagittarius Rising*.
11. Personal communication, Great War Forum, 9 March 2018.
12. Fry, *Air of Battle*.

237

13. Details of 60 Squadron aircraft flown by DVA are derived from Joe Warne's tables published in '60 Squadron, a Detailed History: Part 5', *Cross & Cockade International*, Vol. 12 No. 1, 1981.
14. E.g. *Cross & Cockade USA*, Vol. 22 No. 3, 1981.
15. Alex Revell, *No. 60 Squadron RFC/RAF*.
16. A member of the Great War Forum, 'Topgun1918', confirms that there was a short-lived Roland DI, a single-seat version of the CII, of which about 20 were built by Pfalz Flugzeugwerke. It was, however, criticized for its performance and downward view and, although not impossible, it is very doubtful that it saw much (if any) front-line service. That DVA's Nieuport was damaged in the encounter makes the Roland even more unlikely.
17. C. Shores, N. Franks, R. Guest.
18. Personal communication, 17 July 2017.
19. Andrew Pentland, www.airhistory.org.uk/rfc.
20. Alex Revell, personal communication 6 April 2018, quoting Mary Cobley.
21. Vol. 11 No. 2, '60 Squadron, a Detailed History: Part 2'.
22. D. Grinnell-Milne, *Wind in the Wires*.

Chapter 4
1. Scott and Warne, *Sixty Squadron*.
2. The aerodrome at Lympne, near Hythe on the Kent south coast, was set up in 1916 as an acceptance point (No. 8 Aircraft Park) for aircraft returning from and being delivered to France.
3. Sir Gordon 'Bill' Taylor GC MC, *Sopwith Scout 7309*.
4. Balfour, *An Airman Marches*.
5. A liquid-filled magnetic compass, the lubricant at this time being mainly alcohol, hence the nickname.
6. Arthur Gould Lee, *No Parachute*.
7. John Bradley, PhD thesis.
8. Air Board Technical Department: Aircraft Instruments, 23 July 1917 (RAFM R001943).
9. Ralph Barker, *The Royal Flying Corps in World War I*.
10. *No Parachute*.

Chapter 5
1. Extracts from Veterans' Day keynote speech to Oregon State University Reserve Officers Training Corps and personal correspondence, November 2016.
2. Arthur Gould Lee, *No Parachute*.

NOTES

Chapter 6

1. 'Sopwith Camel Part 1', 22 April 1955.
2. 'Fighting Breed', 30 November 1951.
3. Major W.G. Moore OBE DSC, *Early Bird.*
4. Communication to the author via Major General J. Gilliland, 1 April 1985.
5. Lewis, *Sagittarius Rising.*
6. *War Birds: Diary of an Unknown Aviator* [for author attribution see Bibliography].
7. J. Hamilton-Paterson, *Marked for Death*, p. 66.
8. Analysis by Rob Fletcher from raw data kindly supplied by Mick Davis.
9. Sortie dated 12 August 1917: C. Cole and E.F. Cheesman, *The Air Defence of Britain 1914-1918.*
10. Lewis, *op. cit.*
11. Personal correspondence, 16 April 1991.
12. Cole and Cheesman, *op. cit.*
13. Remarkably, two Camel pilots of No. 70 Squadron had made an experimental night flight in France on precisely the same date, in an unsuccessful attempt to attack German aircraft that were bombing St Omer (J.M. Bruce, 'Sopwith Camel, Part 1', *Flight*, 22 April 1955).
14. The well-known claim that this also tended to lubricate his own internal system has recently been tested and found wanting: http://www.meridianinstitute.com/reports/transdermal.pdf.
15. Appreciation to Dodge Bailey for extensive technical information. See also Andrew Nahum, *The Rotary Aero Engine* (Science Museum, 1987).
16. Lewis, *op. cit.*
17. *Cross & Cockade USA*, Vol. 13 No. 3, 1972.
18. Netheravon was a training and forming-up base on Salisbury Plain; Waddon (Croydon) and Chingford were airfields within the Greater London area.
19. Personal communication, March 1985.
20. Carson, *Flight Fantastic: The Illustrated History of Aerobatics*, pp.52-8.
21. *Motor Sport*, March 1930. Stewart became a leading light in post-war aerobatics. Editor of *Aeronautics* in the 1960s, he co-founded the Lockheed Trophy aerobatic contests and acted as chairman of the judges.
22. *Cross & Cockade International* Vol. 24 No. 1.
23. 'A Yank in the RFC/RAF', Vol. 41, No. 3, 2010.
24. Knight recollected this erroneously as a BE.2c.
25. *Cross & Cockade USA*, Vol. 13, No. 3, 1972.
26. Personal communication, March 1985.

Chapter 7

1. Ray Sturtivant and Gordon Page.
2. Letter to *Popular Flying* magazine, December 1937.
3. Appreciation to 'Frogsmile' for extensive insights into military uniform and clothing.
4. *Open Cockpit*.
5. Personal communication, 8 May 1985.
6. Extract from address by General The Rt Hon. Jan Smuts PC OM CH DTD ED KC FRS. Smuts was twice prime minister of South Africa, and his vision of a League of Nations was the forerunner of the United Nations of today. See full address in Appendix III.
7. Accounts derived from *Popular Flying*, October 1937 and *Flight*, 27 May 1955.
8. The original illustration in *Motor Sport*, March 1930, may be seen at https://www.motorsportmagazine.com/archive/page/march-1930/27.
9. Oliver Stewart, *Aerobatics*.
10. Norman Franks, *Fallen Eagles*.
11. Squadron Leader H.T. Sutton, *Raiders Approach.*
12. For Anthony Arkell's MC citation see https://www.thegazette.co.uk/London/issue/30713/supplement/6359.
13. This was one of three Gothas in whose demise he was reported to have assisted during his Home Defence duties.
14. Stewart, *Words and Music for a Mechanical Man.*
15. Another Armstrong appears as one of the US flyers, but he is easily identified.
16. *War Birds: Diary of an Unknown Aviator.*
17. Letter, 25 June 1920. Bishop's memory let him down here (e.g. 'Brooklyn' rather than 'Brooklands'), and it was certainly impossible that DVA's flight underflew all the Thames bridges from Hornchurch to Weybridge. Probably they skirted London, called in at Hounslow, and picked up the Thames at Richmond.

Chapter 8

1. Appreciation to the website *From Camel to Hawk: A Diary History of 151 Squadron,* www.151squadron.org.uk, which includes valuable first-hand recollections unrecorded elsewhere. The website is dedicated to G.D. Kelsey, DFC, who served with 151 Squadron in the Second World War.
2. Letter, 25 June 1920.
3. NA Kew, No. 151 Squadron Combat Report AIR/1/1227/204/5/2634/151; appreciation to Trevor Henshaw for supplying all these combat reports.
4. Some reports have given the night of 6/7 July for this action, but the date given here is confirmed in his DFC citation and other sources.

5. NA Kew, No. 151 Squadron Combat Report AIR/1/1227/204/5/2634/151.

6. R. Vann, 'Nightfighters 1918: A History of 151 Squadron', *Cross & Cockade GB* Vol. 3 No. 4.

7. NA Kew, No. 151 Squadron Combat Report AIR/1/1227/204/5/2634/151.

8. DFC citation.

9. Pilot recollections, *From Camel to Hawk* website.

10. DFC citation.

11. NA Kew, No. 151 Squadron Combat Report AIR/1/1227/204/5/2634/151; *Above the Trenches; Fall of Eagles.*

12. The incident was described more fully in his DFC citation, Appendix II.

13. Letter, 25 June 1921.

14. Pilot recollections, *From Camel to Hawk* website; cf. the victory shared with Tony Arkell and Albert Stagg on 19/20 May 1918 (above, pp.154–6) when DVA was with 78 Squadron.

15. NA Kew, No. 151 Squadron Combat Report AIR/1/1227/204/5/2634/151.

16. Personal communication, 1989. Victory also confirmed in DFC citation and *Above the Trenches.*

17. NA Kew, No. 151 Squadron Combat Report AIR/1/1227/204/5/2634/151.

18. *Sopwith Scout 7309.*

19. *Cross & Cockade USA*, Vol. 13 No. 3, 1972.

20. T.J.C. Martyn, *Aviation Adventures: The True Story of the World War 1 Royal Flying Corps Pilot Who Founded Newsweek.*

21. Franz Immelmann, brother of Max, *Immelmann: The Eagle of Lille*; Frank Courtney, *Flight Path* [Courtney saw Immelmann's combat turn for himself].

22. *Cross & Cockade USA*, Vol. 3 No. 2, 1962.

23. *Words and Music for a Mechanical Man.*

24. Described in *Flight Fantastic*, pp. 65-8.

25. Hiram Bingham, *An Explorer in the Air Service.*

26. It was a victory for his squadron, not for DVA personally. See page 173.

27. *An Airman Marches.*

28. F.D. Tredrey, *Pioneer Pilot: The Great Smith Barry Who Taught the World How to Fly.*

29. Letter, March 1920.

30. Air Marshal John Salmond (later Marshal of the Royal Air Force Sir John Salmond GCB CMG CVO DSO & Bar), 22 March 1924.

Chapter 9

1. Bouvincourt is still in use as a civil airfield today: the Aérodrome de Péronne St Quentin.

2. NA Kew, AIR1/865/204/5/514.
3. Bowyer, *Sopwith Camel: King of Combat*.
4. Personal communication, May 1985.
5. *An Explorer in the Air Service*. An even less likely claim is that Armstrong made a fatal misjudgement 'barrel-rolling through a Handley Page hangar' (Underwood, *Aerobats in the Sky*).
6. *Great Aircraft*.
7. *Air of Battle*.
8. *Sagittarius Rising*.
9. On arrival in France it had engine 52760/101768, but at the time of the crash the engine number was 51059; appreciation to Mick Davis for this information.
10. *Great Aircraft*.
11. *Into the Blue*.
12. Personal communication, March 2018.
13. Acknowledgements to Mathew Craig and www.prcraig.com, the website created by Peter Craig which commemorates his uncle, Lt George Robert Craig MC.
14. Moore, *Early Bird*, pp.139-40.

INDEX

INDEX

INDEX

247